Political Girl

Political Girl

Life and Fate in Russia

MARIA ALYOKHINA

with Olga Borisova

Translated by Emily Eccles

Beacon Press
Boston

BEACON PRESS
24 Farnsworth Street
Boston, Massachusetts
www.beacon.org

Beacon Press books
are published under the auspices of
the Unitarian Universalist Association of Congregations.

28 27 26 25   8 7 6 5 4 3 2 1

This book is printed on acid-free paper that meets the uncoated paper ANSI/NISO
specifications for permanence as revised in 1992.

Typeset by Jouve (UK), Milton Keynes

Library of Congress Cataloging-in-Publication Data is available for this title.
ISBN: 978-0-8070-2428-7; e-book: 978-0-8070-2429-4; audiobook: 978-0-8070-2430-0

The authorized representative in the EU for product safety and compliance is
Easy Access System Europe 16879218, Mustamäe tee 50,
10621 Tallinn, Estonia: http://beacon.org/eu-contact.

.

Contents

It is inevitable: one day, the prison gates will open, and you will walk through them. However, this does not mean you have truly left the category 'prison' and entered the category 'freedom'. The true gates – the ones in your mind – can only be unlocked by you.

1.

Putin Will Teach You to
Love the Motherland

'I don't want to leave because of Putin's amnesty!' I scream at
the whole of the North.
The North – the smoking area of penal colony no. 2
Amnesty – an act of charity
Putin – a Russian dictator
Me – a girl in a green coat with the tag still on – a political.

political girl

21 February 2012. We performed the punk prayer 'Virgin Mary,
Banish Putin' in the Cathedral of Christ the Saviour. Protesting against Putin's dictatorship and against using the Church to
sanctify it.

They jailed us, Pussy Riot, for two years for a desperate
scream on the eve of the 'election' for the President of Russia.

Convicted – Alyokhina Maria Vladimirovna
Born 1988
Article 213, Part 2
Sentence – 2 years
Start of sentence 04.03.2012
End of sentence 04.03.2014

The black Volga arrives at the train station. I get out. Three large, chequered bags, a red pigtail and my green coat is all that is physically left from prison.

The loudest criminal case in Russia has spread across the news. The whole world has learned about Pussy Riot.

the loudest ones

'So, what is the first taste of freedom like? Come on, we want to know how it feels? What are you going to do? What plans? Tell us! Tell us what your plans are?' I need to come up with a plan. To visit the human rights defenders who came to see me in the penal colony. To tell them that I haven't forgotten about what I saw behind bars, that I won't abandon the people who remain there and will tell everyone about them. I need to buy a phone.

I set off fireworks near the colony. I promised the girls a display to celebrate. Red splashes against a night sky.

red splashes

The crowd that's excited to meet you at the Moscow railway station today will tear you apart online tomorrow. You are a bad mother. After two years in the penal colony, you haven't gone straight home to see your son.

Would they judge me if I were a man?

The first time I go home, I'm with a cameraman. Just for an hour. I need to go to a press conference. I need to say that we are going to fight for the rights of prisoners. The first time I take my son Filipp into my arms. He is six years old. A photo is taken. A video is being recorded. Mum is nearby, she's anxious. Everyone is worried. Me too.

Meetings, cells, halls, tables with microphones, cops, bars, planes, arguments, new people, papers are all mixed up together with little Filipp. There he is by the Christmas tree. There he is with a sparkler. In a café. In the kitchen.

bad mother

The trial against Pussy Riot 'witches' became a convenient launchpad for a wider witch hunt that propelled the country onto its traditional path. If you are against the political authorities, then you are against everything Russian, against the family and against everything sacred. 'Feminism is a mortal sin,' argued a lawyer speaking for the victims, the cathedral security guards, at our trial. During the two years of my imprisonment, the views of our courtroom have expanded to encompass all of Russia.

you're the headline

It is our first interview after two years serving in the penal colony. It's night. Nadya and I are lying on a bed in a hotel in a Siberian city, a telephone lies next to us. The voice on the other end belongs to a presenter from a prominent liberal radio station who asks, 'How are you doing, girls?' We tell him at length about how we and the hundreds of prisoners we have met have fought for our rights. All around us is quiet, there is only icy winter outside, it is a little like a fairy tale until the host says, 'Stay with us for a commercial break!'

We stay on the line. Almost a second later, the presenter has started talking again: 'Pussy Riot have been released, but the heated debate surrounding their provocative action has not calmed down over the last two years, and now, dear listeners, we invite you to vote – who do you think Pussy Riot really are: blasphemers or martyrs?'

'If you think they are blasphemers, dial 1,

'If you think they are martyrs, dial 2.'

And I think to myself: 'Is this really the freedom we wanted?'

stay with us

I regained my so-called 'freedom' at the end of December. The amnesty to save face in front of the West – a VIP amnesty – cuts our sentence by two months. The reason is the 2014 Winter Olympics. Putin has grown tired of answering questions from foreign statesmen about Pussy Riot. The issue of us 'hooligans' needs a solution, so as not to spoil the celebrations.

And still we spoil the celebrations. We go to the Olympics to perform a protest action. It's then that I understand and feel that everything has changed, that we have left prison and arrived in a different country. There is no way back. Putin's third presidential term, which is now six years, and the year 2014, become a point of no return. For everyone.

point of no return

For Putin, the Olympics is the latest operation to return Russia to greatness. Russia must win. So 'Operation Result' is conceived, a joint effort between the FSB and the Ministry of Sport.

> *'People are celebrating Olympic champion winners, but we
> are sitting crazy and replacing their urine.'*
>
> – Grigory Rodchenkov

Grigory Rodchenkov, the director of the national anti-doping laboratory, named in an international investigation for concealing positive drugs tests of Russian athletes and destroying urine samples, developed his own signature cocktail in honour of the Olympics. He was given a laboratory and fifty people for the task. The cocktail 'Duchess', a mix of three forbidden substances, was given to athletes in an alcohol tincture. Whisky for the men and Martini for the women. The secret services were left to deal with the urine. Each sample bottle was numbered and designed so the cap would break if the bottle was opened illicitly. The Anti-Doping Commission in Sochi consisted of a hundred international experts who strictly controlled the process and guarded their facilities 24/7.

operation result

The Russian FSB found a way out: a small hole in the wall, covered by a piece of furniture. Each night Rodchenkov and his entire team of Russian experts would pass the sample bottles through the hole to the neighbouring room with FSB officers standing by to take them. Later the same bottles would be returned, looking untampered with, with clean urine.

Putin will give Rodchenkov the Order of Friendship.

winter olympics in the subtropics

Putin wants to demonstrate 'Russian greatness', so the Sochi Olympics are the most expensive Olympics in the history of mankind.

Twelve billion dollars was the amount Putin pledged to spend on the Olympics and this figure already exceeded all previous Olympic budgets. In the process 12 billion becomes 50 billion, a sum that Russian hospitals and orphanages can only dream of.

construction of death

Migrant workers are brought in to build the Olympics. They are promised good wages, are given fake registrations, and when the time comes to pay them, a cop turns up and they are deported. Then a bus arrives and unloads a new batch.

Groups of police, the migration service and the administration are operating in the city. Cossack units are helping them too. The Cossacks mock the visiting construction workers. The police organize extrajudicial violence, detainees are held in inhuman conditions, beaten and locked in garages. Human rights defenders are forcibly removed from police stations.

A group of workers threatened to strike – they were told they were fired. Two were immediately arrested. The electrician Mardiros Demerchyan was first beaten for several hours in the police station and then raped with a metal crowbar. After that, he admitted to the theft of an electric cable. There was no theft. After the torture, Mardiros lost his mind.

putin will teach you to love the motherland

A week before the games close, we fly to Olympic Sochi to make our action. We are sure we'll all be detained en route. We fly out of Moscow, a large team of twelve people on four different flights. They might detain some of us at the airport, but there is a chance that a few of us may make it as far as Sochi.

It seems there are more FSB officers than residents in the Olympic town. The sellers at the official hot-dog stalls are no lower in rank than a junior lieutenant in the security services.

At the airport's exit I smoke a cigarette with Nadya. Immediately we are surrounded by uniformed policemen. They demand our documents.

– What're you doing here?
– We haven't done anything wrong.
– You're not allowed to smoke here. You'll have to come with us.

If you are an activist, then most likely you are put under 'surveillance control'. The special services will have eyes on any ticket you buy within an hour or two of purchase. They will receive an auto-alert from the 'Wanted Route' database, created in the early 2000s. We are expected. We do not hand over our documents. We argue. We're leaving.

surveillance control

We rent a car. We're going to check out the first location for the Pussy Riot video. On an empty road at night, our car is stopped by a special forces soldier in camouflage. The usual AK-47 on

7

the shoulder and the routine statement: 'There is an All-Points Bulletin out on you.' In less than half an hour, a police squad of two puffy men in acid-green reflective uniforms appears on the road. They claim the car is stolen and the Pussy Riot activist who is driving it holds a fake licence.

– Are we free to go or are we detained?
– No, you can't leave, but you aren't detained!

We are detained. We are released at 4 a.m., and they take the legitimate driving licence away without any explanation.

welcome to sochi

We stay in Hotel Malachite. Thirty metres from the sea. We sleep a couple of hours. Soviet-style furniture, swirling patterned blankets, the windows are covered with a green reflective film. As soon as you connect to the Wi-Fi, your email is hacked.

At 8 a.m. we swim in the icy Black Sea of February. It's our first shoot for the Olympic music video. We don't know if we will be able to film anything in the city. So we start here. A police car pulls up to the empty beach. Operatives get out of it. For twenty minutes, they silently film us on several cameras. Girls in balaclavas squealing from the cold and diving in and out of the waves.

icy black sea

At noon, on the way to the next location, we are stopped by an FSB border detachment. They take us in for interrogation. Our cars are escorted by the political police, Centre E cops – a real motorcade of cars from different special services.

We're detained for not having permission to be in the 'special border zone'. The officers can't tell us the parameters of this special zone. And this is not surprising, because almost all the Olympic facilities are located within it. So anyone exiting the main stadium could be detained for trespassing in the 'special zone'.

They detain us. For the next twelve hours, we are under arrest in a military unit near Abkhazia, former Georgia. They lie to our lawyer that we are not here.

border zone

After twelve hours of being interrogated by the FSB border guards, we are walking to supper. A night café with leather sofas. Kharcho soup and Olympic ice hockey on TV. We are the only diners on the second floor. A guy in a dirty T-shirt with black greasy hair and a bottle of vodka sits down next to us. He starts to drink it with an obvious swagger. He already knows our names.

– Girls, let's have a drink together! the guy says by way of introduction.
– Yes, let's! we cheerfully agree.
– What shall we drink to?
– To the Russian revolution, of course, I answer.

I would love for the thinly disguised agent to drink to the revolution. A second man appears at the next table. No less greasy. He begins to bully 'our guy', and as 'our guy' is 'with us' he asks for our protection. Police agents are trying to drag us into a fake fight, desperately pretending to be café visitors. We pack up and leave, they try to catch us up. There are no less strange types hanging around the crossroads near the café. Everyone is looking at us. 'Well, go on then, hit me! Hit me!'

one of the greasy ones yells at us, but we're already jumping onto the next bus.

There are security cops everywhere. Unmarked cars are following us, suspicious men are at every junction, in uniform and in plain clothes. Anyone who gets on our bus at the next stop could be a security operative.

cop town

Two a.m. We are filming on the outskirts of Sochi near the Olympic mascots: Leopard, Bunny and White Bear.

We are very lucky that the smiling man posing between the Leopard and the Bear turns out to be a tourist and not a grinning cop.

Under an atmosphere of total control, the resort town which I used to know has turned into a secret facility that is divided into sectors and squares. I only want one thing: not to spend the rest of the night in a police station. I quickly take off my coat and start jumping, boxing in the air, shouting the words to the song.

below the church

In the morning, we board a city bus and get off in the centre of Sochi. We can't go by car because it has a flat tyre. 'We'll get them at the port,' a 'passer-by' mutters near us. Fifteen minutes later, a bald cop in a leather jacket runs up to us.

– You must come with us to the station.
– What for?
– Your hotel has been robbed. You're all suspects.

The security cop has a typical donut face, he gets constant calls from his colleagues while we stand there. He repeats, 'Yes, I understand, but I'm alone here. Yes, yes, I understand. But I'm alone here. On my own! I'm standing below the church.' We are on the steps that run from a white church to a garden. Pedestrians pass by indifferently. Cypress trees stand calmly by.

theft of the century

- What theft?
- A theft in the hotel. You are suspects.
- Who?
- You.
- Do you have any orders?
- No, no orders, but you are all under suspicion.
- This looks like a provocation.
- What kind of provocation?
- An obvious one.
- An obvious provocation???
- What rights do we have as detainees?
- Why do you ask? You know this is Russia?

torture without meaning

What can the operative-donut really be thinking as he makes meaningless comments one after the other? It is obvious that he does not know who we are. He is surprised that after a couple of minutes we call our lawyer and hand him the phone to find out the 'circumstances of the theft'. 'Are you from an NGO?' the donut face asks. A rank-and-file cop from the Criminal

Investigation Department who was sent to detain 'suspicious persons' does not even reflect on what he is doing. He is 'just doing his job' and is 'fulfilling his boss's orders', the fuss around the Olympics is an extra stress for him, unpaid overtime. And then there are lawyers and cameras in his face, and all he wants is to get these girls to the station as quickly as possible and go home to his wife. In this situation he is not a sadist, not an ideological warrior against evil, he has not done anything wrong, he is simply working.

'What kind of rights do you think you have? After all, this is Russia,' he said. This should be a headline in all the Western newspapers. For many months, the international media has bought the story that Russia is a loyal defender of human rights, but this is so far from the truth. The West pretends to believe Putin's hype, and that what is happening to us is nothing more than a minor event.

what rights?

– If you refuse to do what I ask and leave, I'll be forced to call for backup, according to the law. And then we'll all be delayed, I'm sorry, girls.

His backup eventually finds him, and we are surrounded by twenty people with phones, black jackets, pointy boots, of varying heights, different faces, different hair, but somehow they still all look the same.

'We're not detaining you, we'll just have a chat.' They twist our arms, forcefully throw us into avtozaks* and take us to the

---

* Paddy wagons.

police station. They break Nastya's camera, she bites one of the cops. No one can explain to us what room the theft took place in or how they found out exactly where we've been staying, given that they've detained us on the street.

we'll just chat

They've locked us in the police assembly hall and then dragged us out roughly one by one for questioning. Everyone's screaming. Nadya is trying to prevent a local activist from being hauled away, Nastya is trying to stop me from being dragged to interrogation. No one wants to go in without a lawyer. They grab my hands, shove me along the corridor, push me down the stairs.

The cops in Sochi need us to stay quiet, or better still for us to leave altogether.

After five hours, we leave the police station. It's raining. At the entrance there is a huge crowd of journalists with umbrellas. We put on balaclavas and break through the ring of press, chanting lines from the song 'Putin Will Teach You To Love Your Motherland'. A pack of journalists runs after us down the alley. People fall, cameras fall.

We go to the Emergency Room for them to check our injuries. The doctor and nurse say they know exactly who we are. They refuse to give Nastya an X-ray, and Nadya is told that her 'scratches' are from a cat.

manus manum lavat

Three Cossacks are waiting for us at the Malachite Hotel. They won't let us pass. Cossack patrols were used over a century ago by the tsars to suppress popular discontent. Their return seems symbolic.

- Why did you even come here, sluts? You're not wanted here!

Our lawyers Popkov and Peter manage to get inside the hotel and retrieve our belongings. David, a local eco-activist from Sochi who fought illegal construction for the Olympics, suggests we move in with him. So we do.

His house on Sochi's outskirts, which looks like an unfinished holiday cottage, turns into a squat. We take turns sleeping on a bed with a broken leg.

yellow mimosa

The cops from Centre E pop up here as well. In black suits carrying shopping bags. Cops go back and forth on the street outside and pretend that they are just out for a stroll. Our car's tyres are let down again. We think about how to leave without being detained.

We go out the back way, through gardens, past garages, over fences. We jump over mimosa bushes. It is February, but yellow mimosa is blossoming everywhere.

blue wall

We are travelling to the blue wall, with 'Sochi-2014' painted on it, near the port. Here we will shoot the key moments of the video. We are in a Russian café hut on the embankment, Centre E cops sit at neighbouring tables. More and more of them arrive. If we do not leave now, we will be detained again. We get going.

Between the hut and the promenade is a red carpet. You could imagine that you are at a film festival, only that bearded Cossacks, not paparazzi, line up either side of the carpet. They shout 'Fuck off to America' at us, they carry whips. They're clearly not going to hand over any kind of film award to us. The Cossacks follow us along the embankment to the blue wall. Sochi-2014 – an inscription several metres high. We throw off our jackets and begin to sing.

red carpet

– GAS! GAS!

I can't work out who is shouting.

The Cossacks spray us with tear gas. They beat us with whips and twist our arms. They pull off our balaclavas. Nastya's hair is torn right out. The metal tip of the whip hits her along the spine. Nadya is pushed to the ground, and with a guitar neck they smash the face of Lyosha in a yellow dress. They beat even those who are lying down. The bearded Cossack who didn't let us get past into the hotel yesterday takes Peter aside and sprays him at point-blank range with pepper spray.

The police, smiling, watch the bloody carnage. We scream in pain, but we keep on singing. In a matter of minutes, the huge advertising hoarding for the Olympics has become the background for public punishment.

public punishment

'We didn't beat them, we taught them,' the Cossack who beat us will say. Instead of jail time, he'll get the Governor's public protection. The crime, which has three main protagonists – the victim, the criminal and witness-cops – will never be investigated.

And where're the others? The Cossacks are beating us, the cops are watching, the cameras are filming – but where's everyone else? People are walking past. What do they think? 'It's not my business'? But they're beating women. Screams can be heard throughout the street. 'Maybe this is a movie?' 'What if it's not a movie?' 'Then I will get it too.'

There's always a choice: to intervene or to pass by. Most people pass by.

sochi-2014

'We should take off our Kubankas and hats, as Cossacks did in the old days in honour of heroes, for the authors and performers of the song "Putin Will Teach You To Love The Motherland". Young people, unlike most of us, have the courage to point out to the President of Russia the shortcomings in his work and the toothlessness of his local officials'

– Grigory Uchkurov, Cossack

The only Cossack who publicly supported us and identified those who had attacked us, Uchkurov, will be excluded from his Cossack host.

wipe away the blood

We wipe away the blood, apply bandages and wash away the pepper spray. Nadya pulls the guitar out of the rubbish bin. One ambulance takes Peter to the hospital for his burnt eyes.

No one makes a record of the chemical burns. FSB vehicles are parked near the hospital.

David goes shopping for new hats. Dima buys scissors. I sit opposite Nadya in a café and try to understand what has happened. The balaclavas are lost. One was snatched by a Cossack, it stuck out of his pocket. I just sit and stare at my phone or at the wall. If someone asks, 'Is everything okay?' I quickly answer, 'Yes, everything's okay.' I have never been beaten by bearded men. I don't know what else to answer. Nothing is okay. But we have to carry on. Because we care.

carrying on

We are going to shoot the last episode. The five Olympic rings on the central square. The surveillance stands, without shame, by the rings. But it doesn't matter. They're not hitting us – that's already a bonus. We shout out the words and dance. The Leopard mascot notices us and spontaneously joins in. We are dancing together.

At night, we edit our Olympic video. We all have bruises, swellings, cuts, torn-out hair, we are knackered, but we keep editing until the morning. Early next morning, we have the premiere and a Pussy Riot press conference.

I don't have a second to think about what's going on. I have to edit the footage. Splice the bloody heads next to the grinning cops. My face and my friends' faces contorted in pain. Our first protest after two years in prison. I don't have a second to think about how this protest looks. I don't feel frightened. I don't feel anything at all. I'm not even sure whether the screaming girl in the video is my friend, and the other girl with terrified eyes is me.

do it yourself

Half an hour before the press conference, the hotel refuses to provide the room we booked and gives us an idiotic reason: that a pipe has burst and they cannot turn off the fire alarm. The meeting with journalists spontaneously moves outside to the entrance of the frightened hotel. There will be no big screen, so we put the laptop on a chair and the words of the song come out of the speakers.

> Putin will teach you to love the Motherland
> Motherland
> Motherland
> Motherland

life is so good

A pro-Kremlin chicken squad appears in the crowd. One pink cockerel and several gopniks* are waving raw chicken carcasses in the air. 'We like sex with chicken!' they shout referring to us. One of the guys tells a CNN journalist, 'Life is so good in Sochi that there is no need to protest.'

---

* Gopnik derives from GOP, literal translation: Urban Contempt Society, made up of aggressive young men.

When the guy dressed as a cockerel is asked why he doesn't also like to have sex with a hen, after all he is also a chicken, he proudly replies, 'But I am a cockerel!'

We do not know where the young gopniks with chicken legs came from. They probably don't know anything about Pussy Riot. They were hired to break up our presentation with a guarantee that they wouldn't be detained by the police for it. A city operating as a 'special facility' does not permit random provocations.

a keepsake

We are on our way to the airport – time to return to Moscow. The taxi driver recognizes us and takes a photo as a keepsake. We stop for lunch. We leave the café and find out that, while we were having lunch, two FSB officers approached the taxi driver, forced him to delete the photo and asked him to come with them for a conversation.

faithful dog

The doping scandal with the Olympic urine tests will be exposed in two years' time. Athletes will be banned from performing at the next games under the Russian flag.

> '*I was a faithful dog. I was needed in Sochi.*
> *Everything was reported to Putin. To believe that he didn't*
> *know is stupid.*'
> – Grigori Rodchenkov

The head of the laboratory, Rodchenkov, will request political asylum in America. Two of his colleagues will be found dead under unusual circumstances. Rodchenkov will be part of the American Witness Protection Program. For several years, Russian propaganda will expose him as a swindler and a liar who sold his homeland for thirty pieces of silver.

> *'Everybody with an open mind could see the face of a new Russia: efficient and friendly, patriotic and open to the world'*
> – President of the International Olympic Committee, Thomas Bach

new face

21 February. Two years ago we were on our way to the Cathedral of Christ the Saviour, for which they sentenced us. Now it's to another Moscow court to support people who were sentenced after us, the defendants in the Bolotnaya Case, who held the largest protest against Putin. Seven people will receive prison terms of two to four years.

People of all ages gather near the court to support the political prisoners. One can't hold back the tears, another argues with the stone-faced cops; they come in groups and on their own, politicians and ordinary people. And yet Western correspondents are nowhere to be seen. These people who sacrifice themselves to get to the truth are not visible through the kilometres of Western media newsprint about the Russian Olympics.

> *'We are not being tried so that we can be judged fairly. They've made us protagonists in a spectacle of punishment.'*
> – Aleksei Polikhovich, sentenced to 3.5 years' imprisonment.

spectacle of punishment

The police push people away from the court, divide the crowd into sections, extracting the most active and throwing them into avtozaks. People bunch together in clusters – if you're in a group, it's more difficult to pull you out and detain you.

When the 2nd Riot Police Unit starts coming for Nadya and me, our cluster instantly forms a ring around us and does not let the cops near. People stand with their backs to the police, exposing themselves to blows, just so we are not detained.

glory to the heroes

The next day, 22 February, the revolution in Ukraine triumphs. Deposed President Yanukovych flees to Russia.

Immediately after the closing of the Olympics in Sochi and the victory of the revolution in Ukraine, the 'Russian Spring' kicks off. In a few days the annexation of Crimea will begin.

2

The New Face of the Country

– Bon appétit, you bitches!

March. Nizhny Novgorod, 6 a.m. We get off the train and go for coffee. Immediately a group of young twenty-year-old gopniks flies into McDonald's and surrounds us. They are wearing down jackets and St George's ribbons. They are holding chicken legs and a jar of glue. One of them is holding a sign: 'Dirty whores, get out of town.'

– Get the hell out of here, bitches!
– Get out of town, whores!
– Get the fuck out of our town, fuckers!

Ten people are standing over our table. They are yelling at us to go 'back':

– To America, bitch!

They also have syringes in their hands, and in the syringes there's Zelenka, green ethyl alcohol, used as an antiseptic in Soviet days. It should not get into the eyes. One of them runs up and spurts a syringe. Aiming at the eyes.

happy meal

A large iron glue can flies towards me. It hits my head. Painful. And very noisy. I didn't even have time to wake up. I touch my forehead, look at my palm and see blood. The can pierced my head. There's blood on my hair too. Blood and Zelenka.

I don't think about the blood, I tell the camera why we came. 'We came to Nizhny Novgorod to visit the penal colony. Prisoners there receive just 200 roubles a month. We are here to support them.'

Tasya is holding the camera, she has an ocular burn that will lead to complete loss of vision. And Nadya has a burn too. I have concussion. The police, whose station is around the corner, take forty minutes to get to us. The ambulance travels at the same speed.

The attack will not be investigated by the cops, because they have masterminded it. Nizhny Novgorod Centre E Colonel Trifonov 'Trishka' announced it on his Twitter the evening before our arrival. The attack, ten men beating up several women, he called 'disinfection'.

Immediately after the attack, he posts photos of our faces covered in Zelenka and blood – it is his man who was filming at McDonald's.

green light

While Russia invades Ukraine, the authorities give the green light to create violence within our own country. The number of Nazi groups increases. Gopniks with St George's ribbons calling themselves patriots attack and beat up anyone who disagrees with the new 'patriotism'.

What are you going to do if someone hits you in the head in a café in broad daylight? Will you complain to the police? Not an option – the police are responsible for it. Will you fight back within the limits of 'permissible self-defence'? Not an option – you will be put in jail and the attackers will be ignored.

mama with a bandage

My son Filya is six years old and at kindergarten they're celebrating International Women's Day on 8 March. Boys in white
shirts read poetry to their mothers and grandmothers.

I am the only mother who attends wearing a strange ban-
dage in my green hair.

> We may be small in stature,
> But brave as soldiers.
> Our beloved homeland
> We'll defend
> To guard the sunshine of happiness.

I don't think about the fact that children learn poems where
boys are soldiers and girls are princesses who need to be protected, which is wildly absurd on 8 March– a day celebrating
the struggle for women's independence. I just listen. I'm just
glad to see Filya whenever I want, and not once every three
months in the penal colony's room for three-day family visits.

I think about the young men who beat us up in Nizhny
Novgorod, who also went to kindergarten and told their
mothers that they would defend their motherland.

revolution on television

In the penal colony, scraps of real news would reach us, but we
had to fight for it. The censor wouldn't let a newspaper through,
the guards would take away a magazine, they would burn letters.

Once the Head of the Culture Department handed me a

magazine with a review of the newly released film *Nympho-maniac*. All the pictures neatly cut out from the text. The prison authorities considered the photos of Charlotte Gainsbourg with two black men to be indecent.

November 2013. When the revolution in Ukraine starts, I am still inside. There is a TV in every barracks. Russian propaganda turns the unrest in central Kyiv into a reality show. The goal is to portray the protesters as marginal. To show that this protest is an insignificant story that would lead nowhere.

The civil protest turns into a revolution. Ukraine's pro-Russian president, Yanukovych, despite talks with Europe, signs agreements with Putin to join the Eurasian Customs Union.*

Putin lowers the price of Russian gas for Ukraine – a small price to have 'his man' in the neighbouring country. People feel cheated and march to Kyiv's Independence Square – the Maidan. Ukrainian flags are raised next to EU flags. The Maidan is becoming crowded with barricades. The main square of the capital turned into a tent camp. There are so many people that it is impossible to ignore them. Ukraine is choosing to abandon its Soviet legacy in favour of a European path. Ukraine refuses to follow Russia into the past.

And that is exactly what Putin cannot forgive.

operation gifts of the magi

The Gifts of the Magi are sacred relics. Gold, frankincense and myrrh. It's said they were presents for newborn Jesus.

---

* Ukrainian President Viktor Yanukovych has allegedly signed an agreement with Russia including Ukraine's commitment to join the Customs Union in the near future, the *Voice of Russia* reported, citing British journalist Edward Lucas, international editor of *The Economist*.

For the first time in 500 years, the relics leave Mount Athos in Greece.

January 2014. 'Orthodox' oligarch Konstantin Malofeev pays for the voyage. With Greek church elders, he loads the relics onto a private jet. The Gifts make a tour of the capitals of Russia, Ukraine and Belarus. The tour enjoys the blessing of the Russian Orthodox Church. The consignment flies to Moscow for Christmas, to be displayed in the Cathedral of Christ the Saviour.

gold as a gift to the king

Initially, Crimea is not included in the relics' route, but by order of the Patriarch, the plan changes in a day. At the end of January, the Gifts arrive on Malofeev's plane to the Ukrainian peninsula.

The Crimeans come to pray, unaware that they are participating in the Russian intelligence operation 'Gifts of the Magi'. FSB pensioner Igor 'Strelkov' Girkin is responsible for the security of the relics.

incense as a gift to the high priest

Recruited priests conduct church services 'for peace'. They are collecting mattresses so they can later house the Russian military in the church grounds.

While people queue to see the relics, the delegation that has arrived with the Gifts is discussing the annexation: they plan to lower the Ukrainian flag and to raise the flag of 'independent Crimea' in its place.

myrrh as a gift to a mortal

A boat with the Holy Gifts and icons then motors alongside ships in the Black Sea Fleet. The Gifts are brought on-board the Russian warship *Moskva*, where the missile cruiser has a 'private chapel'.

Under the cover of the relics, the Orthodox Chekists are testing the ground and gathering intelligence so they can present Putin with an entire peninsula.

gifts of death

February 2014. The Ukrainian revolution is winning, Yanukovych gives the order to shoot at protesters. Special police force Berkut opens fire. Hundreds are wounded, 107 people are killed. But the protest doesn't stop.

Putin orders Russian troops to block military bases in Crimea.

Russian military block entry points to the city.

The head of the Crimean Tatars says that the Crimeans will not allow a split Ukraine and announces a protest. Separatists and the Cossacks come to the protest, with tear-gas canisters and iron spikes. On their jackets are St George's ribbons – emblems of imperial loyalty. So that pro-Russians can recognize 'their own'.

st george's ribbons

Like the British red poppy, in Russia they came up with an emblem to mark the end of the Second World War. St George's ribbon is a symbol of victory. Putin loves to talk about victory:

'We are a great nation, we defeated the fascists.' He doesn't like to talk about the American tanks on loan, or about Western allies. No mention of the Soviet Union being an aggressor and ally of Hitler at the start of the war. In Russia the slogan 'Never again' becomes 'We can do it again!'

never again we can do it again

In 1944, Stalin mounted a genocide of the Crimean Tatars. Tens of thousands were put into wooden wagons and forcibly evicted from Crimea. Thousands died on the road from starvation and typhus. The Tatars have been fighting for the right to return to their native land for decades.

Russia where, according to a 2015 opinion poll, more than half of the population approves of Stalin, will never become a motherland for a people who survived genocide.

Putin will not forgive the Crimean Tatars for resisting annexation. They will be given immense prison sentences, they will be kidnapped, tortured and killed.

polite people

Following Putin's order, a Russian Navy boat with 200 gunmen in green uniform, without insignia, arrives in Sevastopol. They seize state property.

A pro-Russian government is formed in the captured parliament building.

Russian flags fly on edifices.

At night, Russian gunmen seize airports.

The head of security at the airport says his men were 'politely asked to leave'. The quote ends up in the media, pro-Kremlin bloggers are busy – photos of Russian military men with flowers and kittens with the hashtag 'polite people' go viral. Propaganda shifts up a gear; the winners of the revolution on the Maidan are called Nazis, 'polite people' are called liberators.

polite fascism

Troops march across Crimea on Forgiveness Sunday to the words of the Patriarch: 'I hope that Ukraine will not resist.' The police march along Manezhnaya Square in the centre of Moscow, to throw into avtozaks people who say out loud 'No to war.'

State employees are urgently rounded up. Teachers are ordered to the central square to support the troops. To support the war.

At anti-war demonstrations, words fly out of police loud hailers that reveal a hidden division in society that could be worse than a civil war.

'Citizens, do not obstruct the passage of other citizens.' There are those who have an opinion but do not have the right to walk through their city, and those who have the right to walk thanks to their political silence.

divide and conquer

– Don't tell the media what's happened! We'll be
victims for ever.

March 2014. Mordovia. A land of penal colonies. A land of watchtowers and fences, where the regional emblem could be a barbed-wire fence, where half of the population wear prison uniform and the other half wear epaulettes. And everyone votes for Putin – 92 per cent.

The border zone between night and day. The night train left us on the strip of asphalt and turned its wheels onward. An empty platform. They've attacked us again.

They ran up to the steps of our train. Cut to: our faces, hair and clothes are covered in a stinking mess. Nearby – on the platform – empty plastic bottles. I don't want to tell the media about this. We don't want to become public punchbags.

We shake ourselves off, move on.

an argument

This is where Nadya served her sentence for 'Punk Prayer', and we've both come to support the prisoners of her former penal colony. We sit in the visiting room for seven hours to hand over food for the prisoners. The guards look at us as if we're not here.

Guards for generations: wearing their blotchy blue uniforms, they torture behind the walls; in the same uniform they go to get sausages. Their uniform sticks to the skin. They recruit children straight out of school, these children also put on uniforms. Maybe exactly the same ones.

Behind the fence, in the office, there hangs a stick with an iron knob, the stick is called an argument. They beat female prisoners with it. They beat them if they don't sew 'the norm'. The prisoners must sew police and army uniforms. Twelve hours a day, six days a week. For a few dollars a month.

barbed-wire region

A Lada car the colour of an aubergine driven by chubby Centre E cops is following us. We film them, they film us.

We laugh. We drive along the barbed-wire fences. The wire fences stretch and stretch and stretch. There are forests upon forests. Fences and more fences.

Mordovia is all forests, tears and prison zones. And barbed wire.

what's so funny?

We sit in a half-empty café. New gopniks in leather jackets and black hats run in. They're holding green syringes. Nadya leaps under the table. Two thugs with drunken faces grab me by the hair, turn me around and squeeze the syringe onto my face. Zelenka flies into my eyes.

'SO HOLLYWOOD!' yells Peter, seeing my green face. And I want to cry for the first time. Not because I'm in pain – it was much more painful in Nizhny Novgorod.

I feel like crying because I couldn't fight back. I didn't even try.

hollywood

The summoned cops arrive in droves. We go outside. I hold out my hand to one of them. He's embarrassed.

— It's not polite to shake hands with a girl.
— Why not?

Pink walls, small light bulbs, bright artificial lettuce leaves. A syringe with Zelenka left on the table.

They take our fingerprints. For what? It is a meaningless and insincere process. Our honest accounts of assault will become dead letters on that explanation form, it will sit on the dusty shelf of a police major. And you, a uniformed cop, the major's subordinate, are filling the form in and you know it. When you are writing these dead letters, is there any guarantee that you are actually alive?

march for peace

15 March 2014. Moscow. A protest rally against the annexation – March for Peace. The organizer is Boris Nemtsov – a tall, charismatic man with black curls. A politician from Nizhny Novgorod who knows how to speak and make people fall in love with him, one of the leaders of the Russian protest. He takes the stage:

> *'I'm a patriot. I don't want this war. I don't want to see Cargo 200* arriving in Moscow, Yaroslavl, Nizhny Novgorod. Our mothers, wives and children crying – I don't want that. I don't believe we have the right to behave this way towards a friendly country. It's impudent, it's vile and most of all, it will hurt Russia.'*

Thousands of Ukrainian flags wave in the centre of Moscow.
Hands off Ukraine!
The Crimean occupation – shame on Russia!
Russia and Ukraine without Putin!

* Body bags.

forgive us, ukraine

Nadya and I walk on to the stage. A green strand of my hair flutters in the wind. I speak into the microphone.

'We get beaten up all the time. We are constantly being doused with Zelenka. Russian citizens are being chased out of the squares, people are being detained for 'No to War' slogans, people are being detained for holding peace signs. How can a referendum at gunpoint be fair and legitimate?'

referendum at gunpoint

A 'Russian election' is held in occupied Crimea. They need to legalize the seizure – have a 'referendum' in which Crimea will 'declare its independence' and be annexed to Russia as an 'independent territory'.

Armed checkpoints, no observers. Ballot boxes are handed out in halls packed with people in camouflage. Even before the polling stations close, Russian flags are already hanging on the buildings.

The muzzles of Russian machine guns, Russian Cossacks' horses, the concocted results. They called it a referendum. A day later there is a ceremony in the Kremlin. They called it accession.

shot in the heart

In the Kremlin, champagne is being poured, while in Crimea, Russian special forces fire at an observation tower. The tower turns into a sieve. A Ukrainian lieutenant in the tower falls down dead. The bullets have hit him in the heart.

Igor Girkin commands the raid.

The lieutenant-cartographer, who remained to defend the unit, was Serhiy Kokurin. He was the first to die during the Russian annexation. He was thirty-six years old. He left behind a pregnant wife and a child.

medal to grow into

The Defence Minister awards medals 'for the return of Crimea' to Russian military personnel.

On the medals, a map of the peninsula and the start date of the operation – 20 February 2014. On that day, the Berkut riot police shot protesters on the Maidan and Yanukovych was still a legitimate president. The military occupied the peninsula a week later, and the 'referendum' would be held a month after that.

The occupation of Crimea was being prepared since the Maidan revolution began.

fifth-column cult of victory

Those who disagree with the annexation will be declared national traitors.

A fifth column.

Putin and his propaganda are switching to the language of war. And it doesn't matter that it was used over half a century ago. It's necessary to convince people that the Nazis are back, and we are about to defeat them again. The cult of victory is becoming the new consensus.

enemies are everywhere

'Russia is the only country capable of turning the US into
radioactive ash.'

– propagandist Dmitri Kiselev

Cold War rhetoric is coming to life on Russian TV screens. Propaganda repeats on the hour: enemies are everywhere – external, internal, various! And they all want to destroy Russia. They are among us – they must be denounced, they must be forbidden to assemble on the squares, they must be mentioned regularly on television, and if they don't understand – they must be beaten.

radioactive ashes

Putin needs war as an idea, because people don't really live during war – they survive. He needs to force them to survive. So that people do not resent their situation too much, Putin claims they are essential for the great victory.

Many Russians are caught up in the imperial euphoria of the 'return of Crimea to its native harbour'. Putin's popularity rating is rising. Propaganda tells the nation every day that Putin has 'restored historical justice'. Dissenters begin to leave Russia. Food prices soar. The West imposes the first sanctions against Russian officials, against those who participated in the annexation. No sanctions against Putin himself.

our country's tanks

– Why are your country's tanks in our country and no
  one protests about it?

All of a sudden, you take hold of a microphone after two years
in prison and the only thing you want is to be the voice of
those who have no voice.

The end of March. Tallinn. A panel. We talk about political
prisoners. A boy, very young, about nineteen, takes the microphone and asks: 'Why are your country's tanks in our country
and no one protests about it?' The boy turns out to be a journalist from Ukraine. It makes me feel terribly ashamed. Ashamed
of my helplessness, of the helplessness of everyone around me.
And I say, 'The couch the Russians are sitting on has become
too comfortable, that's why no one is getting off it.'

heavenly hundred

We fly to Ukraine. To the city of victorious revolution, Kyiv.
To see everything with our own eyes.

The Heavenly Hundred – that's what they'll call the 107
demonstrators shot by the Berkut riot police. On the fortieth
day after the shooting, people are bringing flowers. We also
bring some – red carnations. Along the roadside, thousands of
lamps with lights inside.

Flowers, posters, barricades of tyres, tents and fires alight
in barrels. How to convey this sense of deep respect to the
strangers around us, our kindred spirits, to those who actually
succeeded?

Anyone who found themselves on the Maidan falls in love with this honesty. A huge banner hangs on the Christmas tree:

We love the Russians – we hate Putin

the european union is concerned

April 2014. The European Parliament, Brussels. We are in formal blouses. Around us are politicians in suits.

We demand sanctions for the Kremlin thieves responsible for political repression and aggression in Ukraine. We call for the blocking of the Western assets of hypocrites who have been robbing the country for years and putting the money in Swiss banks. Here they buy yachts and villas, here they give birth to children and here their children study – and at the same time they call on their TV propaganda channels for missiles to be aimed at – here.

The politicians in suits listen to us and nod. But they're not the ones who invited us to the parliament. It was Werner Schulz, a German dissident, who invited us. He did not wear a suit – he walked around in jeans.

'Thank you for your fight,' you will say, you will shake our hands and smile compassionately. Today you listen to us, and tomorrow you will talk to the Kremlin that imprisoned us. You will talk as if they are not thieves and murderers but the Russian State. Maybe an unpleasant one but still legitimate. Businesslike, serious Brussels. On Monday – an audience with disabled activists; on Tuesday – a conference on climate change; on Wednesday – negotiations with dictators.

deeply concerned

We are here to show that Russia is not Putin, Russia is us too. We want to have fair elections, we want to be friends with Europe and we do not want to live behind the Iron Curtain. The less Europe knows about how Russians live and the more Russians are left alone with propaganda, the worse it will be for everyone.

We need to talk about crimes so that they do not remain in the dark. The more torture and atrocities happen in the dark, the more terrible the people coming out of this darkness will be. People who have lived in a dictatorship for years, who have been exposed to the poison of propaganda for years, will show you hell on earth when they get their hands on weapons.

iron curtain

'Believe in a free future,' says Paul McCartney, and asks us to pass these words on to the young people in Russia. We promise to do so.

When Sir Paul's handwritten letter landed on the judge's desk in Berezniki calling for my release from prison, I liked the look on her face. 'File it,' she said, as if nothing had happened.

As we stand in Sir Paul's studio, 'boards of shame' are being erected in occupied Crimea. They are stands with photos of traitors of the homeland. 'Agents of Western influence' says one of them. Our photos are in the bottom right corner. Eight years later, at the start of the full-scale war, all the people in the pictures will be pushed out of the country, thrown behind bars, or killed.

a free future?

Putin does not stop at Crimea. Taking advantage of the fact that a new government has yet to be elected in Kyiv, Putin hastily tries to tear Ukraine apart, to take away the entire eastern region – Luhansk and Donetsk in the Donbass.

The same Igor 'Strelkov' Girkin commands a pro-Russian parade.

> *'The question is to secure the rights and interests of Russian and Russian-speaking citizens in south-eastern Ukraine. I would like to remind you, using the terminology of tsarist days, that this is Novorossiya.'*
> – Vladimir Putin, 17 April 2014

On the same day that Putin is playing Tsar, Donetsk residents come out to a protest rally – 'Prayer for Ukraine'.

On the same day, the West seats Russian and Ukrainian representatives down at the negotiating table in Geneva.

Foreign Minister Lavrov doesn't want to go but agrees after the West threatens to impose an oil embargo on Russia.

don't mention the war

'Victory for Russian diplomacy', they call the agreement made in Geneva.

No mention of the annexation. No word on the withdrawal of the Russian FSB, army intelligence and the special forces.

Seven hours later, the parties sign a resolution that doesn't guarantee the return of Crimea or peace in Donbass. In a week, Russia will send troops to 'exercise' on the Russian-Ukrainian border.

vanity fair

We fly to Washington, DC. Downtown is filled with people in evening dress. There are lunches and brunches everywhere, sunshine, American aristocracy, officers, CNN hosts walking around the garden and eating little burgers, a red carpet in a hotel, long dresses we call curtains, a glass of champagne in every hand. The essence of luxury. Passport checks at the entrance.

We will meet senators the next day. Our meeting is organized by Bill Browder, the billionaire who traded his business for a war with Putin when a Russian prison killed his lawyer, Sergei Magnitsky.

magnitsky's list

Magnitsky uncovered the biggest theft from the Russian budget, a criminal case was opened against him, they tortured him to death in a prison.

After his death, the criminal trial continued. Against the will of the relatives and common sense. A man in a robe read the verdict to an empty cage. A cage in which a living person had recently stood.

empty cage

Neither Magnitsky's death nor the fraud will be investigated. But Browder achieves sanctions. 'The Magnitsky List' is the first sanctions list against Russian officials and judges. And it's an example for us.

We spend half the night making a list of people to sanction. Peter runs around the hotel at night looking for a printer.

The meeting with US senators and congressmen is in the morning. I am desperate for sleep. On the way there's a Ukrainian demonstration. Capitol Hill. A reception for us in an office and posing for a picture. Senators say the word 'pussy' in a meeting room called 'international relations'. To us, 'hill' sounds like 'hell'.

capital hell

Today is the 6th of May. On this day, back in 2012, people marched at the biggest anti-Putin demonstration ever. Senators study the faces of the Russian judges, on our list, who sent protesters behind bars. I want them to know – millions of people across Russia did not choose this power.

We demand sanctions.

A serious room with a round table. Massive red curtains. Red carpet. Red armchairs. My eyes catch sight of a huge mirror in a giant gold frame. I look at myself in it and think about my life in Russia. Beatings, Cossacks, Zelenka, cops – what a huge difference between all that and the girl in the suit and glasses looking back at me.

girl in the reflection

We have lunch with some Chinese dissidents. The restaurant is full of politicians and lobbyists in suits. The dissidents show us their multi-page report on Chinese prisons.

They tell us: 'We have many cases where prisoners are killed to be harvested for organs,' and ask, 'What problems do you have?'

At this moment it seems like we don't have any.

green light / red light

I spent my two previous birthdays behind bars. In 2012, a helicopter flew over the Moscow pre-trial detention centre all evening. On it was a red light, and I sat in my cell and looked out of the window as the light made circles in the sky. At midnight, fireworks suddenly went off and the helicopter started flying faster, like a frightened insect. For some reason it gave me a real sense of celebration.

In 2013, in the distant city of Berezniki, in penal colony no. 28, I was sitting in the isolation ward of the medical unit. After a hunger strike, I was alone with a padlock on the door. From my small room I had a view of the old wall of the tuberculosis unit. Girls waved and smiled at me from its windows. For some of them, sick with a serious strain of TB, the hospital will be the last place they see. Stacks of old boards were piled in the courtyard; velvet tracksuits were drying on clothes lines.

It was hot and quiet. I was called into the visiting room. I sat with friends and drank black tea from plastic bottles. They were showing me pictures from an exhibition by the artist Slonov. One was with a green man and rifle. The exhibition was banned.

Now, on this birthday in 2014, there are many more green men with rifles and they are guns for hire.

For this birthday there are no prison bars – there is music and celebration. We are celebrating in the same place where we rehearsed 'Punk Prayer'. We are discussing the new reality of Russia. Of the last three years, this birthday is the hardest.

3.

Russian Spring

– So, how is it on the outside?

I'm sitting on the outdoor terrace of a café. People walk by. They're strolling and smiling. The summer sun is shining. Street musicians play songs, some of which I grew up to. The Arbat is a pedestrian street, but I'm not far from the metro and I can hear cars driving by, the sound of cars and songs mix in one ear, and I hold my phone to the other and answer:

– It's not going so well, to be honest.
– Why?

call from the colony

A prisoner is given fifteen minutes to make a call.

– What can I tell you? Not so well because they annexed Crimea, because they started a war, not so well because they now beat us up. Not so well because I just got back from Norway and the prisons are idyllic there, and the more I saw of it, the more I realized that it'll never be like that with us, that's just how it is.
– Come on, it's great. We got Crimea back!

This is Olya – the friend from my penal colony. Another 'political girl'. Olya, a member of Limonov's National Bolshevik Party. Now back in prison for fighting back against

Nashi members who attacked her outside the Tagansky District Court. One lot came to the court where Limonov's trial was with eggs and tomatoes, the other lot with rubber-bullet guns. Olya was one of the other lot. Several years on the federal wanted list. She went to church for a christening. Olya – Orthodox. Arrested on her way out of church. Three and a half years.

– What're you talking about? It's the beginning of the end, it's just not fair, I say.

I'm on my third cigarette. 'I built a bathroom in the penal colony,' she replies. People continue to pass by, musicians play, cars go by.

who are we, russia?

The peaceful collapse of the unpeaceful USSR was a chance for Russia, which retained its vast territory, to become part of the European world.

Putin inherited a country that was only ten years old. Millions of Soviet people suddenly became Russians. They didn't even understand what that meant. And while the former national republics had a clear identity, Russia didn't.

If we are no longer the Soviet Union, then who are we?

we are not pitied

Putin is unleashing war in eastern Ukraine. The Kremlin calls the war 'Russian Spring'. Propaganda presents it as a national idea – the birth of a new, genuine Russia.

Finally, for the first time in our lives, Russia can do something. There's no shame. We are no longer to be pitied.

we are great

The same scenario: pro-Russian feeling intensifies. Lobbying agencies and pro-Russian organizations, created by Russian special services, are activated and 'referendums' are organized.

Two Ukrainian cities, Donetsk and Luhansk, have now been renamed Donetsk People's Republic (DPR) and Luhansk People's Republic (LPR), carving them out for Russian occupation.

'self-proclaimed republics'

At 'referendums', people are asked whether they are 'for' or 'against' independence from Ukraine. There is no 'independence from Ukraine', those who vote 'for' want to be in Russia. Not the Russia that currently exists but the Russia of the past – the USSR. They want to revisit the wonderful past, where everyone was together and defeated the fascists. Propaganda allows them to be 'together', and, by the way, there are still 'fascists' around – they haven't gone anywhere, it turns out they've never been completely defeated.

fascists, by the way

Donetsk, a city of millions, is half empty. People are fleeing. From occupation, from poverty and isolation, from Russia.

They are leaving their homes, their businesses, their jobs. Those who remain are getting used to war, expecting they are about to be allowed entry into the 'Russian world' they were promised, not realizing that they are already living in it.

At the same time, the Moscow curators of the Donbass are cynically discussing 'their' region.

> – *Sash, tell me, what are people living on in your city? Are people working? Is anything functioning– factories etc.?*
> – *Not much is functioning.*
> – *Not much, huh?*
> – *Every day less and less.*
> – *So everything is falling apart bit by bit, right? Soon it'll be a total humanitarian catastrophe, right?*
> – *Absolutely true.*
> – *So it's just going be one big refugee camp, right?*
> – *Yeah.*
>
> – phone intercept of a conversation between Surkov and Borodai

The 'republics' are curated by Putin's legendary aide Vladislav Surkov.

A grey cardinal, the Kremlin's ideologue, devil's advocate or simply a Moscow curator, Surkov is a rare official with lively but incredibly cynical eyes. Black hair, peppered with grey, expensive suits, luxury cars and friendships with creatives.

For Putin he invents the ruling party 'United Russia'. He also creates 'Nashi' – 'activists for Putin'. They are dispatched to disrupt opposition rallies.

> *'Exporting chaos is not a new thing. All empires do it.'*
>
> – Vladislav Surkov

exporting chaos

The Kremlin makes Muscovite Alexander Borodai prime minister of the DPR, and Muscovite Strelkov becomes the DPR's defence minister.

They have been friends since their youth. Both participated in the war in Chechnya, both were reporters for the newspaper *Zavtra*.

Both work for the Orthodox oligarch Malofeev. Both were involved in the 'Gifts of the Magi'. While Strelkov wass guarding the Gifts, Borodai was doing PR for the annexation.

donetsk field of experiments

'We did warn not to fly "in our sky",' writes Girkin on his page. And then deletes the message an hour and a half later.

On 17 July, a passenger plane, Boeing MH17, is shot down from occupied territory. On board, 298 people. Flying from Amsterdam to Kuala Lumpur. No one survives.

The missile hits the nose of the aircraft. People die in the air and the dead fall into a field.

The plane didn't crash, it didn't 'break apart', as the Russian news will say – it was shot down from the ground. By a surface-to-air missile system, 'Buk', donated by Putin.

Propaganda calls the place where it happened 'eastern Ukraine'; the term 'Novorossiya' is forgotten for the evening.

> *'If it really is a passenger airliner, it is not us who did it.'*
> – Alexander Borodai

'buk' complex

The Buk anti-aircraft missile system is being transported back to Russia. Overnight.

Russian propaganda is approving ten parallel versions of who shot the Boeing down. Putin blames Ukraine for the disaster. This is typical of the Russian authorities – they wash their hands.

To me, it's clear that the Boeing was shot down by the Russian army. The Buk originated from Kursk, together with the crew of the 53rd anti-aircraft missile brigade.

Responsibility for the murder of nearly 300 innocent people lies with the supreme commander of the Russian army, Putin.

Only after eight years will the court at The Hague make a decision.

Strelkov will be found guilty of killing 298 people. He will be put on the international wanted list. They won't dare find Putin guilty.

crucified boy

Over the summer, Ukrainians retake most of the occupied territories and surround the remaining ones.

In Russia, on the main state-run channel, the evening news carries a story: a brown-eyed blonde newscaster tells us that the Ukrainians, having returned to Slavyansk in the Donbass, crucified a small boy. Almost immediately it becomes clear that this is fake. But many people, having heard on television about the execution of a child by 'Ukrainian Nazis', will sign up to volunteer for the 'militia'.

festival of dangerous ideas

August 2014. Sydney Opera House. We are speaking at the Festival of Dangerous Ideas.

We call on Australia not to invite Putin to the G20 summit in November. We also say that if the summit aims to fight corruption, it would be more appropriate to invite Alexei Navalny.

mediazona

September 2014. We are opening a media outlet in Russia. It's called Mediazona. Journalists who were fired for refusing to write about the annexation of Crimea as an accession come to work here.

Mediazona's office is a brick house that looks like a garage. It's located at a winery, a centre of contemporary art. We go to Ikea at night to buy furniture.

The opening is at the Guelman Gallery; in a few months the gallery will be shut down after exhibiting Ukrainian artists. I'm printing out huge letters and sticking them on the wall. Mediazona. Nadya invites a photographer. We order pastries.

Mediazona will write about violence in penal colonies, police stations and the courts. Because the real Russia is in the courts and in prison.

institute of politics

They ask us to give a lecture at Harvard. The students tell us they don't want lectures. Students want stories. We have a lot of stories. Here's another one.

A huge hall full of people. The plan is to speak, answer questions and go to a dinner that the students have prepared for us.

The first part goes according to plan, we move on to questions. A guy in the balcony takes the microphone and says: 'I'm here illegally.'

bouquet for the conductor

It turns out that recently the conductor Vladimir Spivakov, who supported Putin in 2014, was invited to perform at Harvard.

This guy from the balcony came to the concert with two bouquets, which were confiscated at the entrance – the flowers were yellow and blue.

After the concert, he came on stage and said to the conductor, 'You make a habit of being silent – silent when Khodorkovsky was imprisoned, silent when Navalny was tried, silent when people were shot on the Maidan, but I'm insanely glad that you've now found the strength to support the occupation and annexation of Crimea!'

Spivakov jumped up, hissed and was one step away from hitting him. The audience booed the activist. The Harvard guard twisted him round – the audience applauded.

bravo

Harvard sued the guy. The court banned him from campus. But he knew the back routes. He ended up on the balcony and said, 'I know they'll arrest me.'

– What police? What arrests? Come to the students'
dinner with us.

We meet on the stairs. Walk towards dinner. Several cops
surround us, handcuff him and take him away. They arrest him
at the exit. So no one witnesses it. Dinner is set up in a room.

– We have to get the guy out, Nadya says to the
students. This is Pussy Riot after all.

We take plates, put all of the food onto them, and set off for
the police station.

The evening streets. People walking with plates. That's us.
Russians, Ukrainians and a high-school student, Ariella. Honours students had refused to come with us.

dinner at the police station

No one wants to let us into the station. I ring all the bells at
once. The door opens. But they still do not let the guy out.

– My dad's a lawyer, says Ariella.
– Call him!

At midnight, her dad is already in his pyjamas. But he comes
when he hears that Pussy Riot are at the station. Release at 4
a.m. It's a super-late dinner.

The next day we met with the university administration.
'How can it happen,' we asked, 'that the only person who
came out to protest against Spivakov ended up behind bars?'
They couldn't find an answer.

a topol is not afraid of sanctions

After the annexation and the war, the West excludes Russia from the G8. They are fighting Putin's regime with sanctions.

Propaganda paints the sanctions against Russian officials as a new Western attack. Against the whole of Russia, against every Russian.

In the starter pack of propaganda merch, T-shirts with pictures of missiles and nuclear warheads with the slogans 'A Topol is not afraid of sanctions' and 'Don't make my Iskander laugh' are displayed on market stalls across the country.

enemy cheese

Putin is banning the import of Western products into Russia. He calls it counter-sanctions. Russians will be banned from eating French cheese and Norwegian salmon. And they explain that it's all because of Western sanctions. Many people will believe it.

While ordinary people aren't allowed to eat enemy cheese, the procurement department for the presidential administration is bursting with forbidden delicacies.

There are jokes and memes about 'contraband', which now means Italian cheeses and Spanish jamón. 'Belarusian Parmesan' appears on the shelves as a substitute.

import substitution

The Kremlin announces import substitution – a trend towards isolationism.

'Import substitution' is becoming a popular term. Billions of dollars of Russian budget funds spent by enterprising officials to create copies of foreign goods, which in reality amount to new labels being stuck on goods bought through AliExpress – domestic know-how.

Cheese that has been illegally imported or stockpiled is confiscated. A year later, by Putin's decree, it will be bulldozed. Rusty diggers will crush edible, unspoilt products.

Poverty-stricken pensioners will look on sadly at the 'war on Parmesan'.

just like in russia

– Come on! Come on, hurry up, run! I shout in Russian
   to the three dazed Danes.

October 2014. I and a team of Danish journalists have arrived back in Nizhny Novgorod. To my penal colony no. 2. The gates are open, there are no guards – they haven't been informed we are coming. After a few seconds, we run out of the car with bags groaning with food and dive into the colony's internal courtyard.

– Just like in a movie! say the Danes.
– Just like in Russia, I reply.

I've come to testify against those who attacked us with Zelenka earlier in the year.

How could you be in the city where you went to prison and not visit it? Impossible. So I stand in front of the barred window and ask the guards to pass on the food and arrange a visit. I ask for a visit with Yuliya, one of the three girls who revealed the truth about the colony when I was there.

Yuliya tells me what has happened at the colony in the last ten months since I got out. I learn how the prison guards bullied my friends, how they trampled on the food I gave them, how books disappeared. Some of this I already know, some of it I'm hearing for the first time. I'm struck by the lack of anger in the voice of a woman who has nothing. A woman whose food was taken away and trampled just because it came from me, a woman with whom nobody was allowed to communicate, or even to approach.

- I'm kind of like an enemy of the people to them, she says, and laughs.
- I am too, I reply, and we laugh together.
- It's worse for you! she objects. You have thousands of them out there. I only have these guys – she nods at the prison guards – we've got used to each other.

punks in parliament

The entrance to the UK Parliament has X-ray machines like an airport. There's also a garden with old trees, but none of that matters because we're late and don't know where to print out statistics of deaths in Russian prisons.

The hall where the hearing is taking place is filled with people: politicians, journalists, even Lords. Half of them are looking at Twitter and the other half are not always successfully fighting sleep. Until this moment we had never seen a living Lord.

- Thank you for inviting punks to the Parliament, Nadya begins, and the hall instantly wakes up and laughs.
- Magnitsky wasn't the first to die in prison. Prisoners are dying. There're more than 1,200 prisons in our

country. Prison doctors don't have access to medicines and they don't want to treat prisoners. Even the terminally ill aren't released to die at home. As long as Putin is in power, nothing will change. Human life has no value in Russia. Is it not like that here?

We move on to talk about migrants. Then about Assange. General bewilderment slips across the faces of the politicians.

prayer for political prisoners

In Cambridge they call us to church. The church, like the whole university, is surrounded by gardens. It's romantic. Vladimir Bukovsky lives here, a Soviet dissident whose life would make a great road movie of prisons.

We've come to the service just to listen. We sit quietly in the pew. On the ceiling, thin stone stems blossom into stone flowers. The priest begins the prayer:

– Today we pray for prisoners of conscience, political prisoners who are behind bars all over the world.

Maybe it's because this vaulted Gothic beauty was not blown up by the Bolsheviks and not rebuilt by bandits. Or maybe it's because of the priest, who prays to God instead of serving the KGB. Or both.

I want to cry. Later. At the time, I just listen. Then I see this church as a foreign place in an alternative reality. I want to cry because the Church that put us in jail didn't stop at repression through imprisonment. Russian priests pour holy water on Russian missiles while real Christians in Russia pray in their kitchens for political prisoners.

i can't breathe

My plane lands and I call a taxi. Moscow. It's cold. So cold you want the ground to swallow you up. I'm home.

- You must be tired, the driver asks me gently. We're stuck in traffic and he wants to talk to me to stay awake.
- Yes.
- What do you do?
- Russian prisons, mostly.
- What?

That's when I start laughing. How do you explain it in a nutshell?

The escort guard taught me to talk about myself in just a few words. While leading you through the colony to work, they will definitely ask you something. And you have to answer briefly. Quickly. And simply.

- I was imprisoned for a political song. Now I defend prisoners' rights.

Your response should be no longer than a tweet. Answers are often stronger than statistics.

Statistics in modern Russia say that President Putin is supported by 84 per cent of the Russians. The rating went up after the annexation of Crimea.

in the middle of a compulsory war

- What do you think about Crimea? I ask the driver.
- I usually holiday in Turkey. But I don't have time this year. I've got to work.
- No, my question is about Putin: was he right to annex Crimea?
- Who the hell knows?

We drive up to Victory Park, a memorial complex built in honour of Soviet victory in the Second World War. Tanks, cold stone sculptures of Soviet soldiers. State workers are brought here for pro-Putin demonstrations.

To the last rally under the slogan 'Peace in Ukraine', they brought children. Ukrainian children, refugees from the occupied Donbass. They're lined up, given carnations and made to recite poems about parents who were killed by fascist bombs. The fascists in these poems were soldiers of the Ukrainian army.

The largest news agency in Russia, RIA, regularly compares Ukraine with Hitler's Germany. Dozens of news agencies do.

victory park

- I don't listen to the news, says the driver. There's only war. For as long as I can remember we have been at war: Chechnya, Georgia, now Ukraine.

For Putin, it is easier to rule in war than in peace, so war has become compulsory. It is tiresome to have to account for corruption, police brutality, dysfunctional education and healthcare. Domestic policy is easier when it simply divides the world into allies and enemies:

Have food prices gone up? – Western sanctions.

Low doctors' salaries? – thank America.

The main method of Putin's foreign policy is expansion. And the main language is the language of the Cold War. The world has also learned that language:

– Are you from Russia? strangers ask me abroad.
– Yes.
– Why is your country attacking Ukraine?
– It's not the country that's attacking. It's the president we didn't elect.
– Do they really ask you that??? My taxi driver is puzzled.

what do you really do?

Doctors are protesting after mass job cuts in Moscow hospitals. 'Our city is sick, its authorities are sick.' Neither the media nor the authorities react. The Russian news feeds are full of pictures of Putin visiting an interactive exhibition of Russian tsars, against a background of regular attacks by 'patriots' on 'traitors'. Their war exists separately from the real problems of the real people who live in Russia.

– So what do you really do? the taxi driver continues as we pull up to the house.
– Prisons. Prisoners' rights. Well, and a little bit of politics.

He looks at me in disbelief. He looks at me with no clue as to what I'm about, what this is all about. I'm home.

icy fairy tale

Night. I'm going to the 24-hour sports store for hot ice and warm trousers. Tomorrow is the rally. An unauthorized protest in front of the Kremlin and the coldest night of the year, according to the forecast. We need to prepare.

The eve of New Year's Eve. 30 December.

navalny's brother

The Kremlin has passed a sentence on Navalny's brother. They jailed a man for three years, just for the fact that he, Oleg, is the brother of the country's main opponent. The verdict was handed down suddenly, especially for New Year.

Despite the cold and the general hopelessness, people still go out to protest on Revolution Square near the Kremlin. The crowd are separated, pushed back, people are seized, packed into avtozaks and taken to police stations.

While people are being dispersed by OMON riot police, others nearby are rushing home with gifts.

After a couple of hours, everyone who hasn't been taken away in an avtozak moves off to drink in bars. The police cordon is removed from the square.

the coldest night

There's a bauble at the edge of the square – a giant Christmas decoration. A huge bauble. Ten kilometres of LED lights.

I go into the bauble. There's an entrance and exit at the sides. Two friends are already there. None of us wants to leave.

It's absolutely freezing. Minus 25 or less. Bottled water turns to ice in ten minutes. We take selfies and post them on social media. Other people appear. Peter arrives. People bring us bread and hot food. We take it in turns to do push-ups. First one at a time, then two, then three. To stay warm. Journalists start writing about us.

we're in a bauble

Cops are surrounding the bauble. They walk around it, freezing. When they get very cold, they go to the avtozak to warm up.

We run for tea in a Japanese café. We make posters: 'While Navalny's brother is in jail we are in the bauble.' We take turns holding them.

No, none of us expect Navalny's brother to be released just because ten freaks decide to spend the coldest night of the year in a bauble. But we stay there anyway.

senseless and merciless

so this is freedom. russia unleashed a war, the army shot down a boeing, bags on heads, zelenka in the eyes, what is your favourite band? heroes never die, why are you detaining us?

radioactive ashes, ripped-open stomachs, get out of town you dirty whores, russian spring, fireworks near the penal colony, fifth column, we are great, shot in the heart, thank you for your fight, can I take a selfie with you? our country's tanks, never again, traitors to the motherland, prisoners of conscience, the region of barbed wire, we will bring it all back, peace march, cargo 200, how much are you paid? 86 per cent, fascists by the way, will russia be free? blinding light bulbs, maria, what happened to your eyebrows? i can't breathe, the word war is not just a word but a new type of reality.

cold

Hot ice is a great thing. You get a bag, put it on yourself and it's warm. I just love myself for buying those bags.

I'll remember this night as the best night of the year. The absolute best.

At 6 a.m. our icy fairy tale is packed into two avtozaks. Two avtozaks for a few frozen people. We're glad we didn't leave. Through the bars of the avtozak's window I look out at the stone walls of the Kremlin. And it is the most honest view.

4.

Political Girl

1988, the height of Perestroika. In a maternity hospital on the Arbat, my mum, Natasha, learns that she's had a baby girl. Me. There's no way to find out a baby's gender before birth, so there are two baby-grows in the wardrobe – pink and blue.

I was born in the Soviet Union, a country that was built over seventy years. By the time I arrive, it is on the verge of collapse. Everyone can feel it. People start talking about repression and the mistakes the USSR has made. Government sessions are no longer meetings of identical, unanimous, half-dead men. The whole country listens to radio broadcasts of these meetings.

While Mum is on maternity leave, the Soviet Union ceases to exist.

warm bread

I don't go to kindergarten. My grandmother looks after me. She dyes her hair with henna and wears a blue dress. We go to the spring for water and to the bread factory for warm bread. My grandmother is a baker by profession. She started out in a regular bakery, then became head of the baking department, and then I came along.

When guests come, Grandma bakes pies with cabbage and potatoes. I like to climb trees – all of them, but especially tall and difficult ones.

candy candy

1995. I'm seven, and for the past four years I've lived in a new country – Russia. There are privatization auctions, there's a war in Chechnya, and they're rebuilding the Cathedral of Christ the Saviour, blown up by Stalin – but I don't know any of this yet.

I'm sitting in the living room, waiting for my favourite cartoon, 'Candy Candy', to begin. Instead, there's breaking news, they're announcing that journalist Vladislav Listyev has been murdered. I have no idea who he is and am upset that my cartoon isn't on. But I understand that something important has happened, people seem bewildered, there is tense music, and they're talking about an investigation.

My first school is a boarding school. Yellow walls. A large football field with birch trees along the edge.

I'm there because Mum is raising me alone and she works, so she can't pick me up during the day.

cola in bottles

A few times, our school receives humanitarian aid from the Americans. That's exactly what they call it, 'humanitarian aid'. I don't understand why they're helping us. We seem to have everything we need. A big lorry pulls up to the entrance and they unload crates, from these crates they hand out Coca-Cola in glass bottles.

I'm friends with boys and with trees. I play on the football field, while I tell the birches everything I can't tell my friends or mum. If someone offends me, I tell the birch tree, hug it and cry. The birches have names that I've given them.

After school, I'm taken to swimming lessons. My grandma is diagnosed with cancer. I give myself tasks – forty laps and the cancer will go away. I swim and swim. But the cancer doesn't go away. My grandmother dies as I finish primary school. On New Year's Eve.

home economics lessons

The year 2000. I'm twelve. The 21st century has begun. A young KGB officer, Putin, comes to power. The *Kursk* nuclear submarine sinks to the depths.

I'm in secondary school. In the fifth grade we start having home economics lessons. Boys and girls are separated for the first time. We girls are made to sew oven gloves. Oven gloves for hot dishes. The boys are sent to hammer in nails. And make stools. I don't understand why this is happening, what for.

Why we need to read books – I understand. Why we need to sew oven gloves – no idea.

– Why oven gloves?
– Not your concern.

They're telling us that a woman's place is in the kitchen. A kitchen with oven gloves. I start getting bad grades.

a woman's place – the kitchen?

2002. I'm fourteen. Terrorist attacks shake Moscow, Russia joins the G20, and Russian group t.A.T.u. is making waves in the West.

Eighth grade. I'm transferred from my beloved yellow

boarding school to a mathematics gymnasium. Mum wants me to have a good education. She graduated from school with a gold medal. She graduated from Moscow State University with honours. Saving on everything wherever possible, Mum hires tutors – teachers from the gymnasium – to get me admitted to their school. But I don't want to go.

To get to the gymnasium I have to take the metro. Cold. Boring. No friends. The first two lessons I simply sleep. The thing I like most of all about this gymnasium is watching the fish in the cafeteria aquarium. My only friend is Malka Genrikhovna, an elderly Jewish woman who is my French teacher. I skip three out of four classes. Instead, I listen to rap and t.A.T.u. behind the garages with a girlfriend from my old boarding school.

My mum is asked to withdraw me from school.

yellow pages

I don't want to go to school anymore, I hear that you can get home-schooled through a psychiatrist. In the 90s and early 2000s, every home had a 'Yellow Pages' directory. A massive book with thin yellow pages listing phone numbers and addresses for everything imaginable. I find the address of a psychiatrist.

- I want to be home-schooled.
- You can only get home-schooled if you have a diagnosis.
- Then give me a diagnosis.
- We can only diagnose you in a mental hospital.
- Then admit me to a mental hospital.

mental hospital no. 6

Late autumn, an ambulance drives down Leninsky Prospekt. I count the meaningless white stripes on the window, hum 'Pure Morning' by Placebo under my breath, and dream about how I'll proudly tell people that I was in a mental hospital. For real.

Every door behind you is locked with a key that looks like a window handle. It's as if they've ripped off all the door handles and now carry them round in their white coats.

For the first few days in the admission ward, I turn all the mattresses. They have messages from previous girls: 'Hang in there', 'I want to go home', and something about mum. On one mattress, there's a diagram of the nine circles of hell, meticulously outlined several times with blue ink.

something about mum

In the admission ward, you stay for a week. As it comes to an end, one evening, they bring another girl into our room. Her name is Lisa. She has pale skin, white hair and a cautious expression. She looks like a fox.

Her story is very different from the others.

She tells it indifferently, detached, as if it didn't happen to her. Lisa woke up one morning and took several strips of sleeping pills. Her hands tremble as if she just pulled them out of a bucket full of hatred, and now she's looking at them, unable to understand what happened. She tells me how she once stabbed a classmate with a biro for no apparent reason, how she used to go to church, and how now she knows nothing. Neither about herself, nor about the world around her. We become friends because I don't know either.

third acute

I'm transferred to the third acute department in a different building. When they move you, the orderlies walk close to you, one on either side. Some patients are tied to the orderlies by the wrist.

The metal door opens with a beep sound. The whole ward is a long corridor with colourless walls. They put a gown on you, take your belongings and lead you to the classroom. The desks are arranged in three rows, and there are worn-out couches along the walls. A care worker does the register. It's almost like a regular school. Except the girls don't listen attentively. They are led by the hand walking in circles or lie half-asleep on couches. When you listen to their conversations, they fall apart mid-sentence. When you look in their eyes, they're either dull or unnaturally bright. I'm not prescribed any medication for a week.

Every day the doctor asks how I'm feeling. Only later will I realize how lucky I am. Usually the doctor speaks to you once upon admission, then gives you unidentified pills for several months and, eventually, discharges you. My doctor is a young trainee, attentive and conscientious. We sit opposite one another in the hallway at tables usually used for eating. The dim sunlight barely filters through the curtains, he asks some questions and writes things down; it seems like he's following a plan. And I'm interested in how this plan looks. After another two weeks, he prescribes treatment.

aminazine

The treatment room is just big enough for a table and a couch, and it always seems to be in semi-darkness. They prescribe me

Aminazine injections. After the first injection, I step into the corridor and the orderlies move slowly – so slowly that I don't want to watch them and listen to them. I want them to grow into the floor, turn into stone and close their eyes. I could never have imagined that one shot could drain the will to live out of you so quickly, replacing it with nothing. Like the air you breathe is one mass of dust and you are an old, forgotten sack, dumped in the corner.

For several days, I move by holding onto the wall from the bed to the couch, from the classroom to the ward.

Aminazine is a tranquillizer. It's usually given in tablet form. Small white ones and large red ones. It's also administered by injection, in the event of serious disobedience. I'll never be able to say that those injections were just treatment. Before them, I couldn't imagine that medication could change something inside you. Change your perception of the world, terrify you so much that you're ready to do anything, absolutely anything, everything-everything, that you're told to do, to stop them injecting you like that ever again. When, through the constant murky fog of sleep, I try to think, all the thoughts and feelings that come to me seem to be heavily shaded in grey: dark grey, light grey – the only thing I can do is think about the shades of this grey indifference, mixed with inexplicable inner pain.

shades of indifference

If you catch a cold, you end up in an isolation room. It's small with two beds and a narrow gap between them leading to the window. I think that if there's a loneliness that can squeeze you like a lemon until only toxic acid remains, it's this loneliness created by the isolation room. I spend entire days staring out of the window. No one walks through the hospital yard. In the evening, the orange streetlights come on, I'm not even allowed to eat with the others. I write letters – long ones, dozens of pages, in diagonal handwriting – and bury myself in books. For the first time, I read Bulgakov's *The Master and Margarita*.

The window in the isolation room has a different kind of grille, it's a fine metal mesh. When I have no strength left to read or write, I examine the tiny holes in the mesh, mentally unravel it into thin wires and, using sheets, climb out of the window.

video rental

2005. In Russia, Putin's glamour blooms – oil prices are rising, and so is the standard of living. No more queuing for groceries. The Kremlin creates a pro-Putin youth movement called 'Nashi', professional provocateurs for fighting the opposition. The only oligarch who defies Putin, Mikhail Khodorkovsky, gets fourteen years in prison.

I get a job at a video-rental store, I don't have enough money otherwise to buy CDs. I hand out flyers at the metro, for just a couple of dollars an hour, but for this I get a card. It allows me to rent video tapes at a discount. I watch films.

Lars von Trier. Kubrick. *Bonnie and Clyde* – thirty times. *The Piano Teacher* – fifteen times. *Trainspotting, Eyes Wide Shut, Requiem for a Dream, Lost Highway, Show Me Love*. I fall in love with cinema. Life starts to feel like a movie.

I think, 'Would this phrase of mine make a great line in a movie?' Words from classmates, teachers' remarks – they all sound like lines from an unmade film. Even textbook paragraphs I assess – how would they sound in a movie?

white-collars and street comrades

My last school is in Krylatskoye District, where the first president of Russia, Boris Yeltsin, lived.

I call my classmates 'white-collars'. For accuracy. At fifteen, everyone has already decided what they will be. Or their parents have decided for them. I don't want that. I want to live interestingly. To change the world. How, exactly, is unclear.

I go to the Arbat and meet punks. They play the guitar. I take a hat and collect money. This is called 'asking', from the English 'ask'. Punks and hippies – I call them street comrades – teach me a lot. They teach me that you can be different and not be bullied for it.

At school, we memorize Pushkin's poems; punks memorize songs by Egor Letov, Viktor Tsoi and Yanka Dyagileva. On the street they shout for 'changes'! – but at school no one demands changes. No one.

history lessons

To get from the metro to school, I must cross a square. A small square. On weekends, there's a market here. And on 9 May a 'festival' is held here. A celebration of Victory Day in the Great Patriotic War, as it is called in Russia. 'The Second World War' is used much less often. On this 'holiday', a truck with camouflage netting arrives. The truck's loading area is filled with green urns, in the urns are buckwheat with meat and sweet tea. Military music plays. A microphone is set up in the centre of the square, elderly war veterans are invited to speak.

At school, we are told to write essays for 9 May. We write

about how great our country is, we are a great nation that defeated fascism. We are not told about the Gulag, the execution squads or the repression of dissenters. Although we memorize poems of those executed by the authorities.

In my essay I write: 'A festival of hypocrisy. What victory are we celebrating if the "victors", the veterans, live in poverty? I don't understand why I should praise Stalin and his victory.' I get a bad grade.

big blues borscht

I leave home to join the hippies and punks. I live in the Hotel Ukraine. Some of these apartments were given to cultural figures for their contribution to promoting the USSR. One of the hippies, named Buratino, is the son of such a cultural figure. He turns his father's apartment, bequeathed by the regime, into a 'commune'. A 'commune' is a place where you can crash or stay the night for free.

We sing songs in the metro, and with the money we make we buy port wine. We listen to blues and cook borscht at night.

From the Hotel Ukraine, along Ukrainian Boulevard, I walk to my last classes of school. I want adventure and have no intention of enrolling anywhere.

hitchhiking

After leaving, I hitchhike south to the forest reserve of Utrish.

Hitchhiking is a test of endurance. You stand by the road with your thumb out. Cars pass by, cars don't stop. One hour, two, three, four. When a car finally stops, it isn't picking up the same person who stood by the road four hours ago.

I travel to Utrish – ten kilometres of ancient forest along the coast in the mountains. Junipers that are thousands of years old. Discarded grates that can be placed on stones to make a fire beneath. Food is cooked on these fires. Singing hippies. Someone threw away a book by Kant and I read it in a hammock.

Utrish translates as a 'rift'.

utrish

2007. I am eighteen years old. I return from the Utrish forest pregnant with Filipp. I take a test – two lines. I had never thought about having children before, had never dreamed of it – but now a person is going to be born. And he will teach me a lot.

- How many pregnancies have you had before? asks the nurse.
- None.
- How many abortions?
- None.
- Are you lying to me?

The maternity ward is on the outskirts of Moscow. It's the fourth or fifth hour of contractions. The pain is hellish. 'Why is this nurse so mean?' The thought spins in my head. More pain. Why doesn't she believe me? More pain. And then, as if on fast forward, a twisted blue-and-white cord. And the baby. Filipp.

I see the level of maternity benefits available, and the figures terrify me. I am a girl from Moscow with an apartment, a mother, and the father of my child has not abandoned me. I can't stop thinking about those who have none of this. The child allowance is just over 50 dollars a month. That wouldn't even cover nappies. I can't yet understand why things are this way, but I want to figure it out.

i want to figure it out

2009. Sergei Magnitsky, the lawyer who exposed massive corruption among state officials, dies from torture in prison. On the 31st of each month in Moscow, there's a Strategy-31 rally in defence of Article 31 of the constitution, which guarantees the freedom of assembly. Each month, the riot police detain the participants.

I no longer want to hand out flyers or work as a courier. I find a job as a peculiar kind of journalist. I don't write anything. I'm given a basic phone and sent to various events. My task is to remember or record what happens and dictate it over the phone. From my dictation, a news writer writes the news.

Russian troops capture 20 per cent of Georgian territories in three days. I am sent to a generals' press conference. I am sent to the opening of the largest 'cultural cluster', Vinzavod, and several exhibitions held there. It's like peeking into different lives. The event that stands out the most is the opening of the Marfo-Mariinsky Convent in central Moscow.

The church is fenced off. Entry is by pass only. There is a queue of pilgrims at the entrance who have come from another city. I have press accreditation: I am allowed in. Inside, there is row upon row of chairs, women and men dressed in expensive suits and dresses. At the pulpit, a priest. The priest and Moscow Mayor Luzhkov. Cameras line the walls with floodlights. I can't understand why it feels so disgusting, but I want to leave quickly. I remember everything and leave. I see how a huge two-metre-tall security guard at the entrance is dragging one of the elderly pilgrims by the scruff of her neck. She just wanted to see the opening.

- This is so unfair! I shout into the phone. She just wanted to see the new church.
- What else was going on there, Masha? Dictate it.
- Don't you get it? It isn't a church.

remember what happens

I like journalism, so I try for university. I go to see what an exam is like and accidentally pass it. In Moscow, there are only two universities where you can study on weekends. I have a young son and I need to pick him up from nursery. I'm taught by poets. I dream of working on catastrophes. Writing about wars, for example.

Between lectures, I read a news story: they want to cut down my favourite forest, Utrish. I jot down the addresses of two environmental organizations. The first organization tells me, 'We can't help you.' I head to Greenpeace.

- Hello, I'm Masha. They want to cut down my favourite forest. How can I stop this?
- Here are some petition forms. Collect 5,000 signatures against the logging and come back.

I write a post. I organize a meeting at the metro station. Three people come to it. We start gathering signatures. We explain why it's important to stop the deforestation of an area 1,500 km from Moscow. That no one knows about. More people come to the next meeting. Within a few weeks, I return to Greenpeace with 5,000 signatures.

— What's next?

— You can organize a protest.

pickets with a pushchair

To organize a mass protest, you need to get permission from the prefecture. I take the metro to the administrative building. With the pushchair up and down the stairs. At our pickets, there's hot tea, placards and hippies in multicoloured trousers. I'm one of them. I have a portable stove, a small metal camping kettle and good ground coffee. I adore coffee and have no money to spend on eight cups in a café. Hot tea is brought by anarchists from the 'Food Not Bombs' movement.

A young journalist from *Novaya Gazeta*, Nastya Baburova, comes along to one of the pickets, she writes an article about the forest. The next day, Nastya and her colleague, lawyer Stanislav Markelov, are murdered by neo-Nazis in central Moscow. He was killed for defending anti-fascists. And she was killed for writing about them.

I meet other people who care about the forest. Within six months, it is already a fully-fledged movement. Pickets in dozens of cities. It takes ten years. Ten years of pickets, petitions, signatures and acts of protest before the forest is designated a protected area where villas for officials' wives cannot be built.

You can achieve something if you find people who believe in the same things as you do. So does this mean I do politics?

hotel ukraine

The bass player – my friend from the boarding school – becomes a member of the art group 'Voina'. One evening she calls and asks if I can help them get onto the roof of the Hotel Ukraine.

'Okay. A roof is a roof. I can't say why over the phone. It's an action, I don't know what kind yet.'

I say that Buratino can open the roof for them.

On the eve of October Revolution Day, 'Voina' project a pirate skull and bones from the roof onto the White House, the Russian government building, with a green laser.

Later, they come to my protest. Nadya and Peter. They stand out from the crowd of colourful, relaxed hippies. They shout slogans near the metal fence surrounding the picket. They look like professionals, like activists from the cover of a magazine. They say they practise political art.

'Do you want to document an action?' one of them asks me.

garage near the uni

They live in a garage and I go to prepare for an action there. This will be the first action I've ever experienced. And the first one I'll document. I know nothing about performance art or contemporary art.

Nadya meets me at the bus stop. She's wearing a red chequered shirt, jeans, and has a bob haircut. Nadya doesn't say a word as we walk. They call the garage 'Palace'. It's a metal box no more than two metres wide. A bookshelf in the corner near the entrance. They steal food from the petrol station nearby. Around us – only forest. I come with a video camera.

I'm studying journalism taught by writers and poets and I'm an environmental activist who organizes pickets. At the pickets, no one talks about art, and in poetry seminars, no one talks about politics. But here, in the garage, they create political art, and I like the sound of it.

The curators of the exhibition 'Caution! Religion' have been charged with extremism. 'Voina' is planning an action at their trial.

caution! religion

The action involves an improvized group, 'Dick in the Ass', singing 'All Cops Are Bastards' in the courtroom.

First, the host announces the performance, and then the group, who look like ordinary people in the public gallery, suddenly jump onto their chairs, pull out a guitar and amplifier, and start to sing.

The police try to catch everyone, throwing them out one by one from the courtroom, waving their batons, but they can't get to anyone. One officer chases one of the group to the bus stop but eventually gives up.

He pretends to have done his job.

It all works out. No one notices the guitar or the amplifier smuggled through the metal detectors.

I like it.

acab

One of the Voina members, Vor, declares himself the undisputed leader. Machismo, a 'power vertical,' the suppression of any dissent. Voina splits into two factions.

One leaves for St. Petersburg.

The other stays in Moscow.

Here, Katya and Nadya form their own feminist punk group, Pussy Riot. With no leaders and no machismo. They record their first song in a children's playground. They look for members. Tasya and Vasya will film them.

Peter is behind the Moscow curtains.

Anonymous members come. In bright, colourful hats – balaclavas. Anyone can join.

Anyone can be pussy riot.

children's playground

2011, and I'm 23 years old. Putin announces that he's running for a third presidential term. The 'elections' are looming. This third term will be a point of no return, though I don't know it yet.

I'm sitting in my friend's kitchen, the bassist from Voina, now with Pussy Riot. I am listening to a Pussy Riot song. They're planning a new action. I say I'll join.

free pussy riot

Sasha becomes a close friend.

Sasha is from a small provincial town, Kemerovo. In the prosperous oil-rich 2000s, no one there is interested in politics. Sasha moves to Moscow. Against the backdrop of the stolen 2011 elections, everyone starts talking about protest.

Sasha sees our 'Punk Prayer'. State media desperately tries to paint us as blasphemers. He hears our words, and they resonate with him.

Sasha comes to the Tagansky court; inside – we're on trial;

outside – people are singing, dancing and inviting passers-by to a 'court festival'. A little girl is drawing with coloured chalk on the asphalt, she and Sasha draw a river – a river of freedom. They draw a circle around the police van and declare it an island, saying that if the cops step outside, they'll get their feet wet in the river.

'They're looking for you! Run!' someone shouts to Sasha, and he runs. He turns around and sees a crowd of police in grey uniform, followed by a crowd of journalists with cameras, and behind them, a crowd of activists chanting, 'Run!'

Sasha is detained for the first time in his life. Two people are already in the avtozak they throw him into. An Orthodox activist from the movement God's Will, and his victim, a female activist he slapped for supporting us. The two of them argue about God for a long time. She says God forgives everyone and everything, the Orthodox activist disagrees.

god forgives

– Masha, wake up! Wake up, Masha!

Where am I? Who am I? Morning. A covered balcony. How and when did I end up here? On the sofa on my friend's balcony.

Autumn 2015. The girl who is waking me up is Olya. She's just turned twenty-one. Black curls, a kind voice, holding a jam sandwich.

She dreamed of being a theatre actress. But then she became a cop. No joke. At nineteen she joined the police to investigate crimes and fight for justice. Like Debra Morgan from *Dexter*.

What she sees in reality is far from the 'justice' in the movies. They call her Barbie, extort money from migrants, threaten them with deportation, demand bribes, cheat on their wives.

2014. Putin annexes Crimea, and her 'colleagues' in uniform support him, seeing him as a 'real man'.

Three weeks before New Year's Eve, Olya resigns. 'Tomorrow, I'll clear out my locker and hand in my handcuffs.' She becomes an activist.

becoming an activist

February 2015. Boris Nemtsov, the leading voice against the war in Ukraine, is murdered in central Moscow, near the Kremlin. A shot to the chest. Ordered by Ramzan Kadyrov, the leader of the Russian republic Chechnya.

Russia and Ukraine sign the Minsk Agreements. Ukraine is forced to sign a document that legitimizes the Kremlin's puppets in the occupied territories.

Olya moves to Moscow. A city seen as a survival game by everyone who settles there. She has already met those continuing Nemtsov's work and carried out a protest of her own. She did it in the police uniform she'd worn to work only recently. An action against the 'law of sadists', which allows prison guards to use batons and electric shockers whenever they 'deem necessary', a law that legalizes torture.

And here, in this apartment, we're randomly meeting for the first time, she wakes me up and I'm crying in the kitchen.

I'm crying because I don't know what will happen next, because I don't know who I am, because I'm lost.

– Stay, I'll figure something out! I tell her.

And I take her to the apartment where it all began, where we recorded Pussy Riot's songs.

death to putin

Supporting one another is what saved us over those years. It saved us many times. It's like a painkiller. Yes, we were sort of pioneers – the first political prisoners in Putin's Russia. What kept us from losing our minds and giving up was that support. The support of those who, waking up in freedom, remembered those of us still in prison. It's as if countless beams of light extend from different points, into a cell or a barracks, to someone who is there now and must not give up. And that's how stars are born. Stars of conscience, preventing the country from collapsing.

While we were on trial, Ukrainians stood outside the Russian embassy in Kyiv every day. Now it's my turn.

Kyiv. Spring 2016. We go to the Russian embassy for a protest in support of Ukrainian political prisoners – Sentsov, Afanasiev, Kolchenko. It's organized by my friend Eva.

Olya and I put on balaclavas. Olya – a blue one; I – a white one. We stand in a line with Ukrainian activists.

The embassy windows are boarded up.

On the black metal fence, someone has written in white paint: 'Death to Putin'.

5.

Remember Means Fight

2016. Los Angeles. I meet Nadya for supper at the Mexican café. With us are nonbinary journalist Alli from Mediazona and the music producer who supported Pussy Riot and left Russia in disgrace, Sasha C. The TV is announcing the US election results. Between the main course and dessert, the oligarch Donald Trump is declared the winner.

The result doesn't come as a surprise. Maybe it's because I've lived a long time in Russia, where bad news always exceeds acceptable limits, and because I've met many apolitical people in the West.

Democracy is not handed down to people for ever by God but was fought for by those who lived before you. If you don't respect it and continue fighting, it can easily collapse.

democracy under threat

The American elections are the main drama series on Russian TV. We don't have our own elections so let's watch someone else's. The majority is with Trump – he mocks the left and reveres Putin. He is one of ours.

On the day of Trump's victory, the chief Russian propagandist, Margarita Simonyan, drives around Moscow with an American flag flying from her car window. 'They deserved it today,' she tweets.

After a year of touring with the Belarus Free Theatre, I am returning to Russia.

'Return Crimea to its home harbour' is already annoying people – the partial isolation of the country, sanctions, price hikes. People are often talking about banned salmon rather than greatness. And they joke about forbidden cheese.

nothing sacred

The hundred-year anniversary of the Russian revolution. The revolution which no one mentions. The state is afraid of the word 'revolution', spending huge sums on the promotion of the monarchy, teaching people that the tsar is a good thing.

It's the West who are talking about the anniversary of the October revolution. Hundreds of stories in the Western media. Russian propaganda is silent. The word 'revolution' cannot be allowed into the present. It's scary. Revolution is in the past. A long time ago.

remember means fight

Every year on this day we gather at Pushkin Square and walk along the boulevard.

On this day – 19 January – journalist Nastya Baburova and lawyer Stanislav Markelov were killed in the historic centre by neo-Nazis.

Crossed-out swastikas and rainbow flags, young anarchist human rights activists and musicians. They walk together to the place of the murder. And bring flowers.

The main slogan of this march is 'Remember means fight.'

anti-fascist march

The boulevard is covered with cops. They are randomly scattered near the metal detector through which the marchers must pass. At the same frame stands a woman with pieces of paper. She is counting how many people actually pass through – she is a 'white counter' – an alternative to propaganda, which regularly underestimates the number of participants.

I am not alone. The White Counter woman shouts to the police:

– Grab him, he is a provocateur
– Don't. He is with me, I answer.

My companion in the big black coat, Dima, is the founder of the God's Will movement, Orthodox activist Dmitry Enteo. He covers his face with his hood. He is embarrassed.

He used to attack this kind of march. And then he met me. And I said that if he does not walk peacefully with me along the boulevard, then I will not see him anymore. And he decided to come.

The woman looks at me for a few seconds and says, 'Masha.' It seems that this is all she can say from shock, but after waiting and thinking, she adds, 'Is it you?' It's me.

it's me //out of frame

After the march we go ice-diving. I dive into the icy water. And then I go on the first tour of my life. A tour of America. With the Riot Days show based on my book.

– Do you think we'll be able to perform in Russia? I ask
  in sunny Albuquerque.
– OF COURSE, YES! says Olya.

Performing in Russia is more difficult, but difficulties are cool. Throughout the spring, we ask friends and strangers, wherever possible, to host the Pussy Riot show.

'Mash, it's true, the book is great, the video is cool, but they'll shut us down.'

'Mash, the idea is super, but for some reason the director refused.'

'Mash, well, Pussy Riot, you know . . .'

We know that there are people in Russia who want to hear this story. And as long as these people exist, as long as it is needed, we will tell it. One person does say yes – the owner of the Art4 gallery.

– Are you coming? I ask Dima.
– I don't know.
– Come on, you have to take me there!
– Where?
– To the show!
– To your show?
– To my show!

Fifteen minutes later, Dima and I are riding a scooter. Without helmets. Without licences.

My mother's eyes, the eyes of those who waited for me to get out of jail. The eyes of strangers. Needles of silence are scattered around the performance and prick the air. When people start clapping, the needles expand and make everyone stand together.

ode to joy

One summer morning I wake up to the doorbell. Olya is standing on the threshold. Olya, my friend from prison. Holding a cardboard box. I ask, 'What is this?' She says, 'A gift.' The box is moving.

We carry it into the apartment. We put it on the floor and open it. Three ducks come out of the box. Three little yellow ducklings.

> – This is freedom, equality and brotherhood, Masha,
>   Dima has written – he wanted to make peace with me.
>   I saved them from the restaurant. They will not be
>   eaten.
> – They will live with you, I answer.

A day later Olya takes the box back.

freedom, equality and brotherhood

8 July 2017. Moscow. The Ministry of Justice is a long, white, ugly building. Next to it is the main building of the FSIN prison guards. People came here for the first pickets for Pussy Riot. Right after our arrest. The first Orthodox activists came here to attack the pickets.

Here I am, having been imprisoned in a penal colony, going out with the man who called for me to go to prison. We read the Bible together. In fishnet stockings. With my friends and his friends. For these friends and these stockings, in a couple of months Dima will be expelled from the God's Will movement.

the bible is at the ministry of justice

But for now, I have a rainbow bag on my shoulder. And I am sure that everyone should have a chance to change. They joke about us a lot on Twitter, some curse me and some say thank you for at least trying to give someone a chance. When he showed me how they sprinkled white powder on balaclavas on the day of the trial and then set them on fire, I cried. When I saw the video of them throwing eggs at rainbow activists, I wanted to hit him.

But instead, I showed him our last words in court, which he had not heard before. And I gave him Nemtsov's book.

angel of repression

In another time zone, Ukrainian political prisoner Oleg Sentsov has received twenty years in a Russian prison for protesting the annexation of Crimea. The prosecutor was Poklonskaya. 'Nyash-Myash' is what they call her on social media.

Ukrainian Poklonskaya supports the annexation and immediately becomes a sex symbol and a Russian citizen. Navy blue uniform, navy blue epaulettes, clear bright blue eyes.

She persecutes Crimean Tatars who are not loyal to Putin, labelling them extremists. Searches, arrests, torture, abductions and long prison sentences – twenty to thirty years is the price for protesting the annexation and for not changing position.

firm position

We decide to go to Siberia to stage an action.

For two years now, Sentsov has been imprisoned in Yakutsk penal colony no. 1. A direct flight from Moscow to Yakutsk costs crazy money. So we fly to Krasnoyarsk to travel on by car to the Far East.

The only time I have been to Krasnoyarsk was when I flew

there with Nadya. Straight after we were released from our penal colonies.

Ksenia Sobchak flies to the Siberian city to interview us. She is called the Russian Paris Hilton. Putin's goddaughter, daughter of Putin's St Petersburg boss – Mayor Anatoly Sobchak. Later she will run a fake presidential campaign 'against all' to give Putin's campaign a boost.

putin's goddaughter

She rents an old Soviet apartment, so it looks like an 'intimate conversation in the kitchen'. On our second day of freedom. Nadya and I talk about the horrors of prison, there is tea on the table. I'm very proud that I managed to get hold of payslips showing prisoners' salaries, evidence of the slave-like conditions of employment in the penal colony. But Sobchak isn't really interested; she compares Nadya with Beyoncé, asks about how much the Pussy Riot brand is worth. I often catch myself thinking that she really does look like a cop. I think of asking her, 'Why don't you wear epaulettes? They'd suit you perfectly' – but she gets in there first: 'Maria, everyone is interested in what's going on with your eyebrows.'

everyone is interested

On the way from one penal colony to another, in the transit prison in Nizhny Novgorod, I shaved my eyebrows and drew two thin stripes with a black pencil. By the time she asks the question, everything inside me is already boiling with indignation. I don't understand why eyebrows drawn six months ago are of more interest to this famous woman than prisoners' salaries. But I still don't know how to articulate my thoughts and argue with people the way I had argued with the prison guards. I still don't know how many strange interview questions lie ahead of me, and I just look her in the eye and answer her question with a question: 'What's wrong with them?' Before the interview, we had gone to a beauty salon to get our hair and make-up done. To look normal.

looking normal

Three years have passed and here I am, at the same airport in the Siberian city, but this time the air does not creak from the cold. August, heat, I'm with Olya and Sasha, who are now members of Pussy Riot.

We try to find a taxi driver who will take us to Irkutsk. It's a fifteen-hour drive. One driver finally agrees to take us. 'Let's go.'

We arrive in Irkutsk after midnight. A fifteen-hour car ride leaves our bodies aching. None of the hotels we try to book exist or they have been shut down. We spend the night on Lake Baikal, the deepest lake in the world. Morning is approaching. Cold. Pink dawn. We are sitting in a wooden gazebo with peeling paint. We finally find a welcoming wooden house. We wake up, pack our backpacks and swim in Baikal before our flight out.

morning on baikal, evening in the far east

We find cheap plane tickets to Neryungri. A city that none of us has heard of before. Our plane – the only one in the small airport, funny and Soviet – lands right in a field. We need to find a taxi. Yakutsk is 800 kilometres away.

Talking with the driver is always an important part of the journey.

- Why is the asphalt all broken up on the road?
- They completed twenty kilometres of it, then the
  funding dried up. They bought up Crimea, so all the
  money has been diverted there.

yakutski weekend

We arrive in Yakutsk at the weekend, we don't yet know that a weekend in Yakutsk means closed shops. Road signs show 'To Beijing' as being twice as close as 'To Moscow'. There are Korean stores, advertisements for Japanese manga lessons and Chinese language courses, original Soviet patterns running the full length of panel buildings.

- So what are we going to do? I ask.
- Shall we go and visit the penal colony? says Sasha.

They are already waiting for us at penal colony no. 1. Five employees and even a deputy head of the Federal Penitentiary Service department. On a Saturday.

- But the girl has Pussy Riot written on her phone,
  right? And you are Maria, right? What will you
  be doing here for SUCH A LONG TIME?

We don't even know ourselves how long we're going to be here for, we don't know exactly what we are 'going to do' here. But we don't give ourselves away, we pretend to be confident and, laughing, we leave.

vanilla activists

Summer Yakutsk is covered in smog – everything is hazy, it's hard to see, it's hot. Much like what's going on inside our heads. And suddenly we spot a bridge next to the colony, ideal for an action.

A long piece of beige linen from a fabric store that is luckily open at the weekend. Pink spray cans from a car repair shop. Coloured smoke. We don't know how to use it, but we are glad that we found it during the weekend. Sachets of vanilla – the only remedy against the clouds of mosquitoes. A friend's dacha in the pines – a Russian language teacher, Alena, her daughter Alexandra and red dog Tina. We write – FREE SENTSOV – in their garden, wipe the vanilla all over ourselves.

bridge near the colony

We attach the banner to the bridge across Lake Saysary. We need to set it alight.

- We haven't ever set fire to coloured smoke before,
  Olya says. We need to watch YouTube to see how to
  do it.
- We're on a bridge with a five-metre protest banner
  and the cops can come at any minute, what YouTube?
- And if it blows our hands off?

Crouching down, we google how to ignite coloured smoke and watch videos of anarchists. We put on balaclavas. Yellow and blue – the colours of the Ukrainian flag. Sasha takes a photo. FREE SENTSOV. The fireworks are lit. Cars drive across the bridge and passers-by look back. But they don't detain us. For now. Happy, we return to our hostel, post the video and go to bed.

permafrost

While enjoying our morning coffee, we look at ourselves on the Instagram account of 'Criminal News of Yakutia'.

'We are criminals,' I say. Olya reads: 'Go back to Moscow, traitors to the motherland.' and: 'Thank you, girls!'

Sakha – the republic of permafrost. All houses are built on stilts – otherwise they will sink into the mud.

We go to the Permafrost Museum. A Soviet entrance with a turnstile, empty corridors and stairwells. The large shape of a baby mammoth at the entrance. We go down to the basement for a tour. There are violets in ice cubes on the shelves. The guide says, 'These flowers were frozen by primary-school children.' Left as a keepsake. For ever.

At the end of the basement corridor, in the hidden depths, there's a closed door. When one of us asks, 'What's behind there?' the guide answers, 'Let's go have a look,' opens the door and turns on the light. We freeze. There, in the farthest basement room, Father Frost and Snow Maiden are standing behind the door. A lopsided Christmas tree with one toy in the corner. And nothing else.

– How long have they been in there? we ask.
– We don't know, the guide tells us. Maybe twenty, maybe thirty years.

for ever

We leave the basement. The sun is shining brightly. We go to see the oldest church in the city. An icon wrapped in cloth. Steps.

– Now we'll take you to a restaurant so you can try our Yakutian dishes . . .

Before our friend has time to finish his sentence, we are cut up by a police car, from which real Yakut cops emerge in unison.

– Wow, Yakutsk cops! says Sasha.

This is his first ever arrest.

This is also Olya's first arrest. We spend the next hours in the police station. The gloomy officers are silent, but when they see themselves on Mediazona, they get agitated. 'Who recorded this? How can it be deleted? Where're your phones?'

We won't wait for our trial – the materials of the 'case' will be returned to the police for 'revision'. We go to our friend's apartment in the dark to pack our backpacks. The cop waiting near the block of flats in civilian clothes pretends to be a lost passer-by and, after asking us for directions, doesn't understand that he has given himself away when he walks with us to our floor. He remains on duty near the window, and we watch him from the balcony.

We fly back to Moscow. Direct.

cinema kosmos

Half past five in the morning. Ekaterinburg. Dzerzhinsky Street. A minibus, stuffed with gas canisters, is on its way to the cinema Kosmos. To the main entrance. The driver exits the vehicle and throws a Molotov cocktail at it. Immediate flames. The driver is detained in hospital.

- Where were you yesterday?
- At the cathedral.
- And today?
- I went for a drive.
- Where to?
- The cinema.

The driver was protesting against the screening of the film *Mathilde*.

tsarist spectacle

Mathilde is a film about the affair of the last tsar Nicholas II and the ballerina Matilda. It's an allegory for Putin, who, after a divorce, lives with his mistress.

A grandiose film. Made with state money. The Minister of Culture wanted to make the Tsar interesting, but propaganda takes control. 'Insulted believers' burn posters, threaten to kill the director and to set fire to cinemas.

There are sex scenes in the film. But saints like the Tsar, as we know, do not have sex.

four stars

September 2017. London. The Strand Hotel has four stars, the porter opens the massive glass door for you, you roll your suit-case in and feel you're important. The idea is that you should feel this way, but I've never understood it. Long corridors, trays outside the doors with last night's empty champagne glasses and leftovers under a metal lid. A big metal lid and, more often than not, there's some small stuff inside like a dessert. The lid is a celebration, the lid is a holiday, on a white table on wheels with a tablecloth, and please sign here. Yes, and here.

I will stay here for a week, drink my litre of black coffee in the morning, and then go to media interviews. On the second day, it seems that the corridors of the BBC are the place where I was born. On the third, my brain refuses to decide such simple things as a choice of clothes, so I take several dresses, put them in a backpack and walk around with them all day. One of them is probably better than what I'm wearing, but I return to the hotel day after day in the same outfit I left in.

A friend told me that this is what girls who run away from home in their teens do: carry everything they need with them in one backpack because you never know where you will be tomorrow.

girls' habits

One of the interviews is scheduled for 10 p.m. I wait in the green room for some prime-time TV show. I suddenly decide that I want to wear a different dress. I undress completely and only then realize that a guy is sitting on the other sofa and waiting for the same show. A reserved English gentleman. Unfazed, of course.

I then end up at a book slam – several authors take turns to read extracts from their books. Next people buy the books and the authors sign them. Our book slam takes place in a

London church, the Priory Church of the Order of St John, and the homeless are fed with the proceeds. On Sundays there are services in this church. I approach the pulpit and read from my book.

- Isn't it absurd?
- Why is it absurd? In England, the Church is separate from the state and financially supports itself, the girls from the publishing house tell me.

Can you imagine this ever happening in Russia? Imagine, we'd fly to St Petersburg, we'd stay at the Marriott, all inclusive – pineapples in champagne, ten-course breakfasts, and all this would be 'room service, please', and the next morning an Uber Black would rush us to the Winter Palace (where else) to meet with other writers. There we would raise our glasses to freedom and to Russia – with our guests, political prisoners, feminists from the Middle East. State TV would record everything and then I would read my book in churches and with the proceeds the priests and I would feed the homeless.

god's last hope

- But let me show you what's actually happening in Russia today.

St Petersburg. The imperial capital of Russia. A procession of the cross. A hundred thousand people. Columns of priests in golden robes carrying icons. Banners and candlesticks in the shape of cupolas with crosses are held up to the sky. Cossacks carry portraits of the Tsar and monarchists wave banners saying '*Mathilde* – a slap in the face of the Russian people' and

'A sovereign's honour is the people's honour.' Believers carry photographs of the Tsar's family. Seminarians sing. From the stage, a St Petersburg Duma Deputy shouts into a microphone 'Russia is God's last hope on Planet Earth'.

– Is this a movie? the girls from the publishing
house ask.

trump tower

October 2017. From London to Manhattan, 5th Avenue – Trump Tower. We are on a reconnaissance mission. We have inspected a few bridges, but there's no need for bridges if we have this location. It will be a feminist invasion of Trump Tower – we laugh – also, a display of international solidarity for the release of political prisoners. Either way, it'll be something new – a golden skyscraper with rich people inside, guards outside and on every floor.

At the entrance they search our things. If asked, we are student artists bringing our work to show at an exhibition. Parts of the tower are connected by bridges; the guard on our bridge is too close. We estimate how many seconds it'll take him to run from his post to us. Less than ten. Not enough time to put on our balaclavas, unfold a ten-metre banner, drop it over the edge and scatter leaflets. So the guard needs to be distracted. We send Olya's British boyfriend Dylan.

We print out leaflets – 'Freedom for Sentsov and Kolchenko' – in the shop around the corner from the hotel. We buy colourful second-hand dresses and cans of coloured spray paint. We find everything except fabric for the banner.

difficult children

– Let's use the hotel's sheets! I say. They have lots!
– How?
– Staple them together!

Our American friends and activists, Elly and Kyle, look on in amazement. I thought they'd say something like 'Typical Russians stealing stuff', but they feel they're in a movie. 'Sheets – wonderful,' smiles Elly. 'And, of course, we must have a rehearsal,' she adds.

We staple the sheets together in the square nearest the hotel – the square of Peter Cooper, an American philanthropist and left-wing anti-monopoly activist. He believed that education should be not just for the rich but for everyone and built a school for 'difficult' children. Well, Peter, meet your next difficult children. Here they are – a hundred years later – in your square in the middle of East Village. They are arguing about whether to put plastic sheeting on the pavement so that pink paint doesn't end up everywhere, or just to spray the banner because there's no time.

la mama

In New York I'm acting in two performances a day for the Belarus Free Theatre. Torture on stage. During the break, between questions like 'How are you?', between worrying we will forget something for Trump Tower, I run straight to the square to help finish the banner. We have one evening to rehearse how we will hang it. Where to rehearse? On the stairwell of La Mama Theatre, where we are performing.

We take a stopwatch. We set up the backpack, take out the banner, unfold it – twelve seconds. That's the minimum we need.

– Photographers, you must all stand in different places,
   you must only take photos during the action. Don't
   film us without balaclavas, we instruct the New York
   hipsters.

At the rehearsal, one photographer, instead of taking out his camera when asked and pretending to start filming, starts filming for real. And I, of course, think that something is very wrong here.

– Masha, we're all here to make this work. We're not
   special agents.

we aren't agents

Next day, after drinking coffee for a buck, we arrive at the tower. Of all the possible scenarios – a heart attack, a fight, an epileptic seizure – Dylan chooses the simplest and most fun: pretending to be a stupid tourist. When he unfolds the map, this is a sign for us to begin.

– Sorry to ask, but I'm lost, he says, holding the map
   upside down.

We take up our position. We put the backpack down, take out the sheets and unfold them. We look down, all the rich and successful people lift their heads towards us for a second, and we immediately throw the leaflets. Hundreds of political prisoners cover the floor of the building of one of the world's top oligarchs. Beautiful.

- Who exactly are you? asks the policeman with
  the gun.
- We are activists of Pussy Riot from Russia, I say.
- And from America! Elly adds immediately.
- And what does it say?
- FREE SENTSOV!
- Free who?

They've secured the tower's entrance and exit.

The policeman looks at the photo of Sentsov, at our Russian passports, at his colleagues. They confer in their uniforms, they say:

- We don't want to cause you any problems in this
  country.

this country

A country that considers itself at the forefront of feminism gets a president who thinks it's okay to grab women in any way he deems appropriate.

There is a wave of women's marches.

female voice

In Russia it's not acceptable to fight for your rights in women's penal colonies. I ignored this fact and won.

I managed to defeat the jailers in court, and the sense of justice was tangible and unique.

In the court's judgement of my case in the name of the Russian Federation, it is written in black and white: 'Feminism is a dirty word.' And in *Domostroy* (a book from the Middle Ages), it is written that it is normal to beat a woman.

domostroy

Trump's wife – supermodel Melania – doesn't support the #MeToo protest. She answers journalists in a routine male way: 'Why have the victims remained silent all these years?'

In Russia, meanwhile, there's no first lady. Russia is passing a law to decriminalize domestic violence. If a husband beats his wife, it's no longer considered a crime.

first ladies

'Hey, you, drink up!' Stalin said to his wife, Nadezhda Alliluyeva, during a celebration at the Kremlin. The fifteenth anniversary of the revolution.

'Are you saying hey to me?' she answered, left the table, and shot herself in the heart with a German pistol in the early hours. Nadezhda Alliluyeva was thirty-two years old.

Brezhnev's wife, Viktoria, didn't interfere in politics. A former bodyguard described the role of a first lady in Brezhnev times: 'You are a wife, a housewife, a mother of a family, that is the extent of your duties.'

Andropov left his first wife. His second one went mad.

Nina Khrushcheva knew five languages, but people have discussed why, at a meeting with Jacqueline Kennedy, 'Khrushcheva looks like a grandmother who has just left the kitchen.' No one could call her 'lady', no one could say 'first lady' about anyone at all.

two shifts

Equality between men and women in the Soviet Union is a lie. Everyone was obliged to work, because otherwise they could be sent to prison for 'parasitism'. But women had double the work. They worked at the factory and then went to work their 'second shift' – at home: doing laundry, mopping floors, preparing dinner and checking the children's homework.

The leader who broke the patriarchal system was Mikhail Gorbachev – the last Soviet leader and also the father of Perestroika. His wife, Raisa, busted the stereotype of the 'non-public' wife of a Soviet leader. 'The first time the first lady of the USSR can speak English without an interpreter,' politicians remarked. Western fashion designers noted that for the first time the first lady was tastefully dressed.

– Wife of the head of state didn't exist as a concept. That's why my standing next to Gorbachev was taken as a revolution, said Raisa.

A family in which there was love and equality changed the country so that the whole world became interested in it. Then the Soviet Union collapsed.

we will turn back time

When Putin was asked what he considered the biggest tragedy in the country's history, he answered: the collapse of the Soviet Union.

Putin talks on camera about how important it is to respect

and love 'our women', but he never loved or respected his.

You could not interview Putin's First Lady of Russia – she was hidden, it was forbidden to write about her in the media, any outlet that did would be taken down. After their divorce, she simply disappeared from public view.

it's her own fault

Dictatorship reveals itself in its relations with women. Putin's Russia is the only country in Europe where there is no law against domestic violence, and on TV they say in all earnestness that the length of a girl's skirt can lead to her rape, that 'to beat is to teach a lesson' and that 'she has only herself to blame.' In the North Caucasus 'honour killings' and female genital mutilation are revived as practices.

'Clitoris circumcision' is offered by private clinics in Moscow. It costs less than 200 dollars to mutilate a child.

For years, the Putin regime, wearing the mask of democracy, has been convincing both the people of Russia and Western leaders that freedom is not an empty promise. And many have believed them. But there can be no freedom where women are not allowed to speak. The first opponent of Pussy Riot was the Patriarch, a bearded KGB agent who put on a cassock, who simply could not bear our protest because we are women.

smash the patriarchy

November 2017. We're going on tour with Riot Days around the UK and Ireland, like real musicians. In a red double-decker bus.

– Eight in the morning! Who leaves that early?
– We are a band! echoes from all sides, but mostly from Olya. We're on tour.

The windows of our hotel in Dublin look out onto a wall. On the wall is a memorial to the children who died. 'Somebody's Child'.

Illegitimate children were sent with their mothers to Magdalene laundries.

It didn't matter if your neighbour had raped you or your boyfriend had got you pregnant, either way you were a fallen woman and a sinner. Your pregnancy out of wedlock could jeopardize the family's inheritance and disgrace the local priest. You were separated from your baby after birth. If it was lucky, your baby would be given to a 'prosperous family'. If it was unlucky, it would die of hunger and cold right there. It would be buried in a common unmarked grave.

Hundreds of children and their dates of death at mother-and-baby homes are written on the walls of the institution. The last such 'home' was closed only in 1996.

Illegitimate children are children born outside of marriage, just like me.

somebody's child

I first met my dad when I was twenty years old. My first thought was I must make sure I remember it. The outskirts of Moscow, a residential area, an almost empty apartment, me in a long skirt. We sat at the table opposite each other. Drank tea. The apartment was straight out of a Soviet movie.

Kitchen, balcony, and hundreds of similar houses nearby. This meeting – a missing piece of the puzzle.

'Children from incomplete families' – that's what they said about people like me. I didn't understand and still don't understand why. I grew up with my mother and grandmother. Why is it that if someone left someone else, they call the family of the one left behind 'broken', and why did thinkers around the globe admire and glorify the Soviet Union as a 'social state', when it was no different from religious institutions in terms of women's rights?

a female chorus

Repeal activists come to our dressing room, they talk about their fight to repeal the Eighth Amendment of the Irish constitution, which equates the life of an embryo with the life of a citizen.

The activists tell us:

– Drink a bottle and sit in a hot bath – this is how they
   do abortion in the Republic of Ireland. But this is also
   a criminal offence: up to fourteen years in prison;
   those who have money catch a ferry to Britain; those
   who don't, use this method. Even if you were raped.
   Even if your pregnancy threatens your life.

We listen, frozen. And then they start singing. It's heartbreaking. A choir of very low female voices. A year after this meeting, they will win. Abortion will no longer be a crime for women in the Republic of Ireland in the second decade of the 21st century.

spice girls

We arrive in Manchester – the city of suffragette Emmeline Pankhurst. After the concert, John Robb, the legendary 80s punk with a mohawk, asks me from the doorway:

- What kind of music do you like?
- I grew up on the Spice Girls.
- So you dreamed of going on tour on a red bus?
- I had a videotape of the Spice Girls on tour and an old German TV. Of course I wanted to tour like them. But I didn't know I would have to spend two years in prison to do it.

crickets

'Can you hear the crickets?' She nods. 'Yes.' He – a Putinist and militiaman; she – a journalist who has been taken hostage by him. He raped her in the cellar; she said, 'I love you,' and begged him not to rape her. She ate canned meat like a dog off the floor because he made her. They are both in the bath – white. 'Can you hear the crickets?' 'Yes.' 'It's beautiful.' She takes a brick. They are both protagonists in a Ukrainian play about the Donbass. She gets out of the bath and beats him with the brick.

The year ends – the 100th anniversary of the revolution. My friend Aya leaves prison. She served five and a half years in a Russian penal colony after the case against her was fabricated. I've just got back from a tour, where I saw the last night of the play *Bad Roads* in London. Brutal and powerful. It's evening in Moscow, we are standing on the Garden Ring. New cobblestones laid with scarce state funds. We move to a restaurant.

- Can you imagine, Masha?
- What?
- That the prison guards all went to the war to pay off their debts!

bad roads

Aya – my prison friend. She taught me how to make a facial scrub out of coffee and honey, she made me a carrot salad for the journey from prison to court. They took us out of our cell at 6 a.m. and returned us at night. Every day. She is the person who forced me – me who had walked in circles around the prison yard and taught people Mandelstam's poems – to start running and doing push-ups on the bench.

She is from Turkmenistan – one of the most terrifying dictatorships in the world. Members of the opposition are killed there, foreign journalists aren't allowed in. There's barely any Internet. Turkmens cannot leave the country – it's North Korea but without the nuclear weapons.

turkmenistan

In the 2000s, after another wave of purges, opposition members were imprisoned and killed. Among them was Aya's father. He was killed in prison. At that time, Aya was already living in Moscow and she was warned that she had to immediately escape Russia as a matter of urgency. She fled. To Switzerland. A couple of relatively peaceful years. If living in constant fear can be called peaceful.

In Turkmenistan, a lawsuit was opened against her and

others for the 'theft of the century', for allegedly stealing from the central bank of Turkmenistan. Neither Aya nor her father had ever worked there. The case was used to arrest, without any evidence, the enemies of Turkmen President Niyazov.

Aya could not be extradited from Switzerland to Turkmenistan – after all, it's a dictatorship that tortures and murders. Then the President of Turkmenistan flew to Russia and agreed with Putin that Aya could be extradited to Russia. To Russia – it's possible.

They came for Aya in Geneva. Eight months in prison awaiting extradition to Russia. And then the flight to Russia and time in Detention Centre No. 6, where we met. A 5.5-year sentence – a Turkmen dictator's vendetta paid for by Russian taxpayers.

war on loan

Aya was imprisoned in a colony in Kostroma. Not far from Moscow. She was forbidden to read political newspapers, but one warden, Maxim, still smuggled them in for her. A young, handsome guy, working in the colony one day in three to pay off his mortgage. The rest of the time he worked other jobs to support his family.

One day, Aya noticed that all the male wardens had disappeared. Including Maxim. Two months later she saw him again and asked:

- – Where have you been?
- – In Donbass.
- – What, you went there to kill people?
- – They promised to pay off our mortgages! We didn't kill. We drank vodka.

no film

International Human Rights Day – Aya and I are going to the cinema on the Arbat. In the evening I'm going to read a letter from Sentsov on stage, and before that there's a film about the Donbass war. I warn Aya that 'patriots' may come to the screening and attack us.

The Arbat is filled with police. A search is conducted at the entrance. Even at the British Parliament, they didn't search that much. 'There are police everywhere,' Aya notes. 'How will the patriots be able to attack?' She hasn't figured out yet this is exactly how they do attack.

We take our seats. The lights dim. The film starts. After the first few scenes, people in camouflage burst into the hall. They have five-litre bottles of liquid with them. They start to pour them out on the floor. The strong fumes make our eyes sting.

'There will be no film! Get the traitors out of the hall!' a short middle-aged man in camouflage screams, and sprays the poisonous liquid around.

The police come in, the lights come back on. 'We're asking everyone to leave the cinema!' We're leaving. The people in camouflage continue to run around and shout. We're outside. The last thing we see is a policeman hailing a taxi for the people in camouflage.

This whole 'Russian World' is not truly Russian if there is no war in it. If there's no enemy in it. We came out in solidarity with Ukrainian Sentsov, who Russia called 'the enemy' because of this. Because, after the march for peace, after the assassination of Boris Nemtsov, that kind of solidarity was less and less on display.

6.

Happy Birthday, Executioners

The Kremlin. A grand gala concert in honour of Chekists' Day.

The Cheka – the first Soviet secret police, whose heir is the FSB. A portrait of Dzerzhinsky – the founder of the Cheka – can be found hanging in many offices today. The Chekists have their own state holiday, the day of the Chekist. It's a special one this year. Their eightieth anniversary.

A huge shining FSB emblem and solemnly shining numbers: 1937–2017.

bloody anniversary

On stage is chief KGB officer Putin. He congratulates those gathered to celebrate. His address ends with a minute's silence in honour of the 'fallen heroes who gave their lives for the homeland'.

The Sretensky Monastery Choir sings:

> 'Sometimes it seems to me all the fallen soldiers
> That never came back home from the bloody fields,
> Were not lain somewhere to rest in the earth,
> But were turned into white cranes.'

On huge screens there is a video of the blue sky. The eyes of the generals' wives fill with tears.

The Sretensky Monastery Choir is the main choir of the

Russian Orthodox Church, whose priests were shot by KGB security officers some eighty years ago.

choir for chekists

The head of the monastery is Bishop Tikhon Shevkunov. A bun of chestnut hair, a beard. Looks like a spider. A spider who grabs government funds with its legs while playing the role of an Orthodox producer.

> *'Father Tikhon offered to baptise me. He explained that when you are baptised, all your accumulated sins are washed away.'*
>
> – Nikolai Leonov, KGB general

When Father Tikhon is given the monastery, the monastic choir becomes a real commercial project, a music group. It performs for oil magnates and politicians. For Putin and Orthodox oligarchs.

Shevkunov is a bishop with a film-director background. He boasts of his connections to the KGB. A dizzying career as a priest, who is personally responsible for creating 'Orthodox Chekism' – the state ideology of the Putin era.

orthodox takeover

Putin is building a new empire, and it needs a new Church. The empire in its new form is omnivorous, it does not care what it has for communion, white or red. The Church works according to the logic of the KGB playbook – conspiracy, external enemy, fifth column.

Father Tikhon thinks globally – he expropriates property, rewrites Russian history, places his people in ministerial positions, issues orders to FSB officers, fights the wrong exhibitions, the wrong plays, the wrong films. He understands the importance of culture and history. Images must be created. Clear and correct images.

He becomes a regular guest at the Kremlin, accompanies Putin on trips and supports him.

> *'Our President was right: those who do not mourn the collapse of the Soviet Union have no heart.'*

He was one of the priests who called for us to be imprisoned.

> *'The outrages of the punk group in Moscow's churches are not just hooliganism. It is a new reality of our lives – "velvet terrorism".'*

velvet terrorism

– Are there any sheets? I ask.

The two-storey Airbnb apartment on Marksistskaya Street, chosen by Olya's boyfriend, has instantly transformed into a Pussy Riot production house.

– Yes, here's some, Dylan sighs. And hands over the
  sheets from their bed.

He didn't expect these days would be taken up with an action against the Chekists. And he particularly didn't expect preparations in this kitchen.

Night. We write 'Happy Birthday, Executioners!' with spray cans on the sheet, folding it as we go along so that it fits in the narrow kitchen. Any splashes of paint we remove with Olya's Dolce & Gabbana perfume.

Morning. We meet at the Starbucks on Lubyanka Square. We go to the FSB reception entrance to congratulate the Chekists on their special day. We hang the sheet outside the most paranoid place in the country. There are several security cameras on each corner.

the lubyanka

Lubyanka Square – one of the most beautiful squares in Moscow. A hundred years ago.

After a red revolution, the cosy square transforms into a quarter of hell. All residents, traders, owners are thrown out of their houses, their place is taken by the Cheka apparatus. Led by Felix Dzerzhinsky. Founder of the Cheka. Iron Felix.

clearing the country of enemies

A Chekist is a scalpel. Cold and sharp. The operation that is performed with this scalpel is to cleanse the country of enemies. First the outsiders. Then the insufficiently loyal. Then the loyal, who show insufficient initiative. Then . . . everyone.

Enemies are never-ending. At least as long as the Chekists are around, they're the new aristocracy formed on blood. The people who break a child's fingers in front of her battered mother until she signs a statement.

A new 'secret police' without principles and without pity. You don't have to be intelligent, just devoted. And it should be a passionate devotion. Without limits. Until your heart stops beating.

black raven conveyor of death

GAZ-M1, nicknamed the Black Raven. Seeing it approach, hands begin to shake. The Black Raven arrives – they pick up – they shoot – they transport – they shoot. The shootings never cease. Has the executioner gone mad and committed suicide? His replacement comes on duty and continues to shoot.

Hundreds, thousands a day. Hard work. Professors, poets, priests – the hearts and minds of the country turn into scattered body parts on basement floors. The Chekist must be able to kill, and everyone else must know that he has been endowed with this right. The sacred and unconditional right of an executioner.

happy birthday, executioners

We go to the entrance of the grey FSB reception building to congratulate the security officers. We are rolling out the sheet in the most protected place in the country. And everything seems to be fine. The fact that we manage to hang it without having our faces immediately pushed onto the asphalt is a success. It seems to me that the corner is not straight. I return to fix it. And suddenly I'm surrounded from all sides by plainclothes policemen.

Olya sees me being led away under their arms towards the Lubyanka. Realizing that they simply haven't noticed her, and that they are dragging me and the photographers inside, she begins to follow us. The cops turn around. We look into each other's eyes, and the cops look through her. It's like she's wearing the cloak of invisibility from Harry Potter. She gets into a taxi. I'm pushed into the FSB building with the photographers.

fsb reception

Our white sheet with red letters lies on the floor. The employee asks:

- Do you have relatives who were repressed or something?
- I've been in jail myself.
- For what?
- For the song 'Virgin Mary, Banish Putin' at the Cathedral of Christ the Saviour. Two years.
- What's that, Pussy Riot?
- Yes, Pussy Riot.
- Well, that's a life's commitment.

We spend the night in the police station. I and the two photographers who documented the action. I lie looking at the ceiling – I've not spent the night in a police station before. Various types of prisons, yes, but not an ordinary police station. I really want a cigarette and I ask two of the guards to escort me to the yard. We all go out. Snow falls, the only place it misses is under the metal roof of the smoking area.

One policeman says to another, 'It got bad for me, so I went to church.'

I ask, 'And how was it?'

And he is silent, silent for a long while, and then he says quietly, 'Missed you there.'

a life's commitment

I hardly slept that night. We were taken to the court.

- Were you holding the placard? the judge asks irritably
  for the second time.
- It's not a placard. It's a gift, I say.
- Maria, do you have anything to add?
- No.
- There's no need to smile, says the judge, and leaves to
  make their decision.

In the Meshansky court, I am given forty hours of community service. On the wall of the building next to the court is a portrait of Varlam Shalamov. He spent seventeen years in Soviet camps.

It may seem that stories about executioners from the land of the Soviets are just stories from the past. They are not. The Chekists from the FSB are proud of their heritage. Hanging portraits of Dzerzhinsky in their offices, they often talk about restoring his monument.

According to the human rights organization Memorial, at least 5.5 million people suffered from repression; the current head of the FSB, Bortnikov, calls this 'local excesses'.

local excesses

'In the Soviet Union there were two ideologies – communist and criminal. In 1991, the communist one disappeared. What remained was the criminal.'

So said Alexander Litvinenko, a Chekist who rebelled against the system. He went live on air and said that the FSB was behind the bombings of Moscow apartment blocks in 1999, justification for sending troops into Chechnya, a republic that dreamed of independence. Litvinenko writes a book. They open a criminal case. He leaves Russia with his family.

chekist-rebel polonium-210

A few years later, Lieutenant Colonel Litvinenko is poisoned with polonium-210. The whole world watches him die in a London hospital. In a week, he loses all his hair, loses weight beyond recognition, and his organs fail one by one.

He was poisoned by ex-colleagues of the FSB. Their names are well known. Lugovoi and Kovtun. Lugovoi will become a State Duma deputy and Kovtun a businessman. Bortnikov, as a deputy director of the FSB, led the operation. After Litvinenko's death, Bortnikov will receive a promotion. Within a few years he will head the FSB.

hello

– Hello, you have to come with us.

February 2018. I am the only one being met at this empty airport in Simferopol. The passengers go outside and I go upstairs with five cops – to the office.

Occupied Crimea. Sentsov was charged with attempting to blow up the statue of Lenin near Simferopol's railway station and sentenced to twenty years in prison. We've made actions near his prison, at Trump Tower, and finally have to do one here – at the railway station.

– Take out what you have in your backpack.

The sheet with the word 'freedom', which we painted all night, is taken away. The equipment too. And we have little time to do something about it – where do we get new sheets from and where can we spray paint on them?

– We're leaving now, right now.

From the office I find myself in a car, and I'm driving through the deserted streets of Simferopol with the police. I was supposed to meet Sasha and Olya in the city centre. They were supposed to arrive by ferry.

welcome to crimea

A dirty Russian flag flutters in the grey sky, a huge banner – 'The Republic of Crimea welcomes you' – and four cops in a row are at the pier to greet Sasha and Olya. They put them in a car and take them to the FSB. At the FSB they remove their phones and take them to different offices.

An unshaven, obese boss has had his day off interrupted. He hangs his Bosco jacket on a chair, a souvenir from an official trip to Sochi Olympics. He asks everyone in turn, 'Why did you come here?' and adds, 'We know who you are.'

In the evening, Olya and Sasha take a taxi to Simferopol. Its number plate is recorded by local surveillance.

The next morning, they go out for breakfast, but before they get to the café, they are detained. Again. They're brought to meet me at the drug-testing station. In an old Soviet hospital.

— Pee in a jar and keep the door open, the nurse
  tells me.
— What do you mean by open? I ask.
— I mean, don't close it.

drug tests

It's unclear why we should be tested for drugs. Perhaps we're
witnessing special Crimean methods for intimidating activists.
While Olya sits and waits for her result, she bursts into tears –
she is afraid that something will be added to her sample.

A February blizzard, bone-chillingly cold, constant surveillance. We go out to smoke. In the window of the hospital, I see
a unicorn. In a child's drawing propped up against the glass it
looks at us and I begin to hope for the best.

— The tests will be sent off for analysis, please sign here
  and you can leave, says the nurse.

I sign and see the address where the tests will be sent – a
hospital on 'Chekist Street'. 'Is there really such a street?' I ask.
Both the cop and the nurse proudly answer, 'Yes.'

I find out later that throughout Russia, in different cities,
there are about 1,500 Chekist Streets.

chekist street

The cops take Olya and Sasha away. When their confiscated
equipment is returned to them, all of it is broken and beyond
repair. Not having the passcodes for their phones, the cops

connected a 12-volt charge to them. The motherboards were burned out.

- Okay, we'll meet early in the morning at Starbucks, let's just go there and see what happens!
- There's no Starbucks here, Masha!
- McDuck? Somewhere that's 24/7?
- THERE ARE SANCTIONS HERE, MASHA! says Olya.

Bank cards don't work here, those companies have all left. Russia came here and gave people passports that would never have a European visa stamped in them.

Simferopol Airport is called international, but there are flights only to and from Russia.

punished peninsula

Three local activists are staring at me, and this is the moment when it dawns on me what has gone on that day. My comrades are leaving for home in ten minutes, it's almost night, I have nowhere to sleep, I have nothing with me but a balaclava. I'm in Crimea, where people are removed from their beds for activism or religious beliefs, tortured, locked up for crazy lengths of time, where all the international corporations have left because it is an illegal territory annexed to Russia. This Crimea is no longer a peninsula, and Simferopol is no longer a city. It's a police training ground. And what is covered up, usually submerged under the bustle of city life, is fully exposed here, grinning, and you will always be backed into a corner. I'm feeling desperate.

schoolteacher

— I'll help you, says a voice from the end of the table.

He turns out to be a schoolteacher living far from the city centre in a wooden house – he gives me a sheet and markers. Late at night on the plank floor I write 'freedom' once again, I do not sleep.

In the morning, we go out the back way, jump over the fence, jump onto a trolleybus, straight to the railway station. I climb onto the bridge over the railway line. The teacher takes a photo as I hang the sheet.

FREE SENTSOV

Cossacks burst into the café from where we are posting the photo of the action. Cossacks with whips. Whips whack the floor. The teacher tries to talk and immediately gets smacked in the face. I take out my phone and start recording. The Cossack reaches out his hand and tries to strike me. The teacher asks, 'Is that how to behave with a woman?'

— To me she's not a woman, to me she's an enemy of
  the state.

enemy of the state

Russian agents with passports in the names Alexander Petrov and Ruslan Boshirov check in for the Moscow–London flight. In their suitcase is a bottle of Premier Jour perfume by Nina Ricci. Inside the bottle is Class A nerve agent 234 – Novichok. A poison developed in Russian military laboratories.

The agents travel by train from London to Salisbury. They

apply poison from the bottle to the door handle of Sergei Skripal's house.

bottle of poison

Skripal served in Russian intelligence, but the UK turned him into a double agent. Putin sentenced him to nine years in prison for treason, but halfway through his sentence Skripal was exchanged for Russian spies convicted in the United States. Skripal and his family moved to Britain, where he lived in Salisbury and continued to work for the West. Thanks to him, three Russian agents were exposed. Unforgivable. His former colleagues are on the scene with deadly poison.

Sergei and his daughter lose consciousness outside a shopping centre. They are taken to the hospital and tested. Theresa May makes a statement that the Skripals were poisoned with Russian military poison. The UK identifies Petrov and Boshirov as the main suspects.

the spire of salisbury cathedral

'Of course, we looked into who these people are. We know who they are. I hope that they will turn up and tell us something of themselves.'

– Putin, speaking about Petrov and Boshirov, smiling from the screen

The next day, the country's main propagandist, Margarita Simonyan, releases an interview on *Russia Today*. Two men in sweaters say that they are ordinary tourists, who just went 'to have a look at the famous spire of Salisbury Cathedral'.

The jumper-wearing fans of Early English Gothic architecture are in fact active GRU military intelligence officers. Their fake passports differ by just one last digit. Their real names are Anatoly Chepiga and Alexander Mishkin. They have both been awarded a star from Putin. Heroes of Russia since 2014. For 'Services in Ukraine'.

russia today

Only a few days before the Cossacks and FSB agents had turned forty-eight hours in Crimea into forty-eight hours of hell, and now here I was in Moscow with my son, walking past the court where I had been sentenced to two years in prison. We were going to the library, right opposite the court, to hand in books and borrow new ones. On the day of our verdict, three Belarusians had climbed onto the canopy of this library, put on balaclavas and shouted 'freedom' to us. Pussy Riot. So I looked at the canopy and smiled – this felt like a sort of freedom.

anniversary of stalin's death

I take a speaker, a backpack, a taxi and walk through the snow to Red Square. The anniversary of Stalin's death – 5 March.

Stalin was 'buried' near the Kremlin wall, like most of the ex-leaders of the Soviet Union. The Kremlin is surrounded by graves. In addition to the graves, 115 urns of 'revolutionary figures' were bricked up in the Kremlin wall.

To reach Stalin, you have to pass through the mausoleum –

past Lenin in a glass case. I had never seen Lenin. A dead doll in a suit. If there is a reminder of the revolution in Russia, then this is it. Dead.

For a hundred years, a body with glass balls instead of eyes has been lying in the central square of the capital. A body without brains. The brains are kept separately in a special institute.

I look at him for about five minutes until an old man begins to kiss the glass and cross himself.

mandelstam from a music speaker

On Stalin's birthday and on the anniversary of his death, veterans each carry two carnations to his grave with flags. This is called 'two carnations for Comrade Stalin', although he was far from being a comrade.

Stalin created the Moscow Patriarchate. Turned the Church into a branch of the KGB. All the beloved poets and directors were mowed down by his strokes like grass. The carnations lie in a scarlet mountain, right up to the tyrant's neck.

In my backpack there is a speaker playing Mandelstam's poems, with which he signed his own death warrant. But poets don't die. They turn into words and return for ever to all who remember them.

I turn the poems up to full volume. An old man with a red banner approaches me and asks, 'Which poems are these?' I reply, 'Mandelstam's,' and he says, 'Tell your poet that he got it wrong and that Stalin was not Ossetian, but Georgian.' I say, 'He died from typhus in a transit prison in '38.' The old man says, 'Well, okay then.' It's not okay.

we live with no sense of the country beneath us*

Sea of flowers. Kids' toys. There are lots of toys and they bring more and more. The word 'Kemerovo' is written with glowing tealights.

This is a spontaneous memorial that sprang up in the centre of the capital after a fire in the 'Winter Cherry' shopping centre.

winter cherry

Kemerovo. The first day of the winter holidays, parents go with their children to the cinema and amusement park. A fire starts at the park due to faulty wiring. Fire extinguishers hang a few metres from the fire but are obscured by furniture.

The fire spreads to the cinema. The ticket attendants don't turn off the films and turn on the lights. Smoke completely fills the corridor. Emergency exits are locked.

red hall

People are suffocating. Parents and children remain in the red cinema hall. They decide to wait for rescuers and continue to call the emergency services.

> *'Emergency service.'*
> *'Girl, we're at the Winter Cherry! We're on fire! Why aren't they coming to our rescue?'*

* First line from Mandelstam poem 'Stalin Epigram' (1933).

> *'The rescue services are already on site.'*
> *'There's no one here!'*
> *'Where are you?'*
> *'In the cinema hall! We're all suffocating in here.'*
> *'Please state your last name, first name and patronymic.'*
> *'Girl, you don't understand, we're all dying in here.'*

Everyone who remained waiting for help in the cinema hall will die.

The men are trying to break down the emergency exit in the corridor. It's locked. A father decides to save his eleven-year-old boy. He throws him out of the window from the fourth floor, where the crowd has unrolled a blanket. The boy is taken to the hospital, his father and sister suffocate by the very same window.

A spontaneous rally assembles in the central square. The despair and pain of the residents of Kemerovo. People in tears demand that they be told the truth about the number of deaths. Among them is Igor Vostrikov; he lost his sister, wife and three children in the fire. A bewildered look, eyes red from tears. He demands the resignation of the governor, demands a meeting with Putin.

united russia

The whole of Russia is watching this protest. A video of Vostrikov is going viral. The authorities quickly understand its value. They will get in touch with him. In less than a week he will say, 'What does the administration have to do with it? What does Putin have to do with it? Putin is a Tsar, for better or worse. I have questions about the actions of the emergency services.'

Putin in Kemerovo, laying flowers at the memorial. Followed by cameras. He doesn't meet with the victims' relatives. Vostrikov announces that he is running in the elections for Putin's United Russia party. And after that he disappears. They quietly remove him from TV. He had done what was required.

petting zoo

While building a repressive state, Putin's regime continues to call itself democratic. It's easier to sell democracy. So let's imitate democracy. For now.

The 'crazy printer' continues to churn out repressive laws. One of them is the 'Yarovaya package': it obliges all social networks to store users' data and provide them at the request of the special services. Our right to private communication is guaranteed by the constitution. But officials do not like articles from the constitution.

The FSB demands that Telegram, the messenger app we use, provides the key to decrypting user messages. The founder of Telegram, Durov, refuses. They decide to block the app.

building with a clock

The main FSB building on the Lubyanka. Before the revolution it was built as an apartment block for rent so that people with low incomes who valued comfort could live in inexpensive flats. After the revolution, they gave it to the Special Department of the Cheka. The whole apparatus of Felix Dzerzhinsky moves in.

The block is occupied by hundreds of Chekists. The number of Chekist staff is increasing, the building is expanding. Hotel rooms nearby turn into prison cells for enemies of the people. A prison for the most dangerous. Throughout its existence no one has escaped from there.

During the next hundred years, the Chekists often changed their name but never left the building. VChK-NKVD – KGB – and, finally, the FSB.

What happened there is still classified.

– Imagine dozens of colourful aeroplanes flying directly into the building. Into doors, windows, those dark walls! says Dima.

And I imagined. I created a Facebook meeting. I called it 'Paper Aeroplanes'.

paper aeroplanes

On the page I painted the Lubyanka in pink. I really want it to be that colour in the future. I want there to be a museum of all the hell concentrated in this place – torture chambers and offices, basements, so that all the archives can be read, so that it's clear what happened. But on the outside, it would be pink, so that no one could imagine what was on the inside, no one would believe it at first. Because that is how it is with all nightmarish acts in the world – no one can believe that people can do such a thing.

A lot of people sign up to join our action. I travel to the centre. Sasha and his friends are already waiting in the Starbucks across the road, they have bought coloured paper and are making aeroplanes.

We will live for ever
on the FSB website
and it's eternal spring
in the cold December

Hundreds of paper aeroplanes fly into the gloomy stone colossus of the FSB building. Activists, journalists, former enemies and close friends are making more and more planes. One of the passers-by is a child. The child picks up a plane off the pavement and launches it at the grey block. It is spring. Fifteen minutes later we are all led to an avtozak.

we will live for ever

– They should move the FSB away from this district, Masha, otherwise they'll keep bringing you here, the duty officer at the police station complains.

They don't know which law they should use to press charges. The issue stretches on into the evening and we sit in the police room with one tired, grumpy cop – twelve of us. According to the law, they are not allowed to detain us for more than three hours. But the guys in uniforms are not always concerned with these 'nuances'.

– We will come to each of you to write your statements, the cop says.
– Without a lawyer we won't write anything, I say with a tired smile. We have the 51st.

simultaneous illegal assembly

Article 51 of the Russian Constitution gives you the right not to testify against yourself and your family. If you live in Russia and they wake you up in the middle of the night, it doesn't matter if you don't remember the names of your loved ones, but you must remember Article 51.

We look around at each other, everyone is interested in what we did wrong by launching paper aeroplanes.

'A simultaneous illegal assembly of citizens.'

- This means that, according to the law, we're not allowed to simultaneously assemble on the street? I ask.
- Yes! Phones, power banks, laces, crosses, pretty hair slides – everything needs to be handed over, answers the cop.
- What did we do wrong? protests one of the activists. I won't hand anything over.

They take our things. The activist is led to a cell, shouting, 'I demand a lawyer!'

There are twelve of us. The cell is divided into two by a bar – one section for the boys and one for the girls. On the floor we lay out the containers of food given to us by volunteers and laugh all night long.

- Is being here like being in prison? the guys ask.
- A little bit, I reply.

life like in prison

– I joined the protest because our basic right, granted to us by the constitution, is being violated, says a female doctor who hasn't been involved in activism before.

She speaks calmly, clearly. I continue, but slightly differently:

– Well, I also launched aeroplanes, first pink, then yellow, then blue . . .

The judge smirks, it's the same judge, the matryoshka doll who presided over the day of the Chekist. She will give me another hundred hours of community service to add to the forty she's given me already. I am banned from leaving Russia. In a couple of months, this will be the catalyst for new adventures. We will still message each other on Telegram, as it continues to work very well, regardless of the ban.

go and watch

The British magazine *The Economist* features Putin in a tsar's overcoat on its cover to mark the centenary of the October revolution. It has the title 'The Tsar is Born'. It seems as if only they understand what is happening in Russia.

The main slogan of the new protests is 'Down with the Tsar!' Why? Because Putin isn't only a tsar on the front cover of *The Economist* – he's already a tsar in people's minds.

russian elections

They've installed cameras at all the polling stations. See how transparent we are. We're monitoring. On live TV, state officials from all over Russia shove fat bundles of 'for Putin' ballots into the narrow openings of the boxes.

In fact, Putin has been in power for eighteen years.

he's not a tsar to us

I go to a protest rally – the crowd is already divided into sections. One section is being pushed towards the boulevard. The other – towards the metro. Young men from Nazi groups work hand in hand with the cops. St George's ribbons, kicks; if you kick in response, you'll be shown to the avtozak. A column of avtozaks line the street.

down with chekist power

There are a lot of students. A new generation of protesters. It's not going as far as the Kremlin. Not yet. But they've read the constitution. Thousands of people in different cities across Russia hold the constitution in their hands. The blue book flashes above the heads of the OMON as they beat people. A single organism of brute force. Push back the crowd. Put up a barrier. Detain. Transport.

'Dear citizens, your actions are illegal.'

7.

Stop Gulag

At the Moscow airport's passport control the girl takes my passport, looks at her computer, calls someone straight away and says something in a whisper into the receiver. She tells me, 'Your documents need additional checks.' And then a young man appears: 'I'm from the FSB.'

– Don't be upset, but you are not allowed to leave the country.

Bailiffs have imposed a travel ban on me for 'evading community service'. The one that they have imposed for 'Happy Birthday, Executioners' on Lubyanka Square and for flying paper aeroplanes in the same place.

It's forbidden for me to travel to my own show.

travel ban

If you are politically active, there are multiple ways they can complicate your life apart from a classic criminal case and prison term. For example, a travel ban or a huge fine: if you don't pay it off, then they block your bank account. This all applies to me.

Bailiffs: their mission is usually to catch people who haven't paid their debts or alimony. From 8 a.m. until 6 p.m. they sit in their car guarding the entrance of the building where I'm living. All summer long. They are not allowed to take their eyes off the door, that's why for lunch they have shawarma from the corner shop.

Each morning starts with a powerful knock on the door. This is the bailiff almost breaking into the apartment to force me out to mop floors. Centre E – the political police – have ordered him and his junior colleague to come here.

back door

'Despite her ban, a member of the group, Maria Alyokhina, has left Russia. She is flying to Edinburgh right now to perform at her concert Riot Days.'

– Pussy Riot's Twitter

This is already the third time that I have crossed the border in breach of my travel ban. I've discovered a back door. The bailiffs don't realize that the building has two exits.

This summer isn't only different for me, but it's different for all of Russia. Russia is hosting the World Cup.

Two years later, the US will accuse the former vice-president of FIFA, Jack Warner, of receiving a bribe of 5 million dollars for supporting the Russian bid for the championship.

world cup

Thousands of tourists from all over the world travel to Russia for the World Cup. The country, which has been fed stories about isolation and the need for an iron curtain – a country which for years has heard that it is encircled by enemies – is happy at last. People don't want to be isolated, and they greet their guests with delight.

Hotels are fully booked; Russians rent out their spare rooms. Across the country foreigners are being fed borsch, and learning Russian phrases. People quickly realize that the 'foreign enemies' shown on TV are in fact ordinary people like them. Whether you are in Moscow, Samara or Sochi, there's a foreigner wherever you look. The locals remember their English, long forgotten after leaving school. And they are very pleased when they see a Brazilian or an English person having lunch in their local cafés.

russian happiness

The centre of Moscow explodes with happiness. Everyone is drinking, talking loudly and hugging and the police don't interrupt them. It is exactly how Putin wanted to show Russia to the West – a completely free, hospitable country where there's absolutely no police violence.

Western tourists will not see the new criminal cases, Western tourists will not hear torture in police stations and penal colonies.

Meanwhile, torture has been ramped up.

championship of torture

That same summer, there is a video from a Russian penal colony, where eleven prison staff torture a prisoner stretched out on a table. They hit him with rubber batons all over his body.

We go to the entrance of the Federal Prison Service, FSIN, with large slogans saying 'FSIN = Gulag, murder, torture, slave labour'. When we start sticking our posters onto the wall outside, an employee comes out and tells us to submit all our complaints in writing. We answer that's exactly what we're doing. We've just enlarged the words so that they don't have any trouble reading them. The FSIN employee shakes his head, peels the posters off the wall and mutters about our improper methods.

fsin = gulag

A video showing torture does not show an isolated case of sadism. Torture is routine practice within the system, which turns people into hostages.

The prison system is a meat grinder that destroys human essence.

In my first colony, those who disagree are thrown out of windows, and in the second, they are put in icy punishment cells.

Today, anyone can be imprisoned in Russia. You don't necessarily have to sing a song that's against Putin. We are here to say that torture and murder should not go unpunished.

execution house

Nikolskaya, a central pedestrian street that runs from the Lubyanka to the Kremlin, draws many of the football fans during the World Cup that summer.

People are dancing until dawn, the bars and restaurants are full, you can hear cheerful shouts from tourists and their hopes of winning. Among this carnival is an inconspicuous building that has been shrouded with a painted canvas imitating the façade of the house.

This is an execution house. Here in the 1930s – during the Great Terror – the military board of the Supreme Court of the USSR handed down its death sentences. From investigation to execution. No lawyers, no witnesses. Death sentences were carried out within the day or even within the hour.

Relatives of the executed were told that their loved ones had been sentenced to prison for ten years without the right to correspond.

> *'My name was Tamara. I was a second-year student. In this building, I and 31,455 other people were sentenced to death.*
> *None of us wanted to die.'*

This is written on the poster. We stick it on the fake façade. It has a huge image of Tamara, a beautiful girl with honest eyes. I film the action.

perfumery

The businessman who acquired the building through dubious methods announces that he will open a perfumery in the execution house.

He is planning to sell expensive Western perfume. Designer scents. The mayor is on board – a museum about repression wouldn't be as profitable.

In the basement of this house, innocent people were executed. Their bodies were put in storage boxes normally used for ammunition and taken to the crematorium. The crematorium at the Donskoy Monastery.

composition no. 23

A year later, *Novaya Gazeta*, Alexei Nesterenko, whose father was executed as an 'enemy of the people', and perfumer Alena Tsishevskaya joined together to create an exclusive scent. It came in a container in the shape of a Soviet gun cartridge, in a black box with earth inside. 31,455 of them.

They went to the execution house, no. 23 Nikolskaya Street, and offered passers-by a sample.

> *'Composition No. 23 opens with notes of old papers and ink that were used to sign death sentences. The fragrance of a damp basement is soon replaced by the main ingredient – the easily distinguishable smell of gunpowder – which is gradually overtaken by notes of ash, leaving a bitter aftertaste.'*

notes of ash

The tyrannical will of Putin is such that he has created a cult of the strong leader, the cult of 'the father of the nation'. The memory of the Gulag, information about the victims of the Gulag, the experience of millions of people who were crushed by this system, languish in secret archives. Why? Because the tradition of repression continues, just under a new brand.

In the 90s, a huge statue of Dzerzhinsky was taken down from Lubyanka Square, opposite the FSB building, and a monument to commemorate the victims of Stalin's purges was erected. A stone was brought from the Solovetsky Islands – a symbol from the heart of the Gulag, so that people would remember and reject the terrible history of the Great Terror.

a policeman plays the game

*'Dear friend, you probably know that in Russia there is no
rule of law and any policeman can intrude on your life. The
World Cup gave us a taste of how the police could behave, but
what will happen when the championship is over? There's only
one way to end this – to fight for an end to the fabrication of
criminal cases and to stop them arresting people just like that.
You must decide for yourself, decide what you can do so your
Russia becomes a lot more beautiful. Bye for now, friend!'*

– Pussy Riot statement at the World Cup

During the final of Croatia v. France, four members of Pussy
Riot run onto the World Cup pitch. They're wearing police
uniforms. This is the action 'Heavenly Policeman'. The guys
are on the international news and are taken to a Russian police
station.

The grand finale is completely ruined for Vladimir Putin,
who is watching the game from a VIP box.

pussy riot's demands:

- *Free all political prisoners*
- *Do not imprison people for likes on social media*
- *Stop illegal arrests at demonstrations*
- *Allow political opposition in the country*
- *Do not fabricate criminal cases and detain people for no
  reason*
- *Turn an earthly policeman into a heavenly policeman*

preparation

They trained every day for a week. Each day they recorded their running times in Tagansky Park. Their goal: 40 seconds. At night, they practised in the playground, where they found a fence the same height as a stadium barrier. On hearing a code word they would jump over it.

They tried different code words. They ended up with the word 'Semyon'.

But first, they had to play the role of hipster-type fans. Preparation is a multi-series drama. A hundred potential obstacles and 200 ways of overcoming them. Olya had pink hair. A cop with pink hair is implausible. So they found her a wig.

the final

They go to the stadium. Each of them has a tote bag – inside the bag a police uniform turned inside out, hidden under T-shirts and chocolates. Football fan passport + passport + power bank in crossbody bags.

Preparing for a search. Preparing for questions. Preparing to be asked, 'Why do you have a police uniform in your bag?' And the answer is: 'We are drama students.'

But there are no questions, the police uniforms are not discovered.

They go to the spectator stands. They watch the rest of the first half. At half-time they go to the toilets, chosen by Peter during a reconnaissance of the site. They go into the cubicles. Pull out the uniforms. They put them on over their clothes, so that when they are detained, they aren't stripped naked. They throw the tote bags in the bin. The crossbody bags remain across their chests.

Exiting from three women's cubicles are three policewomen in full uniform, who quickly check themselves in the mirror.

comrade major

They have different ranks: Peter – a major; the girls – lieutenants.

Peter exits the male toilets. He walks quickly, holds his phone to his ear and pretends to speak to his lieutenant colonel. 'How on earth am I going to find her, Nikolayich?' He is holding a printout of an 'urgent task' – it is an 'APB' for a French female journalist whom Comrade Lieutenant Colonel Nikolayich has ordered they find and detain.

urgent task

The most complicated part is to make it onto the pitch. They have police uniforms but no tokens to gain access. They walk there and worry they'll be discovered, but no one asks them any questions. The guards at the pitch entrance for some reason give way to them, a reflex action towards any cop. Only a bald FIFA security guard regards them with any suspicion.

Peter continues his imaginary conversation with the lieutenant colonel and then puts his phone away.

Semyon! Jump. Mischief managed. Everyone is running

forty seconds of total happiness

The guys are handed over to FIFA security. The stands are indignant. A very severe-looking man takes their passports.

'Who are you? What is this?'

'Nothing, just art.'

In the office are white floor tiles and white walls. Peter and Nika are in snow-white parade uniforms. Every now and then, the office is visited by pot-bellied men carrying shoulder bags and men in suits with official passes round their necks.

year 37

Policeman: Give me the handcuffs, for both of them. Who the hell are you? Surname, name, patronymic? So you decided to shit on Russia?

Verzilov: No, we support Russia.

Policeman: Really? Do you know that Russia will now have to pay a fine to FIFA for this?

Verzilov: Why?

Policeman: Fuck you, that's why!

Verzilov: We are for Russia, just like you are, if you are for Russia.

Policeman: You've made Russia pay a fine.

Verzilov: We've not made Russia do anything.

Policeman: Are you insane?

Verzilov: I'm sane.

Policeman: Where did you get the uniform from?

Verzilov: We rented them.

Policeman: You rented them?! Sometimes I wish that we were back in 1937. I just sometimes wish we were. Look how you've shat on Russia.

Verzilov: We didn't shit on Russia, in fact the opposite, we are for Russia.

for russia

On the way to the police station one of the cops even seemed to worry for them: 'Well, if you're Pussy Riot, they might sentence you to prison.' The concern ended when the Centre E cops came. They took their phones. For the rest of the evening, the guys were called 'jesters' and 'clowns'.

They spent the night in a glass cage in Luzhniki police station. No lawyers or food were allowed. The next day they were transported to the court. The court issued a civil arrest. They all got fifteen days' detention. Everyone was relieved it was not a two-year sentence for a crime like ours.

It was the same court that had sentenced us. For 'Punk Prayer'. Six years ago. The Khamovniki court in Moscow.

our court

Why didn't they file criminal charges against them? They'd ruined the match. The Federal Security Service had messed up in front of everyone. But they understood that they could not afford a new Pussy Riot case that might be louder than the last. They imprison people for protesting, just not such well-known people. Not yet.

Put your shoelaces in a carrier bag. Put your piercing in there too. This is Special Detention Centre No. 1.

The detention centre is on high alert. They've warned all the employees that 'some very challenging girls' and 'a very difficult guy' are on their way. They have also warned the detainees. Some presume that they have run naked across the pitch. But after they spent their fifteen detention days there, a guard says, 'We thought that they were bringing in some terrifying people, but you turned out to be so sweet.'

For the girls, this is their first detention. They are eagerly awaiting their release. They dress up. But an avtozak is there waiting for them when they leave detention. 'Shit, it must be a criminal case,' each of them thinks when they see it. No one knows the avtozak's destination. They spend another night at the police station and are driven to the court the next day, where it is planned to give them another fifteen detention days. They don't understand why and they don't know what to expect.

There is one bonus: everyone's phone is returned, and so while they wait in the avtozak outside the court, they can read the news.

> *'In [the Central African Republic] three Russian journalists have been killed. The journalist Orkhan Dzhemal, the cameraman Kirill Radchenko and director Aleksandr Rastorguev. The Russians were making a film about "PMC Wagner".'*
>
> – Mediazona, August 2018

– I was meant to be there with them, says Peter.

pmc 'wagner'

Private Mercenary Company Wagner – Putin's tame mercenaries, trained fighters. They are black ops beyond the limits of Russia, where it is important to execute tasks quietly and successfully. Like in Syria and Africa.

The Wagner Group got its name from its commander, Dmitri Utkin, whose military call sign was Wagner. Utkin is a special forces officer, a lieutenant colonel. His body is covered in Nazi tattoos; he signs internal documents with the symbol SS and greets his boss, Prigozhin, with 'Heil Petrovich!'.

africa

In Africa, the Wagner Group is working to increase the Kremlin's influence. Africa has gold and diamonds, and Putin needs them to keep up with the West. That's why Putin is helping African leaders. Protecting local presidents from local revolutions and supplying arms in exchange for access to resources. Protected by Private Mercenary Companies, which are prohibited by Russian law.

> *'Participation of a mercenary in an armed conflict or in*
> *hostilities shall be punished by imprisonment for a term of*
> *three to five years.'*
>
> – Russian Federation, Criminal Code, 1996, Article 359 (3)

The owner and sponsor of the Wagner group is Evgeny Prigozhin.

Bald, with an angry jaw line, Prigozhin looks like an Orc

from a computer game. Twice convicted, he has committed a wide range of offences: theft, fraud, robbery. He gets out of jail aged twenty-nine. He opens a restaurant. A pretentious restaurant called New Island. One of the most expensive in Russia, a boat on the banks of the Neva River in St Petersburg – Putin's home city. FSB generals, governors, foreign heads of states all dine there. Putin brings George Bush Jr to the restaurant in 2003. So Prigozhin earns the nickname 'Putin's chef'.

putin's butcher

'11 September. Pyotr Verzilov, the Pussy Riot member, was hospitalized in a serious condition.'

– Mediazona, September 2018

Peter was going to fly to the Central African Republic with the journalists. His tickets were bought. If it hadn't been for Pussy Riot's action at the World Cup, if he hadn't spent fifteen days in jail, then he would have also been shot dead in an African field.

When Peter found out about the murders of the journalists, he began to independently research who was behind it. Less than two months after the murders, he is hospitalized.

The doctors don't say what they found in his blood. Pro-government bloggers on a state salary spread the rumour that he has suffered a 'drug overdose'.

Resuscitation. For three days, Peter reacts only with his eyes. On the fourth day, he recognizes Nika. Delirium and hallucinations continue. Peter doesn't know where he is.

charité clinic

With the help of friends, family and God the lord, special transport is arranged for Peter. A private jet takes him to Germany – to the Berlin clinic Charité. Here they treat other poisoned Russian opposition members too.

> '*When I came round, I thought that the head of the Berlin clinic was a prison director, and I saw cats everywhere.*'
> – Peter Verzilov

The doctors in Berlin suspect Scopolamine poisoning – a substance that is contained in the poisonous jimson weed. An overdose of Scopolamine leads to delirium, confusion and very realistic hallucinations. Jimson weed used to be considered a bridge from the earthly to the spirit world.

delirium

One of the few things I regret is that I didn't fly to Germany that autumn. My travel ban was not the reason why I didn't go. The ban didn't stop me when I flew to Ukraine two months' later. But that autumn I ran around Moscow on the phone endlessly talking about Peter's condition and buying winter clothes for Filipp. I couldn't stop asking him, 'Is everything okay? Did you get to school all right? Did you get home safely?' Now I can say that I was frightened. I saw how quickly a person could be reduced to nothing. Any person close to you.

olya slits her wrists

- I know what I can do.
- What?
- Slit my wrists.

I'm travelling on the metro from one end of Moscow to another. The journey takes about an hour. Olya, the one from my prison, is travelling with me. All journey she's been trying to tell me something, but I'm not listening. But when she says the words 'slit wrists' – I raise my head and say:

- Not bad.

Slitting your wrists is one of the most radical forms of protest that Russian prisoners use when all their other attempts – official complaints and hunger strikes – aren't working.

After a few days, Olya goes to an exhibition displaying innovation in torture and things made in prison. Organized by the Ministry of the Interior, the FSB and the Russian Guard. Knight's armour and police uniforms, made by prisoners, handcuffs called 'tenderness', Tasers and shiny new avtozaks.

She jumps on to the roof of a prison avtozak, throws pamphlets into the crowd of cops, makes a speech and slits her left wrist. The blood drips down the white vehicle. Seven streams.

When they take her to hospital, I message journalists. After the tenth text, I start to cry.

selfie from the maidan

- I can't come to mop floors, I'm in Kyiv.
- How can you be in Kyiv? I don't believe you, send me a selfie from the Maidan.

The bailiff can't believe that once again I've flown out of the country despite my travel ban. Here we will stage the final performance of *Burning Doors* with the Belarus Free Theatre in support of the Ukrainian director Sentsov. In a big theatre. Having travelled half the globe, this play is returning home, and soon its hero – Sentsov – will also return home.

He and thirty-four other Ukrainians will be exchanged for Russian war criminals. Sentsov was swapped with a Russian involved in shooting down the MH17. Hundreds of people will come to meet the freed Ukrainians. With flowers, tears and smiles. Sentsov will step off the plane, President Zelenskyy will come to meet him and shake his hand.

The exchanged Russians, meanwhile, will be transported in police cars. No interviews, no flowers, no congratulations. Putin won't come to meet them.

During the full-scale war three years later, Sentsov will join the Ukrainian army to defend the country from Russia.

all our homeland

I return to Moscow. I hand my passport to the border guard. A man in uniform materializes behind her and grabs it.

A man takes me to a room in the basement. My bailiff is there with a whole delegation. Eight people, one has a camera.

There's a pale light in the basement. Outside the airport there is cold November snow. And everything that happened abroad this summer and autumn appears in my memory like bright sparks.

A gilded statue – a theatrical award – the eyes of concert-goers full of tears, laughing eyes, queues of people who have come to say thank you and buy your book, snow-covered Swedish cities that welcome you, which you travel round with the publishers of your book. You listen to the group Army of Lovers, your favourite director, Lukas Moodysson, comes to your dressing room and you talk for four hours. A Greek left-wing politician tells you, 'My mother was the first public feminist in Greece. She bought a bus with her friends and travelled around the country and agitated through a megaphone.' And she adds, 'You remind me of her.'

wet soviet stairs

'No, Maria Vladimirovna, no one is detaining you. Here is the requirement – you go to clean floors tomorrow or you will be given a mandatory attendance and an additional fine. We couldn't wait to see you.'

I have to clean the floors of a five-storey building that is due for demolition. Half of the tenants have already moved out. Eight entrances, five floors. Once they're washed, the stairs need to be photographed and the photographs sent to a woman on WhatsApp. My phone has a photo collection of wet Soviet stairs.

new cleaning lady

I go to the dispatcher's office to get water in metal buckets. One entrance needs about two buckets to clean it.

'They've sacked the cleaner, they don't have the money.' The dispatcher doesn't understand why they've sent me to clean a half-empty building.

If your tap breaks or the lights don't work, if you're stuck in a lift and you need help, you make a call and the district dispatcher answers. This is her. The dispatcher's consists of several rooms which house electricians, carpenters, and plumbers and their tools. The street cleaners also store their shovels there. They are often migrants from Central Asia – they wear blue overalls, receive pitiful wages and work semi-legally.

They were all incredibly happy when they found out that a new cleaning lady had arrived. In other words, me. So I cleaned their rooms instead of the stairs.

140 hours

Torn linoleum and dirt embedded in the floorboards, one sink for all with layers of rust. If you have an allergy to dust, you'll most likely die here. Good that I no longer have allergies.

According to the rules, 'community service' should be for no more than four hours a day. Such rules, evidently, are needed to prolong the pleasure of work. One hundred and forty hours. I won't make it to the next tour.

The dispatcher's is on the ground floor of the building where I spent my entire childhood, where my mother still lives. I travel every day from the other end of Moscow to clean. By the end of the year, I look like a squeezed lemon.

All Russian grief accumulates in a heap and becomes my life that winter.

On New Year's Eve, everyone is running around looking for gifts, cooking and decorating. I also feel some of the festive spirit; the carpenter from the dispatcher's gives me a touching gift – a box of sweets.

'Give them to your son! Happy New Year!' he says.

sweet gift

Again, I go on tour: the first view of each city is from the open door of a van and the last view is from a hotel window, and in between are the hundreds of names of people who want me to sign their books.

I am in another part of the world – in New Zealand.

The country where the suffragettes were the first in the world to win voting rights for women. Some of the chief opponents to this, right back in 1893, were the distillery companies. They did everything they could to prevent female representation in parliament, because women were campaigning to limit the volume of alcohol sold. The fact that reducing drinking was the suffragettes' main priority disappoints many people, but I think the opposite: it's cool to demand less, and then to change the world.

land of the long white cloud

The land of harmony, where if you enter the water, it's like you are entering the sky – there's no horizon. The land of the long white cloud. Aotearoa is the name given to New Zealand by the pre-colonial people, by Māori.

Instead of handshakes and kisses on the cheek, Māori press the tips of their noses and foreheads together – sharing the breath of life. That's how they greet us.

Māori are among the few indigenous peoples who have not only survived but have succeeded in making up a quarter of parliament.

māori

This is a spontaneous tour, organized by New Zealand activists. We are living on a farm, where there are two ponies. Every morning alpacas come down from the hills. When we leave, we drive across the whole island.

'We have more sheep than people here and are proud of it.'

It is the first time we've been invited to perform in a church. A small white church in the city of Nelson. It has wooden balconies. 'Virgin Mary, Banish Putin!' echoes throughout the nave.

The next concert is in Christchurch. We get a call while on the road to be told we should 'watch the news immediately'. For the first time in the history of New Zealand, there's been a terrorist attack.

christchurch

The terrorist entered two mosques with an arsenal of weapons and opened fire on the congregations. He shot people, then went back to his car to change shotguns and rifles and came back to kill the rest. He broadcast the murders live on Facebook.

From his personal point of view. Like a computer game.

Fifty-one people were killed and forty injured.

The first terrorist attack in the history of New Zealand was committed by Australian ultra-nationalist Brenton Tarrant and prepared for two years. In his 'white genocide' manifesto, he accuses liberals and globalists of replacing the indigenous population with Muslims. Tarrant quotes the Norwegian neo-Nazi terrorist Breivik and sympathizes with Trump.

In the evening, we reach Christchurch. We go to the club where we were supposed to perform. I sit on the edge of the stage, take the microphone and speak quickly:

> '*Hi, I'm Masha from Pussy Riot. With all my heart I want to express solidarity with the victims' families. The manifesto that this Australian wrote is full of hatred. I live in a country where hatred is generated by the state. They call us enemies of the regime, enemies of the people. Anyone who disagrees with their policies. Our country is a good example of a culture of hatred. And hatred is a road to nowhere.*'

At the end of the night, I pluck eucalyptus leaves and purple freesias from a vase to take to the mosque. The street is blocked, but flowers are being brought to the crossroads and I also lay my flowers down there.

rip current

We arrive at the coast at dusk – Dima, the journalist Amanda, and I. She joined us halfway through the tour to write about Pussy Riot. The sky is cut with red stripes, there is no one on the beach except us. She questions me:

– You are both so different, how come you don't argue
  constantly?
– We do.
– For example?
– Oh, I wouldn't know where to start.

Our very next conversation turns into an argument about
abortion rights. The sun is setting on the water. I'm going into
the sea, towards the sun. Amanda is coming with me. Dima and
a sign saying, 'It's dangerous to swim here!' remain on the shore.

I dive into the sea over and over again, because the water seems
to remove everything that is haunting me. I remember what it
says on the sign, and don't go far. I surface and notice Amanda
each time, but then suddenly I come up and she's gone. And the
sun has gone. And I can no longer feel the bottom under my feet.
But I can still see the beach – it's not far away and I'm paddling
towards it. With all my strength. I'm paddling and paddling, but
every time I raise my head, the damned shoreline is further away.

They say that if you get into a rip current, you have to swim
into it sideways. It doesn't work. It just takes me even further.
The waves get bigger. My mouth fills with more and more
water. I try to shout 'Help!', but the waves overwhelm my
scream. First my feet start to weaken, then my calves. I realize
that I only have a few minutes of strength left and that's it. The
cold will overpower my legs completely and I won't be able to
swim. I'll drown. The ocean – a dark, cold, merciless thing – will
take me. It's wildly scary. I realize that everything I've been worried about for so long, everything I've been arguing about, it's
all going to end very quickly. I'm amazed at how quickly death
comes. Compared to how long life lasts, death comes so fast. A
few minutes and that's it. I won't see my child again, I haven't said
goodbye to anyone, which is terrible and irresponsible. Why did
I go into the water? There was a sign, and I was told a thousand

times it was a dangerous beach, they told me that lifeguards aren't around after sunset, why did I do that? I have to swim. Every other second I give up, and every other second I try again.

All around it is completely dark, but at one point I see a small white spot. The white spot cannot be the ocean, so this has to be the shore. I'm starting to swim hard towards the beach. I've lost hope, I just have to do what I can. At one point I feel like I've touched the bottom, it wasn't it, but it was like I touched it, and I begin to swim harder, with my last strength, I feel the bottom, I paddle more and more and more.

It turns out that Dima stopped the only person around who was walking along the shore, took his white towel and waved it. When I crawl out, they wrap me in his towel, and the guy says:

– You're a star, you swam right out of there. You must
  be very strong.

I want to tell him that God probably helped me, but I don't have the strength to talk, let alone argue with him.

concert at a factory

We come back to Russia and perform Riot Days in Moscow. We play at an underground activist festival against domestic violence. In support of the Khachaturyan sisters, Krestina, Angelina and Maria, who for many years had suffered domestic abuse at the hands of their father. In the end they killed him. He had put out cigarettes on their bodies, kept them captive at home, pepper-sprayed their eyes, forced them to have sex, cut them with a knife, and when they escaped from him, he called his friends in the police, who returned them home. To hell. At the time of his murder the sisters were nineteen, eighteen and seventeen years old.

freedom for sisters

To perform in Russia is really something. A small venue with concrete walls that used to be a factory, where you are expecting the cops to turn up at any second.

Before this we had organized just two concerts in Moscow.

After the first, they shut the venue down, and for the second they showed up with a search warrant.

In Russia it's people who speak the same language as you who gather together, listen to a story that happened many years ago and suddenly hear it in a completely different way. 'When you did "Punk Prayer", I was fourteen years old.' 'We love you.' It is one thing to hear such words from someone who can write a dissertation on Pussy Riot, and another from a person from Russia, where not a single university offers gender studies.

russian universities

The Khachaturyan sisters are on trial for murder. As are thousands of other women who have resisted domestic violence. Such cases never qualify as self-defence. Although in many cases the women had no choice.

There is no law on domestic violence in Russia. The police do not keep statistics on such cases. No data – no problem. The organizations who do conduct surveys of domestic violence are accused of being foreign agents.

Feminists are waging war against domestic violence. The Church is declaring war on feminists.

family values

Patriarch Kirill and Father Tikhon personally address Putin, demanding that the law be blocked. The Russian Orthodox Church insists that the West should not be allowed to destroy Russian families. Tsargrad – the imperial TV channel of Orthodox Oligarch Malofeev – churns out articles about the terrible consequences of laws against domestic violence in Europe – 'men are expelled from their own apartments'. Ultra-Orthodox militias organize prayer services against the enemy law. The law is blocked.

> *'You have to break a woman over the knee, tear off her horns, bend her, rub her, stuff her in the washing machine . . . A man must break a woman a hundred per cent! Turn her into a real woman. Wash off all the pornographic paint applied to her by modern civilization.'*
>
> – Archpriest Andrei Tkachev

give birth and be afraid

Why do they need patriarchy?

Authoritarian regimes need a 'traditional family'; it's a concept people can follow from childhood. A woman should obey men and give birth. A man should be patriotically faithful to his leader and if necessary be prepared to die for him.

The body must belong to the state. The body of a woman must be deprived of the right to choose whether or not she will give birth. The body of a man must be deprived of the right to choose whether or not to go to war. No one will agree to be just a compliant body in the 21st century, so a system where bodies act within a hierarchy is created.

cycle of violence

Violence has been a principle since childhood. Patriarchal rules condone men using force, according to Church concepts of family – the man is the head of his wife, like Christ is the head of the Church.

In practice, millions of self-deified men systematically beat women. Continuing the cycle of violence, many women pass on violence to the weaker ones – to their children.

Medieval punishment is presented as a 'traditional value' – 'to be put on peas' is essentially torture where a child is made to kneel on dry peas for bad behaviour. The peas are sucked into the child's skin and cause acute pain. This is still practised by Russian families.

Violence happens in families and children's homes, where children are beaten with belts, wires, cornered, dragged by the ears and slapped. Violence happens in schools – where teachers make children apologize on their knees and call them idiots. Violence happens in the army – where soldiers of higher rank humiliate and beat conscripts and practically turn them into servants. After all, they themselves went through such a 'tradition'. Violence is cyclical and contagious. Torture happens in prisons, murders in police stations. Violence becomes the norm. And no one is punished.

I want you to know that there are Russian people who have always wanted and still want to live differently. We are these people. And we have tried to fight for that right.

i/we protest summer

After a year, I completed my community service. I had finished mopping floors. One hundred and forty hours. We go to a gay bar with friends to celebrate. Moscow in summer with dozens of new small places. Nothing is permitted, but everything is allowed. And we love to joke about it.

Moscow is holding elections. For the city parliament – the Moscow City Duma. Independent opposition candidates are not allowed to run. There's a spontaneous protest of about ten people near the Electoral Commission, by the next day they have grown to one hundred.

Moscow elections are not the most significant. A deputy of the Moscow City Duma can hardly influence more than the installation of some park benches, but as long as there are elections it's important to take part.

let them in!

The candidates call a rally. They perform on stage. They say that if they are not registered as candidates within a week, they will come directly to City Hall without permission. And they'll not leave. Twenty thousand people are there.

Alexei Navalny, who proposed the meeting at the City Hall and 'not to leave' is sent to a special detention centre for thirty days. The homes of all the unregistered candidates are searched. They too are detained. Despite this, a week after the rally, on 27 July, people still come to City Hall.

this is our city

Konstantin Konovalov reported that he was detained when he went for a jog near City Hall (27 July, 09.28.)

At the restaurant Armenia on Pushkinskaya, riot police beat people with batons; on the other side of the street protesters broke down the barrier (14.31).

On Bryusov Avenue, a girl's head was smashed in (15.47).

Konovalov – the first detainee of today's rally – was diagnosed with a fracture of the medial condyle of the tibia (16.44).

Boris Kantorovich, who was severely beaten with a baton by a riot police officer on the corner of the Teatralny Lane and Rozhdestven-ska Street, is hospitalized with suspected concussion (19.42).

People are singing the Russian anthem on the square while riot police grab people and take them to avtozaks (20.03).

jog near city hall

In any Western country, to organize a rally you need to warn the police or local authorities. In Russia, in theory it's also like this. But not in practice. In practice, you send an application to the mayor's office, and you are told 'no'. And thanks for the heads-up, a bunch of cops and a cortège of avtozaks are waiting for you.

On the day of any unsanctioned protest, the first thing I do is see how many people have already been detained. When I wake up on 27 July someone has already broken a leg.

I travel into the city centre.

what to take with you to a march

passport
phone
power bank
water
warm clothes

The City Hall is fenced off with barriers, the crowd is split up and everyone has been pushed into the narrow streets. Finding each other on chats and social media. It's not easy, as the jammers are at work. I enter a lane and for a while I move with the crowd, until it is suddenly invaded by a formation of running 'cosmonauts' – the name given to the OMON and the Russian Guard. Because of their helmets. Cosmonauts are splitting the crowd up and blocking the street.

We're standing opposite each other, a wall of riot police facing a wall of protesters. Wall to wall. We outnumber them, but we don't move forward, and if someone does try to break free, then the cosmonauts grab them out of our wall, twist their arms and march them to an avtozak.

And then they move on us. They beat their shields with their batons. And they advance quicker. To intimidate us. To stop us linking arms and force us to run. And we run. From each end of their wall, the cosmonauts detach and randomly grab runners.

I run into a café. It's an expensive café with lots of plants, a kind of café garden. People sit at stylish glass tables and sip signature cocktails. Some sit by the window. Outside the cosmonauts are packing people they've managed to pull out of the crowd into avtozaks.

on the left – a restaurant, on the right – arrest

I find out where the crowd has moved to and go to join them. I leave the metro and go towards a grassy area.

I can see a crowd of cosmonauts surrounding the green. They grab someone from the crowd and drag them across the ground. I run, film them, sit on a bench to send the video to Mediazona. A young girl asks to take a selfie. We take a selfie.

I look up and a Centre E cop is standing over me: 'I'd like a selfie too if that's okay?' I don't have time to answer before he quickly sits on the bench, takes out his phone and presses the side button. Then says to the three cosmonauts standing near him: 'All done, you can detain her now.'

is this our city?

Member of Pussy Riot, Maria Alyokhina, is detained (20.41).

There are twelve of us in the avtozak, I'm the only woman. Also, I'm the only person who has experienced detention before, and time in prison.

On the way to the police station, I tell everyone about the 51st article of the constitution, which gives you the right not to answer the police's questions. I explain why everyone has the right to refuse to give fingerprints when they are detained and answer all their questions about what life is like in a penal colony. Even though we are meeting for the first time, I'm sure that I am spending the evening with some of the best people in Moscow.

Name of the priest who, when the riot police were beating protesters, opened the gates and let them into the church, saving them from detention: Giovanni Guaita.

girl with the constitution

1,373 people are detained on 27 July. Who are they?

They are called the new protest generation. They are mostly aged under twenty. Their whole life has been spent under Putin. They play protest music on loudspeakers, they climb up lamp posts, they are threatened with expulsion from university.

Everyone will remember the girl with the constitution. When a crowd of OMON marched on the protesters, Olya Misik sat on the pavement and read them the constitution, the article on the right to peaceful assembly. A year later they open a criminal case against her for protest graffiti, and she spends one and a half years under house arrest.

> *'A fascist regime never seems fascist from the inside. It seems this is petty censorship, some kind of targeted repression that will never touch you.'*
>
> – Olga Misik's closing statement to the court

new protest generation

The City Hall gives permission for the next protest. It is fenced off with crash barriers, with rows of metal detectors at the entrance, snipers on the roofs of neighbouring buildings. The protest is controlled by cops from the former 'Kyiv Berkut'. The same people who fired on unarmed students on the Maidan found new jobs in Russia.

Music artists join the Moscow protests. Any musician who performed at the rally was put on a blacklist, their concerts across Russia shut down by the police.

People who come out to protest without permission get criminal cases. This is how the Moscow Case came about, the biggest lawsuit since 2012. The investigation team was headed by Rustam Gabdullin, who had also led the Bolotnaya Case. By autumn, he was awarded the Order 'For Services to the Fatherland' first class.

Protest playlist:

- IC3PEAK – Death No More
- Noize MC – Like Common People
- Monetochka – Russian Ark
- Face – Humourist
- Anacondaz featuring Noize MC – Let Them Die
- Pornofilms – It Will Pass
- Oxxxymiron feat. Samariddin Radzhabov – Winds Of Change

queue for protest

The authorities do not issue permits for rallies anymore. But solitary pickets are still allowed. According to the law, any person can stand at any point in the city with a banner. But if another person stands next to them, the picket is no longer a solo one. Even if the second person doesn't have a banner, they will both be detained immediately. So there were queues for pickets. A person stands alone with a banner picketing for a few minutes, then a different person takes their place with their banner or takes the first person's banner, but they don't hand it to each other directly (because then the surrounding cops have grounds to detain you). It might seem like a game, but it's just a Russian protest.

To hold a banner for a couple of minutes, you have to queue. I loved telling foreign journalists about the queues.

- Hi, yes, hello, are Russians coming out to protest?
- Yes, we are, I'll send you a photo! It's a one-person picket, people queue for three hours to hold a sign. I'll explain everything to you . . .

The queue stretches from the Lubyanka to the Presidential Administration. The glazing of its doors is covered with awful reflective film so that no one can see what's going on inside.

All autumn we come to the Presidential Administration as if we are going to work. Someone brings placards, someone hands out warm clothes, someone brings hot tea and coffee, someone takes photographs. The demand to 'Allow independent candidates!' is replaced by 'Free the defendants in the Moscow Case!' Now the unregistered candidates are standing up for those who earlier came to the square to support them.

For some, the solo pickets seemed a futile protest, but they produced a result. Some of the defendants in the Moscow Case were released. They were released only because of the outcry.

you walk by
we stand in line
they serve time

November 2019. The Kremlin. Bolshoi Kamenny Bridge. We've made a huge ten-metre banner with portraits of current political prisoners.

To fix it to the bridge we need to make holes in its corners and at its centre, thread a thin rope through each hole, and attach a metal hook to each tiny rope. The banner should be rolled up, its corners marked for quick identification, so no time is lost in throwing it over the bridge, fastening the hooks to the back of the bridge's railings, and getting out of there. To lose time searching for the right corner of the banner on a bridge near the Kremlin will mean being pushed nose first onto the asphalt and detained.

On the outskirts of Moscow, in the yard, we make holes in the fabric and attach metal hooks to them. A huge banner of political prisoners unfolded on a playground. Some shops refuse to print it. And in a few years, it will be impossible to find anyone to print it.

crime and punishment

Yan Sidorov and Vladislav Mordasov, 'Rostov Case', held hand-written posters in support of people who had lost their homes in suspected arson – four years in a penal colony, tortured.

Ruslan Kostylenkov and Anya Pavlikova, 'New Greatness Case', created a protest chat, met in McDonald's and discussed politics.

Ruslan – 7 years in a penal colony, tortured and raped.

Anya – 4 years' probation. She was in jail, but after a public campaign – house arrest and probation.

Konstantin Kotov carried protest posters and called for 'honest elections' at demonstrations – 1.5 years in a penal colony

Yegor Zhukov had a political blog on YouTube – 3 years' probation with a 2-year ban on web use.

Nikita Chirtsov 'pushed a cop' – 1 year in a penal colony.

Yuri Dmitriev, a historian and expert in Stalinist repression who uncovered the firing range 'Sandarmokh', rehabilitating the names of 6,000 people executed there during the Great Terror – 15 years in a strict-regime penal colony.

*Azat Miftakhov broke a window at the offices of 'United Russia' –
6 years in a penal colony, tortured.*

*Anastasia Shevchenko joined an 'undesirable organization' – 2
years of strict house arrest, 4 years' probation. During house arrest
not permitted to visit her eldest daughter, who was seriously ill in
hospital; shortly after, her daughter died.*

stop-gulag

State terror is not a thing of the past. That's why we went to
the Bridge, to the Kremlin. We demand the release of the political prisoners. We demand the end to repression. We demand
the lustration of people involved in these repressions.

Stop Gulag – freedom to political prisoners!

The fine for the banner – 2,500 euros. I received a similarly
huge fine for sitting on a bench that summer. Of course, I am
never going to pay these penalties and as soon as they hit the
bailiff's desk, I'll be slapped with another travel ban.

But until that happens, I manage to go on tour.

the quill breaks the handcuffs

After one of our concerts – in the city of Ludwigsburg – a man
comes up to me. He says, 'I have a gift for you.' And he takes
out a very beautiful pink pony. The pony has boots and a little
yellow balaclava, and its side is embroidered 'the quill breaks
the handcuffs'.

- It's been waiting to meet you for ages. I made it myself
  seven years ago when they sentenced you in Moscow.

From the stage, we talk about what is going on in Russia, about the new protest generation, police violence, new prison sentences, how we support political prisoners. Nikita Chirtsov, accused in the Moscow Case, is from Berezniki, the town next to my first penal colony.

He received a prison sentence for defending someone at a demonstration. After his arrest, his grandmother, Nadezhda Sergeevna, came to the court in Moscow to attest to her grandson's character. She said, 'When he understood that I was seriously ill, he decided to help me and put his own needs to one side. He lived between Moscow and Berezniki. My grandson decided to be near me as thanks for all that I had given him during his life.'

His grandmother stood in a solitary picket every day. With a diagnosis of cancer. 'Freedom to our Children', said her banner.

grannie hope

We picket and go to the courts until the end of the year. Right up until the New Year celebrations. My kitchen and bedroom are covered in posters, I took them home with me. If you help someone, they become like a family member. My actual family members sometimes ask, 'Who is this?' 'Who is that?' 'Is it true he was sentenced for a paper cup?' and I try to answer, although of course I would really like it if they knew the answer already. Just read the news. Although it is strange to wish something on your closest people that will not make their life any easier.

my russia is imprisoned

New Year's Eve crept up. Filipp asked for two rats as his New Year present. Because the following year was the Year of the Rat. I said yes. He got two baby boy rats. Black and grey.

I remember one New Year when I was in solitary confinement in prison, and the guards didn't allow me to watch a film, and I went to sleep.

And this time on the eve of New Year's Eve, we've realized what we need to do – we go to buy baubles at the store, wait at the print shop at night and warm the lighter that has fallen in the snow.

On New Year's Eve we go to the Lubyanka to decorate a New Year's tree.

new year's tree

We made thirty-six balloons, multicoloured balloons with portraits of political prisoners.

Almost all of them are under arrest, many of them have been tortured, some face up to eighteen-year sentences. One of them has found love, one of them has got married, but they all share one thing – their lives will never be the same.

The Lubyanka is a terrifying place. The building should become a museum, not be a home to Chekists. When the archives are opened and we see how many lives were extinguished within these walls, and when this is taught in schools, there will be a chance that the rule of the strong, and the power wielded by fear and indifference, will no longer hold such sway in Russia.

Because real power does not lie with those who have helmets and batons. Real power lies with those who remain human.

8.

2036

India, Goa, Querim village.

On a secluded beach where there used to be a fishing village, there is a magical place – a temple looking like a multicoloured merry-go-round. It is like something from childhood. Inside is the story of fisherman Ajoba.

Ajoba knew how to talk to dolphins; they told him when and where to fish, so the village became rich. One morning the dolphins told him not to go to sea. Ajoba passed the message onto his friends, but they didn't listen. A storm broke out, and not just any storm, but a superstorm of Varuna, the god of oceans. The fishermen's families asked Ajoba to talk to the dolphins, but when he did they told him it was too late and the fishermen had gone missing. Ajoba asked Shiva to turn him into stone and, by paying this heavy price, his friends were returned.

On the vaulted arches of the temple's entrance are orange wreaths of living flowers, gingerbread columns, magical animals, flags and bells. And at the temple's centre, a stone in a deep cavity – Ajoba, who saved his friends.

Candles and incense are lit in memory of someone who was not afraid to sacrifice his life.

pandemic

I'm sitting on the beach reading the news about a new virus spreading around the world – Covid-19. According to the official version, it came from China when a man ate a bat from the wet market.

The first pandemic in a hundred years. The apocalypse online. Minute-by-minute statistics of hospitalization and mortality. Panic. Empty streets in all the capitals of the world. All flights are cancelled. My flight included.

i yell at the ocean

Time *magazine included Pussy Riot in the list of 100 most influential women for the last 100 years.*
– March 2020

This news for the 8th of March reminded me that although Putin is still there, we showed the whole world what kind of person he is. Our trial clearly exposed Putin's fear of the dissent of ordinary people. Of women. His third term became the point of no return. From then on, Russia, where it had somehow been possible to say anything, became a country where it was better to shut up.

influential women

'We need to keep Putin, as they say, close. If something goes wrong, he can support, help, insure us.'
– Valentina Tereshkova, Russian Duma, 10 March 2020

The first female cosmonaut, Valentina Tereshkova, stands at the rostrum in parliament calling for a change to the Russian Constitution so that Putin can remain in power for ever.

> *'Why twist and turn, why create artificial constructions?*
> *Restrictions on the number of presidential terms should be*
> *removed or the incumbent president should be able to be re-*
> *elected in accordance with the updated constitution.'*

Parliament applauds.

In an hour, Putin arrives with a prepared speech, at the same rostrum, and agrees to be the 'forever president'. By law, he's no longer eligible to run, so the law needs to be changed. Amend the constitution.

why twist and turn?

Putin has effectively been in power for twenty years.

How to become a tyrant, Russian-style?

1. Stage terrorist attacks so that people want the return of 'a strong hand'.
2. Crush independent media, kill journalists who are too brave.
3. Hand out business assets and powerful positions to your friends – they won't betray you. Steal together!
4. Make the Church a loudspeaker for propaganda – your power is from God.
5. Wage war with your neighbours and conquer other people's territories.
6. Shoot down the voice of the opposition – the rest will be scared and silenced.
7. Brandish the undesirable as foreign agents – those who are against you – as traitors and enemies of the people.
8. Poison your main critic – he is too popular.

9. Jail the rest of those who don't agree – any of them
   might plan a revolution.
10. Extend the number of your presidential terms –
    there's still so much to be done.

zero it!

My plane lands in Russia. An 'evacuation flight' costs twice as
much as normal. They meet us in masks and protective suits.
No taxis at the airport. A special bus takes people straight to
the address given to the border guards.

Leave anywhere without a mask – a fine.

Go on a walk without permission – a fine.

Travel somewhere on the metro hoping they won't notice
you – a fine.

Pandemic. Protest rallies are banned, they test out their
tracking systems on people breaking quarantine rules.

Moscow City Hall invested in a facial-recognition system
back in 2017: 200,000 cameras. They used it at protests.

facial recognition

A young, dark-haired security cop is standing opposite my
entrance. She's pretending to take a photograph of a memorial plaque when she's obviously taking a picture of me. Who in
that situation would carry a bright red phone case?

We set off to the river for a swim. Behind us is a car. We
enter the water; the same girl who was at my entrance is there.
She is walking along the bank holding hands with some young
guy. They go up and down the river five or six times in a row.

On the journey home, Filipp could tell the difference between an ordinary grey car and a grey security cop car tailing us. I don't want to contemplate how useful that knowledge might be to him in the future.

how to recognize centre e

1. *They pretend to talk on their phones when they're actually filming you.*
2. *Live in greyish-brown cars parked under your window.*
3. *Wear pointy shoes.*
4. *Walk around in puffy jackets.*
5. *Carry black crossbody bags.*

A tail of cops is following me wherever I go, by car or on foot. Up to three grey cop cars at a time. In each car – two Centre E operatives. We take them to various corners of Moscow. Sometimes until five in the morning. We listen to music. And laugh.

Why are they following me? Despite the pandemic, the authorities are afraid of acts of protest against Putin's amendments.

a package of amendments

Putin is increasing his powers. The package of amendments includes the right for him to personally sack judges and even the prime minister, appoint more senators, and ignore laws passed by the Duma.

The constitution used to guarantee adherence to international law. Now Putin's amendments give Russian law supremacy over international law. That means there's no longer an imperative to pay compensation for human rights violations.

new constitution

They don't talk about it on TV. There's a TV advert where famous artists call for people to go to the polling stations. They say we need a new constitution to 'protect the constitution from enemies', to protect veterans 'from Stalin being compared to Hitler', and to interpret history in strict accordance with Putin's textbooks.

The 'traditional family' will be preserved with the amendment: 'marriage is the union between a man and a woman.'

Even before the vote they are selling the new version of the constitution in the shops. I ask friends to buy one for me.

let it burn

> *'Hello! I am Masha. And this is the new constitution of the Russian Federation. It says that even before any vote, Putin will rule us for eternity. Under the disguise of amendments, we are encouraged to legitimize dictatorship and move away from democracy. I'm against dictatorship in Russia. I'm against corruption and theft by officials. I'm against cops who beat us at peaceful demonstrations, I'm against propaganda that makes us enemies of the people. I'm against torture, I'm against a trial run directly from the Presidential Administration. I am against the fact that our country's traditions are based on discrimination.*
> *I'm against the amendments.'*
> – Burn it!! Olya commands, as she films me on her iPhone.

I put on a yellow balaclava and set the pages alight. I throw the ash into a bucket. For the background of the video we choose night-time Kremlin.

election on tree stumps

The election for the amendments is called 'all Russian' – so that everyone is fully aware that the decision is a national one. The polling stations are organized outside. On the first day of the election, there are thousands of memes – photographs of voters on tree stumps, on rocks, in buses and in the boots of cars.

The last day of the vote – 1 July – was declared a public holiday for the whole country.

2036

Red Square. The final day of the vote. Cops in white ceremonial shirts are peeling eight members of Pussy Riot off the cobbles. They had formed the number 2036 with their bodies. Putin will now be able to remain in power until this year if the amendments are approved.

Each number is a two-person coupling, handcuffed to each other. Handcuffs bought in a sex shop, the pink fur removed beforehand. They rehearsed with a stopwatch.

The action is a homage to the Russian art group E.T.I., who in April 1991 spelled out a three-letter word equivalent to FUCK with their bodies, near Lenin's Mausoleum.

'Get up!' The cops go to them in turn, grab someone by their jeans, drag someone under their arms into the car.

Someone is dropped, someone is being throttled. The sound of the police siren is mixed with the sound of the chimes. The Kremlin clock chimes ten times.

They take everyone to the police station, one of them is brutally beaten. They are released without arrest – the cops were given instructions not to detain anyone on the final election day. Not to spoil the holiday.

amendment day

On this final day of 'voting' my surveillance is tripled. Even though the results will be falsified, I still go to cast my 'no'.

'Elections' in Russia are mostly held in schools. The people who falsify them are ordinary primary school teachers. The 'amendment vote' is no exception. I go with Filipp to the neighbouring school, where a polling station has been set up. Right behind us at the school's entrance are four security operatives. We notice there's another on the street corner.

If I had gone to the action with the others, it would probably not have happened at all. But it still hurts a little. And so I set off to the city centre after voting. A protest rally had been planned there.

protest on pushkinskaya

The constitution has been changed. I arrive and see 500 people on the square. They stand wearing face masks with placards. I take a placard and stand next to them.

The police, surrounding the square, don't detain anyone. Propaganda and bots circulate messages about how great the police are, handing out face masks to irresponsible protesters who came out without them at the height of the pandemic.

Another rally is organized. To collect signatures to declare the amendments illegal. This time the police disperse the protest and open criminal cases against the organizers.

The year that most of the world will remember as the year of pandemic and self-isolation is a year of new repression in Russia – new political prisoners, long prison sentences and queues outside courthouses.

and that's all you can come up with?

On the Moscow–Pskov train. I'm travelling to hear the verdict against journalist Prokopyeva. She's been accused of 'justification of terrorism' for messaging about a seventeen-year-old anarchist, Mikhail Zhlobitsky.

He brought a bomb to his local FSB building in Archangelsk, saying online: 'The reasons should be quite clear – the FSB is the main terrorist. They fabricate cases and torture people.' The bomb exploded in his hands. He died on the spot, wounding three security officers.

I make a placard for Prokopyeva on the train. Almost all the journalists who are in the same carriage as me will be forced to leave the country after the full-scale war starts.

Those who disagree with the war will also be prosecuted for 'justification of terrorism'. If previously enemies were branded 'extremists', now they're called 'terrorists'. Prison sentences are longer, the effect of intimidation is stronger.

fsb – the main terrorist

'People! Do not kill one another' is etched onto the stone at the entrance to the former firing range, Sandarmokh. These are the words of local historian Yuri Dmitriev.

The Chekists had hoped that the grass would grow over the area and no one would find it. Dmitriev did.

guardian of history

Years of excavations and hundreds of hours spent in the archives allowed Dmitriev to rehabilitate several thousand of those killed at the firing range during Stalin's Great Terror. Thanks to him, the terrible words 'killing fields' have been transformed into a memorial.

forest of faces

There were 236 communal pits. Dmitriev exhumed and cleaned bones, he collected the names of the executed in several hand-written books. People finally found out what had happened to their relatives. They started to come here from countries in the former Soviet Union and Eastern Bloc: Poles and Lithuanians, Georgians and Chechens, Ukrainians and Belarussians. They erected monuments. They installed memorial plaques with photographs. Now those who enter the forest can see the eyes of people for whom this forest became a final place.

rewrite history

When Putin came to power, he shut down the archives. This desire to classify everything and hide it is inherited from his Soviet predecessors. The FSB – the successor of the Cheka – started to retaliate against Dmitriev. First, they found local 'historians' to say that it was not victims of political repressions but Soviet prisoners of war that were killed by the Finns during the Second World War.

Then Dmitriev himself is arrested in a despicable fabricated case. He is accused of producing pornography, having been lured out of his apartment while they stole photographs of his stepdaughter, which he had taken to monitor her health.

He is sentenced to fifteen years of strict regime – a death sentence at his age. A week after the break-in at Dmitriev's home, the head of the FSB for Karelia will be promoted and transferred to Moscow.

'I know the fates of so many people who went through this in the 1930s – those who lie under the ground at Sandarmokh or at Krasny Bor. I guess I have a better sense of how they must have felt. Who cares if eighty years have passed? It's the same prison, same walls, same corridors, same decisions.'

– Yuri Dmitriev

same decisions

I travel by train to Karelia with Dmitriev's colleagues and supporters. To Petrozavodsk, for the trial.

The night – I spend in a hostel. I read about Sandarmokh. Two men are sitting with me. One of them asks me to repair his jacket. I am a woman, which means, in his eyes, I must be able to sew. I joke that I even have a diploma in professional tailoring from the penal colony. They realize who I am. I sew his jacket and talk about the Stalinist purges, about Putin and the Patriarch, about how we were not naked in the Cathedral of Christ the Saviour, and the fact that the rainbow flag is important because people are killed for their sexuality. And why I am here. These men are local, but they don't know about Dmitriev's case or Sandarmokh.

– You can read about it while I sew. You live here,
   after all.

An hour later, the owner of the jacket berates the authorities, muttering that he does not understand where all his taxes go. Then he googles Dmitriev. We go up to our rooms at midnight, I have to get up early. At 9 a.m., a car will be leaving for Sandarmokh.

firing range

This place was classified. People transported here to be executed were documented as missing. A police officer, Ivan Chukhin, initiated the search for them when he saw his father's signature on the death sentences.

Birds hardly sing here. More than 6,000 corpses are in mass graves – execution pits. Here they shot people who had been forcibly settled, prisoners from the White Sea Canal construction site, local people. One of the most terrifying stories was the execution of prisoners from the First Solovki Transportation. The prisoners sent here from the Solovki Islands were considered missing, the authorities lied for decades, then sent them here to be shot.

They killed 250 people a night, and before the execution, they stripped them, tied them up, beat them, brought them unconscious to the pits, threw them in and finished them off there.

the living and the dead

The stories from the hell of the past are mixed up with the stories of our present hell, when a historian who dedicated his life to the victims of repression becomes one of those names on a list of the repressed.

Dmitriev spent decades stirring up memories that were uncomfortable to the authorities. A stubborn wise man with a white beard, hollow cheeks and a dog named Witch, he was finding what they had wanted to scrub out. He would dig up the bones of the executed, give them back their names, get to know them and introduce them to others. He brought the dead and the forgotten back into the world of the living.

impossible to look away

'We all know the most genuine sacrifice is being committed here!' screams a guy dressed in a police uniform surrounded by cameras and journalists. He's holding a knife to the throat of a mannequin that says 'truth', 'freedom', 'humanity', and is covered in the names of political prisoners. Then he takes off the mannequin's scarf and cuts its throat with a yellow scalpel. A red liquid sprays from its throat.

This is artist Pavel Krisevich and it is his action near the court, where they are just about to pass the sentence for one of the political cases – the New Greatness Case.

the future of russia – today

A group of Moscow youngsters went to protest rallies and discussed politics in their chat, called 'The Future of Russia – Today'. A black bird with outspread wings – a mocking jay from the Hunger Games – as the avatar. And then the chat was infiltrated by an FSB agent. He suggested renaming it to 'New Greatness' and to create a formal organization. He wrote the organization's charter, rented an office and drove the chat's members out of town to practise shooting. He filmed everything on a hidden camera. And then wrote a report to the police. That's how the New Greatness criminal case came about.

may luck always be on your side

I arrive at the court with the book *Hunger Games* and silver glitter arrows.

That summer we started coming to the courts covered in glitter – I came up with the hashtag #glitteragainstrepression.

Are we crazy or pathetic? Or do we simply care?

Who are we? How many of us? Why are we doing this? And how long can we last?

#glitteragainstrepression

'From time to time, I was overtaken by an attack of wild laughter, which I could not control. It irritated the cops. "Kavkazets" took a yellow bag and put it over my head; it

became hard to breathe. They stretched me out. "Pimple" held me, and "Anonym" first beat my kidneys, and then took a steel kitchen hammer for beating meat and thrust its handle deep into my anus.
After a couple of minutes, they left and "Redhead" entered. He said that I must record a video confession. The text was too long, and I could not remember it the first time. Later, this video made it onto the Internet.'

– Ruslan Kostilenkov

Ruslan will receive seven years in a penal colony – they will make him the leader of a 'extremist organization'. Not one episode of his torture will ever be investigated. As a sign of protest, Ruslan and Vyacheslav Karpov, another defendant, slit their wrists in court.

sacrifice

All of the defendants will be found guilty. They will give three of them long sentences. Parents will cry in the courtroom. Guys in glitter – on the street outside. I will not cry, I'm used to it.

The practice of infiltrating agents to 'uncover conspiracies' has long been the practice of the Chekists, then Soviet NKVD and the KGB. The agents provocateurs penetrated dissident circles, then wrote denunciations, which became the basis for criminal cases. They were accused of creating terrorist cells. A portrait of Dzerzhinsky hangs in the offices of today's security officers. He reminds them what to do.

novichok

'Alexei Navalny was hospitalized with poisoning after an emergency landing in Omsk. He is in intensive care.'

– Meduza, 20 August 2020

FSB officers poison the main opposition politician of the country, Alexei Navalny, with a nerve agent – Novichok. The FSB officers smear military-grade poison on Navalny's underpants in his hotel room in Tomsk. Miraculously Navalny survives the attack; the plane to Moscow where he lost consciousness makes an emergency landing. Two days later, when the scandal has attracted worldwide attention, he is flown to Berlin's Charité clinic, the same place that treated Peter Verzilov for poisoning.

Navalny didn't die – not this time. After a month, he gets back on his feet and starts an investigation with a team from Bellingcat: they want to find the names of the poisoners. They're hacking into the emails of one of the top intelligence officials. It may seem unbelievable, but his mail password is 'Moscow 1'; after the hack it was replaced by 'Moscow 2'. The third time the Chekist replaced his password with 'Moscow 3'. What do you think he changed it to the next time?

moscow 4

Navalny calls his own killers pretending to be a representative of Nikolai Patrushev, the Secretary of the Security Council. Most of the poisoners sense something's up and put the phone down. But one, Konstantin Kudryavtsev, answers all the questions.

Kudryavtsev – who has followed Navalny for years, listened to hours of surveillance recordings of his voice – talks to him directly for over forty minutes. Kudryavtsev tells Navalny that his team 'received the command to work on the underpants'. He gives the names and mobile phone numbers of his colleagues and explains how the FSB covered their tracks. He also gives the reason 'why it didn't work': the plane made an emergency landing in Omsk, where the paramedics administered first aid. After the phone call is uploaded online, Kudryavtsev disappears. Where he is now and whether he is still alive is unclear. Two doctors at Omsk hospital, where Navalny was taken, died suddenly within a year.

laboratory x

Poisoning the regime's enemies is an old Chekist tradition.

The Lubyanka. Behind it is a two-storey mansion. On the second floor – Dzerzhinsky's office; in the basement and in the yard – a place to shoot people. Over several years, the Chekists kill up to 15,000 people here. In the same building, there is a secret 'Laboratory X' – a laboratory for developing poisons. The goal is to find a poison that imitates natural death. And leaves no trace.

Experiments are carried out on prisoners sentenced to death by firing squad. They are taken in Black Ravens from the Lubyanka's prison on 'a visit to the doctor'. Under the disguise of medicine, they are given poison. And they are watched through a special peephole as they die. To see how convincing the deaths are in resembling a normal heart attack. The victims die in terrible agony.

doctor death

Someone is given tea with granules; someone is shot with a syringe gun; someone is injected with a special umbrella, at the tip of which is a microcapsule of toxin.

The chemists in uniform cannot stand it and go on a drinking spree. Two of them commit suicide. The orders are given by Stalin and his chief Chekist Beria. Laboratory X is led by Colonel Mairanovsky – 'Doctor Death'.

The war ends. Stalin begins to have pre-death paranoia. Doctor Death is imprisoned. He ends up in the same cell as the captured Nazi doctor Carl Clauberg. In Auschwitz, Clauberg mutilated and killed women to find an 'easy and cheap' method of sterilization. For example, he injected liquid acid into their Fallopian tubes without anaesthesia.

Mairanovsky will serve ten years; after leaving jail he will be sent away from the capital. When he arrives back in Moscow to ask for an 'amnesty', he will collapse in the hospital corridor. The official cause of death – a heart attack.

poison and heart

I go to the Solovetsky Stone with a placard: 'You have poisons, we have a heart.'

Across the road – at the entrance to the Lubyanka's main building – people are being detained. Not many, ten, maybe twenty.

Why are there so few of us?

When we had the first wave of political prisoners, we protested, but it was not enough.

When Nemtsov was killed, we cried, but no one sought revenge.

We began to congregate at protest rallies – they banned rallies.

We queued for a solitary picket – they banned solitary pickets and queues.

And on that day, a nice warm August summer day, I'm standing by the Solovetsky Stone and part of me just can't comprehend what's happening.

They just poisoned a man for telling the truth, the constitution has been amended – where's everyone? What has happened to us? When did it start?

A long time ago.

Whose fault is it?

Seems like it's ours.

neighbouring dictatorship

A few blocks from the Lubyanka – the Belarusian embassy.

Belarus is a window onto the future. Belarus is occupied by the dictator Lukashenko, for twenty-six years he has imprisoned and killed his opponents. He calls Putin 'my older brother' and, like Putin, he regrets the collapse of the USSR. He introduces the death penalty for high treason. The KGB continues its business as usual, and the opposition is trampled on, often through murder.

But something incredible happens that summer.

almost revolution

It all started when one woman, Sviatlana Tsikhanouskaya, decided to run for president instead of her husband, who had been jailed for criticizing the 'president'. The dictator did not see her as a threat – a simple housewife could not rattle the totalitarian regime. He laughed at the idea of a pre-election debate with her: 'What would I discuss? Meatballs?'

At this point Tsikhanouskaya was already rallying people to huge protests. The whole opposition agreed to vote for her so she would win and free all the political prisoners – genuine elections would be held.

For the first time in many years, Belarusians had hope of bringing down the moustachioed dictator. On election day, queues form at Belarusian embassies around the world. In Moscow, hundreds of people with red-white-red flags – the flags of an independent Belarus – stand in line all day to vote. The queue extends to streets nearby. Passing cars beep their horns in support.

cockroach

Lukashenko wants to look like the 'father of the nation'. 'Batka' – meaning guardian – is a nickname that he is proud of. Every day, the news shows him visiting factories and inspecting crops.

The elections are falsified. Lukashenko creates an 80 per cent victory for himself. But it is obvious to everyone – Tsikhanouskaya had won. Almost a million people protest throughout Belarus. Lukashenko orders a forceful dispersal.

Thousands of riot police fly out of avtozaks and fill the streets. They beat people indiscriminately with batons. The streets of Belarusian cities turn into a battlefield – screams, stun grenades. Shots fired at the unarmed. People hide in courtyards and entrances. The riot police rip down doors. They snatch terrified people and stuff them into cars.

Those people taken to special detention are escorted along

a corridor by cops carrying batons. Reaching the end of this corridor, the detainees can no longer walk by themselves. The screams from the inner courtyard reach relatives waiting outside. Thousands of criminal cases.

long live belarus

We believe in this protest. We find hope in every news line. But our hope is diminishing, and the news is getting darker. Every day we go to the Belarusian embassy in Moscow. We stand across the road, by the church. Candles, placards, red-and-white flags of an independent Belarus.

This is not just a protest against a dictatorship in a neighbouring country. The two repressive regimes go hand in hand. Both dictators dream of reviving the corpse of the USSR. For both of them, a woman is a voiceless being who produces new bodies for the army.

That is why it is important for us to support the Belarusians. On one of the days in front of the embassy, I stand in a chain of solidarity – this is an action organized by Moscow feminists. Dozens of women in white dresses and with wreaths in their hair. The most touching moment – 'Kalykhanka' – the Belarusian lullaby. We sing it in chorus:

> 'Bye-bye, bye-bye
> Close your eyes'

And at the same time, thousands of people in Minsk are burying Alexander Taraikovsky, shot to death at a protest. They carry flowers. There is news of torture and beatings, flowers again, and a chain of girls in white dresses across the street.

chain of solidarity

Lukashenko calls his 'older brother' and asks for military aid. Putin sends soldiers and a team from *Russia Today* set off to Minsk. The Russian propagandists cover stories about brave riot police defending the country from enemies, and activists are portrayed as paid provocateurs.

In Moscow, the police, Centre E officers and Kremlin provocateurs appear at protest rallies for a free Belarus. The ultra-nationalist movement SERB, a puppet army of 'patriots', deface Nemtsov's memorial, attack opposition members with Zelenka, trample on rainbow flags and shove human shit in bags under activists' doors. They work closely with NOD, the ones who attacked us in Nizhny Novgorod.

One provocateur pushes the organizer of the action – Dasha – into a fence. I seize his placard. He whines, 'She's from Pussy Riot! She attacked me!' A cop standing nearby recognizes me. But suddenly he doesn't stand up for the provocateur, he stands up for me. 'Move away from them,' the man in uniform commands.

move away from them

I go to a church kiosk to buy coffee, two security police are following me.

- Will there be any songs today? Will we hear any songs today? one asks.
- The years go by and your jokes never change, I reply.
- Do you know that Belarusians are against LGBTQ? continues the second.

The girl serving at the church kiosk looks out: 'Please don't discuss such things here, take them outside the cathedral bounds.'

out of bounds

We were laughing when we wanted to cry. One protest, a second, a third. One dispersal, a second, a third. If it was a TV show, no one would watch it until the end. The detentions on Pushkinskaya, the avtozaks at Kitai-Gorod, Revolution Square cordoned off. 'Citizens, we ask you to disperse and to not obstruct.'

Tsikhanouskaya is forced to leave the country, she cries and reiterates that otherwise they would have taken away her children. Lukashenko will no longer be called a legitimate president. Her comrade, Maria Kalesnikava, is given eleven years in a penal colony; she refuses to leave the country and tears her passport up at the border.

In exchange for remaining in power, Lukashenko has turned his country completely over to Putin's command. In the future, Belarus will host training camps for Wagner soldiers, a Russian nuclear base and Russian troops firing missiles into Ukraine.

window onto the future

'I wonder if I set myself on fire near the entrance of the local FSB headquarters, will it bring our country even a little bit closer to a bright future? Or will my sacrifice be pointless?'

– Irina Slavina

Irina Slavina is a well-known journalist in Nizhny Novgorod, a perky, proud blonde who founded her own media channel, Koza (Goat), to tell the truth without censorship. She went to protest rallies, published investigations and wasn't afraid to argue.

Her tyres were slashed; she was reported. One fine after another. That autumn twelve security cops break into her apartment with crowbars. They announce that she's a witness in a criminal case. They take all her equipment. Years of experience in Russia teach you that switching from being a witness to a suspect takes a few minutes and one signature. She did not want to go to prison.

'With her action, Mum wanted to get people to listen to her.
It was a cry of desperation and a call to wake up, sent into the
future, to us today.'

– Irina Slavina's daughter, Margarita Murakhtaeva

call to wake up

Under the window of the Ministry of Internal Affairs there is a bench-monument to the police state. Three bronze policemen: a tsarist, a Soviet and a modern one sit on the bench.

Slavina sits between the Soviet and the contemporary cop, ties herself to the bench with a rope, douses herself with kerosene. And sets herself on fire. The last thing she does before she dies is push away a passer-by who tries to save her.

A terrifying death in a matter of seconds. Terrifying for those who are afraid, but not for her. Before igniting the lighter, she writes:

blame the russian federation for my death

Her blood will forever now be on that bench.

A national memorial – candles, portraits of Irina, and many, many roses – will be thrown into black bin bags and taken to the rubbish tip.

> *'The sculptures were paid for with our money, with the money of police officers. There's a piece of each of us in this monument, and I have the right to say that the memorial doesn't belong there.'*
>
> – Alexei Trifonov, former head of Centre E in Nizhny Novgorod

a small part of all of us

The white closed coffin is carried to the applause of the Nizhny Novgorod people. At Irina's farewell ceremony, a short woman with a quiet, trembling voice, who has never met her, comes up to the stage.

'I am very scared of speaking. I am a small person. I am a small resident of this city. I am a small resident of the Russian Federation, who has always lived with my family, in my small house. My life has been good, and I have been afraid to live any other way, and I'm afraid now. I'm very afraid. I am very grateful that Irina did not think only about global injustice. She thought about small people, she thought about me.'

She touches the lid of the coffin and says, 'Forgive me.'

'You were silent while my mother was burning' will be written on a placard held by Slavina's daughter. She will take charge of her mother's media project until the full-scale war, when they make her shut it down. There'll be no criminal investigation into incitement of suicide. People will still bring flowers to a small metal goat, in honour of Slavina's media channel, in the centre of Nizhny Novgorod.

more and more

They say after death there is a white light and a tunnel
And there's something good at the end of it.
If you've been good, then there's good at the end too,
If there is death, there's good after death, so they say,
But it didn't happen like that.
Something died and died many more times in our country
and all over the world –
Not even something, tens of thousands of people.
But there was nothing good afterwards,
It was worse than before, death came into our lives,
death just walked into our lives
and then it just became more and more
and more

9.

Rainbow Diversion

'When it was Pride month in the summer, a rainbow
flag suddenly appeared on a flagpole in the grounds of a
St Petersburg school. The headmistress was very unhappy, she
asked one of the pupils: "Why have you organized an LGBTQ
sabotage here?" I laughed: "You think this is sabotage?
We'll show you what real sabotage is." '

– Sasha Sofeev

rainbow sabotage

We congregate in an apartment on the fifth floor with a gabled window and a balcony looking out onto Chistye Prudy Boulevard. During those years we moved between dozens of such apartments.

It's autumn. The birthday of my close friend Sasha. Nika has baked a cake. We've printed photos from protests, travels and parties and have made an altar of them. Lit candles and turned out the light.

red corner

We danced and listened, we watched and chatted. Ours was like many other gatherings, with one exception. We didn't meet just to celebrate, we met to plan an action.

'Let's divide into groups.'

We turn off our phones, leave them in another room and sit in a circle.

Another birthday is coming up in a week's time. Putin's birthday. We want to congratulate him – to give him a rainbow.

birthday

> *'Do we really want our country to have "parent number one", "number two", "number three", instead of "mum" and "dad"? Have they completely lost their minds over there?!'*
> – Vladimir Putin

Homophobia is the most convenient instrument for opposing the West. The Soviet empire has collapsed. A new country, Russia, has failed to re-create itself. If we are no longer an empire, then who are we? If the question isn't answered, we'll end up being the same country, only much smaller. It's offensive. Putin decided to build an identity 'in opposition to the other' – 'Who do we hate?': the West. The West is rainbow flags, gay parades and men in thongs. The West wants to destroy our traditions. They are on their way to hell and want to drag us there with them.

During his third term, Putin makes homophobia a 'national idea'. He introduces a law that forbids 'the propaganda of homosexuality'. It's a PR law. Just like the law that criminalized offending the feelings of religious believers. Their aim – to make it clear where the authorities stand. To give a signal to society how they should behave. And how not to.

No one knows what 'propaganda of homosexuality' is, not even the lawmakers. In the final version, 'homosexuality' is switched to 'non-traditional sexual relations'. To avoid further propaganda.

gay propaganda

This is Pussy Riot's first action with so many people. We have five targets – key buildings of the regime:

- FSB on the Lubyanka
- Presidential Administration
- Ministry of Culture
- Police station
- Supreme Court

At each target there's an empty flagpole. On each flagpole we will raise a rainbow flag. With this gesture we are saying, 'We are here! We exist and we are not afraid of you! Here is your regime with all its machinery, and here's our flag.'

They will keep telling you that society 'isn't ready yet' for change, until someone starts to fight for that change.

our flag

- Can I be part of an action that supports the LGBTQ community if I'm not a member of it? asks Lucy.

Every target needs a team. We decided to split into teams of three – one to stand below, one to jump onto the shoulders of the first and hang the flag, the third to take a photo to send to the chat. The chat coordinator organizes the photos. Three to a target. Sixteen people.

Everyone chooses the target they feel closest to. For example, Nika immediately takes the FSB. Tim is keen on the Presidential Administration building because he has stood outside in solitary pickets for much of the year. He wants to honour his efforts.

I have also stood in pickets. I also wanted to take the Presidential Administration, and the FSB is already spoken for. I choose the Ministry of Culture. At the other targets you can hang the flag by jumping onto someone's shoulders, but here the flagpole is very high, it's on the grey façade next to the golden letters 'Ministry of Culture of the Russian Federation'. Technically, it's the hardest target.

Lucy says that she also wants the Ministry of Culture and she wants to be in a team with me. We don't know each other well. But we both like that it's complicated.

The flagpole has to be reached by a ladder, two people need to hold the ladder and a third needs to place the flag. And one more is required to document the action. So we need another person.

princess diana

At night, I travel to the outskirts of Moscow, to Lyubertsy, once a dangerous gangland. There, in one of the panelled high-rise blocks, with three cats rescued from the street, lives Diana, a girl who performed 'Punk Prayer', but who managed to escape and not go to jail. She maintained her anonymity for nine years, and it is only in this year that she's decided to reveal her name.

I don't know what it must be like to run from prison. It's probably very scary.

When the guards chased us out of the cathedral, Diana was

the only one who went back to collect our jackets, all hastily thrown down near the altar. As a child, she had dreamed of studying music; her first wages were spent on music college. She became a drummer.

> *'They expect girl-musicians to be beautiful, but I don't just*
> *want to be beautiful, I want to say something.'*
>
> – Diana Burkot

'Will you come with us to hang a rainbow flag on the MinCult?'

'I'll come!'

come out of the closet

> *'Today there is a specific test of loyalty, a pass to that*
> *"happy" world, the world of excessive consumption, the world*
> *of apparent "freedom". Do you know what this test is? The*
> *test is a very simple and terrifying one – it's a gay parade.'*
>
> – Patriarch Kirill

One person told me that we had released evil spirits. That the Pussy Riot action with the anti-Putin song in the church not only meant a prison term for us, it had also strengthened the Church. From the moment we were arrested until we were sentenced, the country heard each day how evil powers were violating our shrines and how those shrines must be urgently defended. That we were those people who provoked a law that carried criminal charges for offending believers' feelings. That if we hadn't 'stuck our necks out', there would be no need for these laws.

That we had provoked repression.

defend shrines

It is impossible to 'provoke repression' in a system that doesn't need it. But Putin's system always needs an enemy and repression will happen anyway. And it doesn't matter if this enemy is shouting about their rights or keeping their mouth shut.

To be silent doesn't mean staying safe; to be silent means buying time before they come for you.

The witch hunt started with us but it doesn't finish there. More 'moralizing' criminal laws. More hatred. Putin needs to be the 'eternal tsar' – the Church provides the 'sanctity' of the tsardom. The union is functioning efficiently.

traditional hatred

At night, we go to buy a ladder. Closer to dawn we make it to an open store.

At dawn we drive the super-ladder to town. It is so long it hangs out of the boot and shudders on each bump in the road. We are shattered. The goal is to get rid of it in an apartment in the centre and sleep.

But there isn't an apartment in the centre. And when I ask on the chat: 'Who can we leave a ladder with?', only one person, Lucy, answers, 'You can at mine.'

We drive to Lucy's. We ring on the entry phone. The concierge buzzes us in. A woman wearing a nationalist party shirt, and it seems she doesn't like anyone at all.

– So many homeless around, she says, commenting on our appearance.

super-ladder

How do you hang an LGBTQ flag on a ministry building with 24-hour security?

We decided to dress up as utility workers. I go and buy orange uniforms with reflective stripes.

Our flagpole is above the entrance. Right behind the entrance door is the guard's desk. When I went on my reconnaissance trip, I calculated that for the guard to get up from the table, walk to the door, open it and stop us would take him less than ten seconds. This is too little time for the action, so we need to look as authentic as possible. Dressing like workers will buy us time.

orange is the new black

We start rehearsing in the morning. We're practising near Lucy's building. A professional climber is training us. We extend the ladder, place it against the entrance porch, climb up. The climber is monitoring us with a stopwatch. As soon as we clamber up onto the porch canopy, a woman looks out of a window below. 'I see you! I know what you're doing!' In fact, we don't even know what we are doing. Each one of us is climbing up and concentrating on not crashing down.

- I know what you're doing! challenges the woman, and she starts to film us on her phone, using a flash
- Look what's going on! she continues to the concierge, who has come out at the sound of shouting. Look what they're doing! I can see exactly what you're

up to, sneaking into our flats and installing your . . .
surveillance equipment!

We quickly fold the ladder up. And go to another yard. The
woman comes after us, but we lose her.

the last night

> *'I don't think it's enough to penalize gays for promoting
> homosexuality to teenagers. They should be banned from
> donating blood and sperm. And their hearts, in the event of
> a car accident, should be buried or burnt as they are unfit to
> sustain anyone else's life.'*
>
> – propagandist Dmitry Kiselev

The day before the action, some of the guys said that they
weren't going to take part. We didn't need to ask why, but we
did need to work out who would be taking their target – the
Supreme Court. We are.

The night before the action we meet in the same apartment.
We write a manifesto and create a partisan chat.

We demand that the government:

1. Investigate the killings and kidnappings of gay,
   lesbian, transgender and queer people in Chechnya.
2. Stop the persecution of activists and organizations
   who help the LGBTQ community.
3. Pass a law prohibiting discrimination based on a
   person's gender and sexual orientation.
4. Legalize same-sex partnerships.
5. Stop the persecution of same-sex families and the
   removal of their children.

6. Repeal the current law banning the promotion of non-traditional sexual relations as it is discriminatory and violates the right to freedom of expression.
7. Make 7 October LGBTQ Visibility Day.

we are visible

Some of us still didn't believe that everything would work out. But at the last moment, the pieces of the puzzle began to come together.

We went into pre-dawn Moscow.

'I report that employees of the 5th department of the Centre for Combatting Extremism of the Ministry of Internal Affairs of Russia in Moscow, within the framework of monitoring the "Internet" channel "Instagram", that is open access, discovered photos of activists of the LGBTQ community together with art-punk group "Pussy Riot", which on 7 October 2020, during the period of 06:30 to 8:00 on the territory of the City of Moscow, held an action-performance with demands by placing LGBTQ flags on various administrative buildings.'

— *Police report*

We need to catch the moment between night and day. The moment when people haven't set off to work yet but the sun is up.

now is the time

We are picked up by a truck. An old truck, like the ones that picked me up hitchhiking and not at all like a taxi. The streets are empty.

We approach the Ministry of Culture in our orange uniforms. Put up the ladder. I hold it on the right, Diana on the left. Lucy climbs up with the flag. Inserts it into the flagpole. The guard comes out.

– Who sent you?

In these kinds of moments, it's important to remain calm.

– Today is Putin's birthday. They told us to decorate.
– To decorate what? What are you putting up there? Is it authorized?
– Of course, it is authorized.

Diana calmly adds, 'We are just doing our job.'

That guard will be fired after the action but doesn't have time to shout, 'Wait a moment!'

We leave the super-ladder around the corner and drive to the next target.

We see cops standing at the entrance to the court we've chosen. What should we do?

Liza suggests on the partisan chat that we go to another court – the Supreme Court. A majestic building with a bronze Themis above the entrance. Probably the only Themis in the world that is not blindfolded. Instead of a sword in her right hand, she has a shield with an Orthodox emblem. The Supreme Court – just the same as an ordinary Russian court. Here there's no justice, instead there's 'telephone law' – judgements are passed after a call from the Kremlin. Exactly the same process as our sentencing for 'Punk Prayer'.

kangaroo court

The team responsible for the police station goes to check the flagpole at the Supreme Court for us. The flagpole is there. The cops are not there. Let's go.

I jump on Vasya's shoulders, install the flag. I don't manage to straighten it out; I worry about that, but Nika messages, 'You're the best!' – and we run away from the entrance, directly to the summer garden. We run and laugh – we did it!

All the targets are covered in rainbows.

we are just doing our job

> *Vasya: I've been detained with Liza. Taken to Basmanny.*
> *Help us.*
> *Sasha: The police are knocking on my door.*
> *Nika: I was detained. 4 cops in uniform + some higher-up*
> *fucker. Find a lawyer.'*
>
> – 'Partisan chat'

The first participants in the action are detained that same evening. The team responsible for the flag at the Basmanny police station are taken to the station where they hung the flag. For the next month, detentions and court hearings are non-stop.

- Mash, can you come and give an interview about the action?
- Let's try! Only don't order a taxi to the entrance but ask it to come to behind my building.

I run out of the house, jump in the car, arrive there, jump out of the car and go up to the studio. This is the opposition channel, TV Rain, that is not shut down yet. We laugh in the dressing room at my level of conspiracy and then go outside for a smoke. A girl from the channel just manages to shout: 'Masha, the cops are here!' And then in slow motion: we run up the steps to the glass doors, the channel's security guard doesn't have the time to press the button to open the doors for us. Two uniformed men are dragging me back down the steps, dragging me along the street under my arms, in plain sight, grappling with me into a grey transit van.

– So fucking tired of trying to catch you, says an out-of-breath cop.

I straighten up my skirt and start to laugh. Loudly. Nobody understands why I'm laughing. The last time I heard that phrase was eight years ago, when Katya and I were captured after 'Punk Prayer'.

so fucking tired

The cops have been monitoring Sasha's home for over a day, bashing on the door, but he doesn't open up. They don't have a warrant or even wear a police uniform. They force the landlord to come to the apartment where Sasha rents a room. They show the landlord a video of the action.

'Do you know who rents your room? Did you know that he is a fag? And that he hangs gay flags around the city with his friends? You didn't know? Why don't you go into the flat and ask him yourself?'

go in and ask

Vasily Vasilyich – a former church worker, an old man with a grey beard, in jeans and a shirt, enters the flat. When he is about to leave, the cops stop the door from closing and open it with force, drag Sasha out, push him into a vehicle and take him to fill in an arrest protocol.

> *'They put me in a minivan and took me away. On the way to the police station, one of the cops told me to leave the country, because "people like you are not wanted here", and that I am "a useless piece of shit".'*
>
> – Sasha Sofeev

Russia inherited homophobia from the Soviet Union. Having sent millions of people to penal colonies, forcing them to survive in inhuman conditions, the country created a 'penal colony man'.

In a male prison, rape is a way to establish power. Male prison is practically a caste system. To rape is to lower someone. They don't talk to the lowered, they don't eat with them at the same table. They fuck the lowered and that is part of the penal colony order. If you're a rapist, you don't lose authority; if you're raped, you become a pariah. That's the prison concept. And half the country lives by it and the whole country knows about it.

common knowledge

The Bolsheviks reinstated the law criminalizing sodomy that had been abolished ten years before, straight after the Russian revolution. Having dealt with their primary enemies, the Soviet authorities took on everyone else.

In 1933, the police raided several gay parties in Moscow and St Petersburg. One hundred and thirty people were arrested. But there wasn't a law to charge them with. So the Chekist Yagoda convinced Stalin that counter-revolutionary ideas were fomenting in these homosexual circles.

'A group of perverts, using their exclusive, closed and deviant networks for counter-revolutionary aims, politically indoctrinate sections of youth, the working youth, and also try to infiltrate the army and navy.'

– Yagoda to Stalin

'We must punish the bastards.'

– Stalin to Yagoda

The Gulag filled up with new prisoners. Over half a century, about 50,000 people were sent to prison camps under Article 121 on sodomy. They were forced to incriminate themselves and confess their love for Nazism and Hitler. And then sent to the most feared places – the Far North or the Far East.

The article on sodomy was abolished only in 1993, two years after the collapse of the Soviet Union. As a new young country, Russia wanted to join the Council of Europe. But unlike other political prisoners, the people repressed under Article 121 were not rehabilitated. No monuments, no plaques.

After ten years – in 2013, with the law on gay propaganda – Putin 'brings it all back'.

back to the future

I leave the police station and travel to another police station. Lots of us are going there to support Sasha – he is the only one who is facing detention days. That's how we spend the evening. There are lots of similar evenings ahead. We hand over food at the police station where he has been left for the night and we have supper in a nearby half-empty café.

– Buy bouquets. I'll give you all of them for 150 roubles.

Somewhere in Western Europe an old woman isn't going into a café to sell flowers but is sitting at a table with a glass of wine. She rides a bike there and shows her friends selfies from her travels. But we aren't in Europe, we're in Russia – we've just brought food to a friend who has been left to spend the night in a cold cell. We watch the old woman who is going from one bar to another on this autumn evening to sell hydrangeas wrapped in paper. Three bouquets are cheaper than a glass of wine.

– Please buy them. The metro shuts soon.

buy bouquets

The average monthly pension in Russia in 2018 is 190 dollars. The same year Putin raises the pension age by five years. The reform doesn't affect the cops.

People who have paid contributions into the pension fund all their life are scared that they won't live long enough to claim their pension. People protest.

Before the war with Ukraine, the increase in retirement age

was the government reform that Russians most wanted to reverse.

I buy bouquets with tears and anger, gather them in my arms and go to a gay bar. I give two of the bouquets to drag queens. I take the third bouquet to the court. In the morning, the court arrests Sasha for thirty days.

generation 20.2

We are detained in different ways: someone is lifted from the street and forcibly shoved into a grey transit van, others are waited for by their apartment doors.

> *'We're in the transit van, there are three cops and one officer. One cop has heard about our LGBTQ action and asks me: "Are you one of THOSE people or what?" The officer answers: "According to my information, Lyudmilla Petrovna likes men."'*
> – Lucy Shtein's Twitter

Lucy 'flag at the MinCult' is taken to the police department, Little Masha 'flag at the police station' is locked up at one of the police stations. Tim 'flag at the Presidential Administration' is detained near the court, where he came to support Sasha 'flag at the FSB', who is already arrested and in detention.

wreaths of autumn maple

Detentions are intertwined with one another, and we have wreaths of intertwined autumn maple leaves in our hands. Bright yellow, warm orange – wreaths of fallen leaves. We weave them in the gazebo near the court. We are not expecting a court decision, we are waiting for Sasha to come to the window so that he can see us all – everyone who came to support him.

Upstairs the guard says to Sasha: 'Get away from the window.' Below the cops say to us: 'Why did you come here? Disperse.'

we will not disperse

A security officer has spent several unsuccessful days at Diana's apartment entrance on the outskirts of Moscow waiting for her to come out. He tries a different method. He sends her a DM on Insta where his nickname is 'hateeveryone':

> 'Three great days ahead! The weekend! Come on out, it won't take long, ask Lyudmila Petrovna (Lucy);
> 'Which police station will we go to?'
> 'Tverskoye, message your lawyer, they should come too. We have to complete the job, as I'm sure you understand.'
> 'Your job isn't a great one. Why don't you find another? Sorry for my lack of tact.'
> 'I chose this path.'
> 'And don't you ever question your chosen path? Aren't there more important things than chasing kids with rainbow flags?'
> 'I'm messaging you online, because you wouldn't even talk to me through your door.'
> 'Your nickname is cool :).'
> 'Thank you.'

The job of cops from Centre E is to create fake accounts on social media, follow activists, politicians, artists – everyone who has ever been noticed for speaking out against the government – to follow and to monitor. To monitor our social media for hours and then write reports labelled 'discovered', 'revealed' or 'please take action'. Usually, their social media accounts are empty profiles without photos and names, with a name like 'igor 015987', but sometimes a personality breaks through.

#hateeveryone

'My dearest and treasured friends! How much I missed
you this week! News from the wide world reaches me only in
snatches – thanks to chats with you, even if fleeting. They only
give me my phone for fifteen minutes a day and they turn on the
jammer so the internet is very slow, but I feel with all my heart
that you are with me! It was so joyful and totally lovely to see so
many supportive people under the windows of the Moscow City
Court, but my happiness was short-lived because the guard told
me not to lean out of the window, and the bailiff dragged me
away, saying that we are not a circus. On top of that, the stupid
Moscow City Court decided to take me out of the back door, but
I still caught sight of you, my lovely friends!
The rainbow sabotage is unstoppable!'
– Sasha Sofeev, letter from Detention Centre No. 2

a thanksgiving evening

Sasha Four Eyes, a pan of glühwein and I are going to the city centre. To a thanksgiving evening for lawyers – that's what we called it.

In the cosy Armenian café Paros, hosted by Susanna Christophorovna, we sit at a long table covered with a cloth in a separate room, to say thank you to our lawyers, who have been running

24/7 between courts and police stations for almost a month. There's not a lot of us left, and it's sad, and soon, very soon, there's going to be even fewer, but for now we take turns, like adults, to give toasts.

other children

Every summer when I was a child my mama sent me to a pioneer camp. One of these camps was by the sea. Palms, cypresses, many different-coloured roses planted along the paths. We lined up in the morning and in the evening. We needed to line up in the square. To listen to the final night concert. The pioneer brigades presented their acts. Jokes, songs, guitar playing, dancing. When we had finished, other children came out on stage.

Together they began to sing a song, 'Little Country' – a song we all knew. Only it was with different words.

> Little Chechnya
> Little Chechnya
> Hear us, Vladimir Putin
> We don't need war.

I didn't know what Chechnya was and I barely understood who Putin was. But I cried.

we won't break, we won't cry, we won't forget

We can't choose where we are born. In some places people can hold hands, build a relationship, bring up a family, and in other places – they kill you. The 'other places' are several regions within your country.

I'm looking at us leaving one by one from the café to go on to somewhere else to continue the night. It took almost a month for them to catch us for the rainbow flags, but if we were in Chechnya, where Russian law only exists on paper, we would no longer be alive.

We hug and laugh. We go to a karaoke bar and sing, not hitting one note. At dawn we sit in McDonald's. We spend the morning in an unknown apartment. Within a few months, this apartment will be surrounded by cops and the girl who lived in it (and all her friends) will leave the country under the threat of criminal trials. But we don't know that yet, and from night until day we're circling each other and, somewhere in this dizziness, Lucy and I kiss for the first time.

After a few days, the Centre E cops phone Lucy's landlord. They tell him that he has an extremist renting his flat. 'The grandad took fright and said he doesn't need these kinds of problems.'

He gives her a week to find a new apartment. And we find one.

apartment for an extremist

That night the Democrats win the elections; young Trump fans and young pioneers from the Biden ranks are locked in arguments in Moscow bars until 5 a.m. Russia passionately discusses the American elections because we haven't had our own elections for a long time.

In the evening, we went to the gates of the detention centre with balloons, fireworks and glitter – a whole crowd of people had got together to greet Sasha. But they didn't open the gates. Sasha didn't come out. The cops took fright when they saw a crowd of multicoloured guys with glitter and drove him away from the detention centre. On the road they threatened that next time he wouldn't be let off with a month's detention and instead he'd face a criminal case.

We order taxis and follow the police car; we don't know where it's going, but our motorcade goes at all speeds. A chain of taxis and car shares block the street and stop at the police station. Here Sasha is taken in, and immediately we get out. With glitter and painted flags of Russia on our cheeks. There will be no criminal case. For now. There will be champagne, music playing from speakers, the great joy of friendship and happiness in the moment. We take a group photo to remember. A year later I look at it and realize that almost no one is left in the country.

10.

Careful Fragile!!

They were catching us as if we were dangerous criminals; we tried to remain alive and cheerful, although it was obvious that this was only a prelude. We were being caught by the cops. Our conversations were more and more about the cops. I could see a life without cops only abroad, but here we were inseparable. So when Rita said, 'I want to propose something to you,' I wasn't surprised. I knew what it would be. An action with a cop at its centre.

She could have been a model but decided she wanted to be an artist and activist. We didn't know each other well, but she had already been detained several times and the cops had treated her like she was a member of Pussy Riot.

I agreed.

attempt no. 1 – national unity day

National Unity Day was thought up to replace Revolution Day. It's not that I am in awe of Lenin's revolution, but in this country the authorities are not only afraid of celebrating it . . . they are afraid of the very word:

the word revolution

For the action we decided to tape a riot policeman to a lamp post by the Kremlin. Rita and I – in Russian folk dresses and national headdresses (kokoshniks) Farhad, playing the role of riot policeman – in a helmet and uniform. Firstly, as the Russians say, 'for the sake of beauty', and secondly, large red words: 'CAREFUL FRAGILE!!' are written on the tape we're using.

Putin's Russia is a police state. Security forces are used to detain, search, handcuff, torture and kill. Stressful work – so the security forces must be protected from harm. Laws, detentions, jailing – the country should learn that you mustn't touch a man in uniform, but he can do anything he wants to you. Pensions, apartments, vouchers for the sanatorium and, of course, praise from the president. Work hard, brothers! Protect the country from revolution, and we will protect you.

morning near the kremlin

Morning. We are near the Kremlin. Behind us a tail of cops. We realize that they must be cops because they're the only ones who can park an ordinary car on a taxi rank without any issues. Plus, some of them are walking right behind us. 'Nothing will come of it today,' I say.

– Well, at least let's make fun of them! Rita laughs.

We run after the Centre E cops filming us and turn our cameras on them. They scatter, all but one – a suspicious type in a hat who for some reason doesn't react to our pursuit and

219

continues to film us. After a couple of minutes, we shout in unison: 'It's TIM! How could we confuse our friend with a cop???'

At McD's. We plan what to do next. Coffee, orange juice and five people – surveillance – at adjacent tables. When a detachment of riot police with batons enters, we run to the toilet. Rita, Tim and I are locked in one of the women's cubicles, we clamp our mouths shut so as not to laugh out loud.

On the metro. We turn around as we leave a metro train somewhere on the outskirts of Moscow. The tail seems to have disappeared.

On the street. Packages of pitta and kefir fall to the pavement. I fall with them. Ten people in uniform are running to the door of the store, they twist the arms of Farhad and Rita, I am pinned to the ground.

At the police station. We take a photo in our dresses and riot police helmet against the background of the cell bars, holding our detention protocols. And we take another photo, at the exit, with our lawyer, it is much sweeter.

attempt no. 2 – national police day

It is National Police Day. This time we abandon the Kremlin and tape our 'riot policeman' near to the main police building. The police building, a chapel, a monument to Lenin – not a bad collection for one square – symbolic.

We meet in a café across the road. There's no mention of any preparations on any chats. We change in the toilets. When we get to the target, all we need to do is throw our jackets off and act. We have someone to hold our jackets – Samar. He, like no other, knows how fragile the riot police are.

'Wanting to cause psychological damage deliberately, with force, he threw a bottle of liquid in the direction of police employees, wishing the bottle to create a sense of danger and fear amongst them.'

– Prosecutor's indictment, Samar's trial, December 2019

plastic bottle

When the protests began, in summer 2019, Samar was twenty-one. On 27 July, he, like many others, went to 'hang out in the city centre', and when the cops started to beat people up and carry them off to the avtozaks, he threw a plastic bottle in their direction. It fell next to the police. Samariddin became a defendant in the Moscow Case, and three of the cops, victims.

One of the three policemen resigned, refusing to testify under oath that he was afraid of a plastic bottle. The others were forced to come to court and testify.

In court, the cops described the irreparable psychological damage and fear that was caused to them by the bottle falling nearby. One of them called this 'a severe rustle that made him fear for his own life'.

Samar spent five months in jail, he paid a fine. They wanted to keep him in prison for longer, but we didn't stop picketing for his freedom. We still remember the memes about a 'severe rustle' and a plastic bottle.

'Someone threw some plastic cup at a representative of the authorities. Threw it. And nothing. Then a plastic bottle. Again, nothing. Then they'll be throwing a glass bottle and then it'll be a stone, and then they'll start shooting and looting stores.'

– Vladimir Putin, meeting of the Presidential Human Rights Committee

we're russians

Metro station Oktyabrskaya. A Centre E cop stands at the chapel entrance. We know how this will end. But we take our jackets off anyway. The Centre E cop directs the cops in uniform towards us. 'Your documents?' – we hand them our passports.

- What are you wearing?
- Kokoshniks
- Why?
- Well, we're Russians, so we put them on.
- Let's go to the police station.

They fill in a protocol based on a non-existent law. After a month, they fine us for the non-existent offence. Rita and I, for wearing kokoshniks in the city centre; Farhad and Samar, for NOT wearing them.

a non-existent law

Sasha 'Pechenka' brings food to the station. In a few months' time, at the height of the purges, Sasha will be fired from his job at a Covid hospital because he participated in a protest for Navalny. He shines a torch on Valentine's Day in support of those whose loved ones are behind bars. Sasha is a Tadzhik. Almost immediately after the protest they will deport him from Russia and will ban him from entering for forty years.

But that was later and now we are leaving the police station in our kokoshniks, the state's propaganda cameras surrounding us, but we plough on and they scatter, flying off like sea spray. The church bells right next to the Yakimanka police station are ringing.

attempt no. 3 – action

Be calm and collected – a third attempt, and we really want it to work. We got up before dawn, checked our surroundings from the balcony, crossed the road and jumped in a car. Calm and collected. The whole car is rattling with the bass. A former village teacher from Ukraine and super-rapper Aliona Aliona shakes the beat about 'mum's soup':

> Mamin soup, mamin soup
> Mamin, mamin, mamin soup
> And papin borscht.

square near the kremlin

In Russian national dress, we approach the lamp post, tie our riot policeman to it and run away. We run along the Kremlin walls, straight to the metro. Someone is chasing us, someone has caught up with us and seizes us by both shoulders, it's Farhad. He unwound himself immediately after the action, took off the uniform and caught up with us. We laugh. Two women in national costume and a bearded man in black laugh in the train carriage, then run to their connection and laugh all over again. Today this trinity are the happiest people on the metro. The people who made it.

a street kid

We order a ton of sushi for a ton of money. We make a real feast. We edit the video, choose the best photos and congratulate one another. After we post the action, Rita and Farhad go home. I say, 'Just don't go on the metro, guys, please.'

Farhad is detained as he steps out of his taxi.

Rita manages to get to her apartment.

I'm in a friend's apartment and am chilling on two chairs until I hear:

'Mash, we have a problem.'

A car of Centre E cops is parked at the block's entrance. And another one is parked across the road by the church. It's clear I need to get out, but how? I write to our lawyer. 'Mansur, please come! Please come and get me out of here.'

He replies: 'OK.'

- We need to dress Masha in clothes she would never choose to wear, says Mansur on the threshold.
- We'll dress her up as a guy, answers Sasha.
- Go and get everything you have, Mansur orders.

Tracksuits, belts, sweatshirts, sweaters – a mountain of clothes are dragged out of the wardrobe. I put on all the clothes I'm told to. After ten minutes, a street kid stares back at me in the mirror. A bright mint sweatshirt, an XXL tracksuit tied at the top with a belt, a beanie and pink glasses.

'Fourth floor,' Sasha dictates as we go down the stairs.

'Third floor – maintain maximum concentration.'

'Second floor – get ready.'

'First floor.'

We leave by the front door, Mansur drives the car to the

gate. With a quick pace to the gate I dive into the front passenger seat and then we are already cutting through Moscow, without a tail. The car of the Centre E cops guards the apartment's entrance for another day.

i'm in the suitcase

We are in another flat filled with people.

'They took a photo right in my face,' says Lucy, who has come round.

Now a cop van is guarding this entrance too. They found me by tracking my phone.

'What are we going to do? How do I get out?'

The suitcase is rolled out of the back room. Yes, they are going to carry me out in a suitcase. The cops will write a protocol, detain me and fine me anyway. But it's better not to do it when they want.

A big black suitcase. With stickers. We think up our legends. Roma and Lucy – a couple who are flying to Turkey on holiday; Olya – a taxi driver who is taking them to the airport.

'Guys, open up, I can't breathe!' I yell, curled up in a ball.

One photo of me in the suitcase is taken near the entrance. I'm being turned. I'm put in the car boot. I'm wasting my last breath to video from the suitcase – I have brought the phone with me so it isn't so dark.

'How are you getting on in there? Don't be scared!' Roma yells.

I've never felt potholes and sleeping policemen quite like this before. The boot opens after driving several streets to make sure there's no tail.

We are finally in the kitchen. Lucy's kitchen, which I already want to call ours. Here in the kitchen, we slept on the floor on a mattress, in the next room we slept on a tiny bed; the walls were renewing themselves and drying out. There are air bubbles in the new laminate from water drops. A supper from nothing on the floor and a colourful blanket by the wall – nothing more is needed. A house with a mural of Bulgakov, who never lived here, and close by, a black cat.

nothing more is needed

After a day, they cut off the electricity. They cut the wires from the outside. It's the simplest way of getting you to open the door and leave – that's what the cops want. They do the same on the other side of Moscow to Rita's apartment. I have no option but to leave. Evening.

They cannot give me detention days because my son is younger than fourteen. It is a strange twist in the law that you can put a mother in jail for several years for committing a crime, but you can't make her serve days in the special detention centre. The cops don't leave the entrance and Lucy shouts at them from the balcony: 'Comrade major, why have you cut the wires?'

Before I exit, our lawyer comes up with another joke. He goes downstairs with the same suitcase which had brought me into the flat. This time it's empty. When he leaves the building with it, the cops immediately run towards him and demand that he opens up the case.

- You aren't permitted to examine my belongings, I'm a lawyer.
- We have operational intelligence that a person is hiding inside it.

– Are you completely out of your mind? Why would I
hide someone in a suitcase?
– We have operational intelligence!

After ten minutes of bickering, our lawyer concedes, 'So be
it,' and opens the suitcase. It's empty. The cops feel like idiots;
we film the whole scene from above on the balcony, laughing,
and then I go downstairs. To be detained.

co-dependency

As soon as I open the apartment's entrance door, the Centre E
cops are drawn to it like a magnet. Several men in dark jackets
and surgical masks. One of them comes up to me.

– We will drive you. Others will do the paperwork.
We've agreed that people will sort out this . . .
unpleasantness, said one of the cops, meaning the
electricity wires being cut. He has his head down,
looking at the pavement.
– Look, Masha, we're all in this together. We sleep, the
police sleep. We don't sleep, the police don't sleep,
says Olya.
– A kind of co-dependency. I laugh.

The Centre E cop is scared to leave us even for a second.
Cars sweep by as we wait on an alley pavement. After a minute,
a police car with a blue light appears and a correctly dressed
policeman in uniform gets out. The Centre E cops explain
to him that this is the person who has been detained and she
needs to be taken to the police station. The cop says, 'Hello',
and I answer, 'Let's go!'

twenty days for rita

They give me another fine. Now I need to work out how to reach Rita. All the time that we have been taunting the police, having fun and kissing, she has been in a flat alone. The cops had been guarding the lift on her floor, ordering in pizza, and weren't looking to leave. She also had no electricity.

It's just a matter of time before she'll be put in the detention centre. I exit the police station and go to her in the apartment so she doesn't have to be alone when they come to detain her. While I'm there she feels ill, so we call an ambulance. The ambulance takes her to the hospital, the cops drive to the hospital behind the ambulance, guard the corridor and, after she is refused treatment, take her to the same police station I left only a few hours before.

The lawyer and I guard the police station all night. They leave Rita to sleep in a cell. The next day the court gives her detention days.

This is Rita's second detention for an action, and her third could easily turn into a criminal case.

three posters – up to seven years

After the Bolotnaya Case's sentence and the annexation of Crimea, the authorities needed to do something about the mood to protest. A new article – Article 212, Part 1 – was added to the Criminal Code: 'Repeated violation of the rules for holding rallies.' One rally – a fine; the second rally – days in detention; and if you take a placard to another one – a criminal prosecution. Three placards – up to seven years.

This was called 'Dadin's Article' because activist Ildar Dadin was the first to receive a substantial prison sentence for three placards. A guy with kind eyes and a placard reading 'Maidan, Russia is with you for your and our freedom.'

> *'They twisted my arms behind my back and hung me up*
> *with handcuffs . . . I hung like that for half an hour. Then*
> *they took off my underpants and said that they would bring*
> *another inmate who would rape me if I didn't agree to end*
> *my hunger strike. After that, they took me to Kossiyev in his*
> *office, where in front of other colleagues, he said, "You haven't*
> *been beaten up enough. If I give the order, you will be beaten*
> *much more. Try to complain and you will be killed and buried*
> *beyond the fence." '*
>
> – letter from Ildar Dadin, October 2016

He was beaten several times a day. They continued to imprison people using 'Dadin's Article'. When the major war began, Ildar went to fight for Ukraine and was killed there.

white chevy

Several times I catch myself feeling surprised. Surprised that I am still with Lucy. With someone who has never loved women before, and it isn't a fact that she does, but she is intensely jealous if I speak to her about someone else.

Middle of December. The renovation is almost finished.

We go to Tim's, to Diana's concert, to Rita's appeal at the Moscow City Court, where I bring milkshakes.

> *'I'm in trouble, but it is fixable. Masha, if you can come*
> *for a week at least, I can manage without hospital, I can*
> *stand the withdrawal. But if you can't come, tell me not*

to wait and not to hope. I won't be offended one bit, I'll
understand.'

– Marina

On one of those days between all this police-entertainment fun, I receive a message from Marina – my friend from the penal colony. She asks me to help her. I find out that she is back on drugs. Marina lives in Udmurtia, in a small village. Lucy suggests we go together and take her to rehab in Moscow.

– We can go by car and see Russia in the snow!
– But we don't have a car.
– I can try to get one, says Lucy. She finds one.

We're sitting on the bed and I like what she's doing – that she's found this white Chevy. When we leave Moscow at night, I like the fact that she wants to wash the car at a car wash. I like a lot of things, but I'm really worried about whether I'm doing the right thing by leaving the city, because Rita's been locked up. Will I be able to get people to bring her food and what she needs every day? I try not to talk about it too much.

russia in the snow

Olya drives for more than ten hours straight. I put some music on – my playlist. Having hitchhiked, I know that a driver shouldn't fall asleep, which means playing music and talking to them. But I and the other passenger are selfish, we kiss in the back for minutes, maybe for hours on end, as if we were being driven by an Uber, not by Olya. But at least we switch on the music. An old Cossack song.

And so the next time we are at war
And so the next time we are at war
I'll charge the incoming fire
On this black stallion of mine
I'll charge the incoming fire
On this black stallion of mine.

The bright warm December sun floods the streets as we drive into Nizhny Novgorod. Peach-coloured trolleybuses ride along the street. If it is 9 a.m. and no one has slept, everything seems even more touching. Or tender. I have a salted caramel ice-cream sundae, which is a rare thing in the Russian depths. I have a pleasant feeling of tiredness and a wish to show Lucy everything.

It's like when you take people you love home to show them your old school or the playground where you used to play. I want to show off this town. 'Look! This is the McDonald's where they attacked us with Zelenka, that time they gashed my head, and here's the Committee against Torture, where I went as soon as I left the penal colony, the best human rights defenders I know work here, they are heroes!' And of course the penal colony. We drive to show her our penal colony.

our penal colony

The cleared snow on the paths between barracks. Firs, birches, pine trees. 'Look! That's where the women line up before work.' We interrupt each other: 'This is my 11th unit, and this is where the mechanics work, and here is where we lined up for morning inspection.' I don't know what Lucy feels about all this, but she's listening intently.

We get back to the car, turn on a song at full volume and make a 'royal' drive by, past the gates of the colony.

fences and walls all around,
fences and walls all around,
fences and walls all around,
how do you like the care of the system?

We drive under the windows of the colony's office, which is directly behind the entrance gates; the bass is pumping. They can definitely hear it. And, despite our sleepless night, it's definitely funny.

care of the system

We stay the night in Kazan. In a Soviet hotel. Lucy and I ask for a room with one bed and laugh about whether this could trigger some sort of 'suspicion'.

In the morning, we go downstairs, where a continental breakfast is promised. What is a continental breakfast Kazan-style? Oatmeal with a knob of butter, two eggs, a slice of cheese, a thick pancake with icing sugar, a plastic cup of yoghurt and tea. Soviet-style tables, a fir tree decorated two weeks before New Year. There's no one else in the canteen and possibly the whole hotel. An owl and a mouse look out from my backpack – soft toys which we bought at a petrol station the night before.

I saved Marina once before, from distant Udmurtia, and I brought her to Moscow so she could come off heroin and so our lawyers could remove her son, Danya, from the children's home. We succeeded in both. Five years later she has had a relapse. Last time I took her by car, by taxi, from one Russian region to another. And when we passed Kazan, a red moon shone. I've never seen anything like it in my life.

Snow, snow, snow, so much snow along the roads. It covers the valley plains, covers the branches of pine trees. There are more and more pine trees covered with snow. Our destination, Marina's Udmurt village of Balezino, is now only a few hundred kilometres away. She sends a message: 'I have been detained.'

russian village

At night, we arrive at Balezino. 'Christ, how do people live here?' we say to one another. But people do live here. Dark streets with broken asphalt, rows of five-storey apartment blocks, and then more rows of those five storeys. Wooden old houses. How many of them have no electricity? Most people don't have a job; to get a job they try to leave for the town. The wages at the factory in the village are about 7,000 roubles. Seventy US dollars. The most popular drug is spice, a cheap substitute for heroin; they buy it on the dark web then find it in geotagged locations – drug stashes – buried in the ground, fixed to pipes with magnets, attached to a staircase. Spice eats up your soul and life. A monumental dependency. Probable death within a year.

We turn off the Avenue of Russians. Park the car. On a small dark patch of asphalt. We walk up to Marina's apartment, to work out what has happened. Liana, her friend, opens the door.

'Make a video of how shit everything is in Balezino,' Liana tells us. 'They sell heroin and spice, even to teenagers, and the cops provide protection to them.' The next day this woman turns in her boyfriend to the police for stealing her phone, so they detain and jail him. No, these people are not exceptions, this is a normal Russian village.

Danya, Marina's son, and his friend are playing on the computer. 'The teapot and tea are here; the charger is there,' he says, seeing that we've come into the flat. A dark-haired, sad boy, who wants to show in every way possible that he is 'sorted'.

– The cops took Mama, Danya adds, and he leaves to
   play in the other room.

in game

We start to go through the papers. Things that have been her life over the last few years. Court cases over the apartment, more court cases. She was fighting for a normal life.

Short hair, big bright blue eyes. The life and soul of the zone, she didn't understand how to survive without the zone, how to survive when you can't find a job because of your criminal record for drugs, because of HIV.

Marina is one of three women who saw injustice and remained quiet about it for years but finally decided to speak to human rights defenders about appalling prison salaries. The price: a full sentence, more years of separation from her child.

Marina went out of range three hours before our arrival. We sit in her kitchen and phone round the police stations, trying to find her. A sphynx cat has given birth to a litter, the young ones are walking around the kitchen and mewing with hunger. A wallpaper with pink roses in the bathroom.

After a call to the police station in a village called 'Game', a cop rings us back. He is not answering any of our questions but is asking his own. He is asking why we have come and where we are going to stay. We find out that Marina has been given eight detention days. In 'Game'. We go downstairs, to leave the village and find a hotel.

windscreen

The windscreen of our car is smashed. One piece is missing, the rest of the glass is covered with a white web of cracks. A dent on the car rear. The brakes aren't working. 'Here we fucking go again.'

Journalists are calling; we tell them that we are here on personal business. 'PERSONAL BUSINESS! NOT AN ACTION!' But it seems that there is no such thing as personal in this life.

We need somewhere to stay. There are no hotel rooms. We drive very slowly. The wind blows through the windscreen and if it blows any stronger, shards of glass from it will hit our faces. The car will be blown off the road. I sit in the front passenger seat because it all looks a little scary. Two cut faces are a little less scary than one.

The only hotel which agrees to take us at five in the morning is in the neighbouring town of Glazov and is called a motel. A motel in the Russian understanding of the word.

motel motel

No blazing sun and ground-floor doors with a huge-wheeled jeep parked outside. A brick, three-storey building in the snow, double-glazed doors, on one panel a blue strip saying 'Motel', and on the other panel too. Just in case anyone forgets where they are, there's a 'Motel' neon sign on the roof too.

They have detained Marina for eight days. We still think we will wait for her, repair the car, meet her out of the detention centre, and the four of us will drive back to Moscow. This isn't going to happen, but we don't know that yet. The sun sets over the detention centre in Glazov town.

comrade keller

In the town of Glazov there are no windscreens for a Chevrolet, so they bring one to us from a city – Perm.

The screen is transported by Olya's comrade, Andrei Keller – a cheeky kid with thin-rimmed round glasses. He wears khakis and has a half-mohawk. He is seventeen years old. He uses swear words to appear older.

We are sitting in the kitchen with yellow walls and a blue frame around the window. We have been told to leave the motel for two days, and we've rented an apartment so that everyone can fit in. A gas stove and carved wooden boards.

I go to the shop – we need to bring Marina a food parcel. Before I go, I look out of the apartment window. I see an old woman in a brown coat and a pink scarf, she's tying a knot on a white sack for a long, long time. There are things in the sack and it stands on a sledge. A small Soviet sledge with multi-coloured slats, the kind everyone had in childhood, we rode them downhill in the snow. The old woman looks up. She doesn't see me, she doesn't see any of us near the window. She looks like she might cry. And none of us know how to help. She lowers her head, takes the rope and slowly drags it through the white snow.

free woman

'Girls, there will be no extension today.' A woman has come to the door of our room in the motel-hotel, she is unhappy that we have been smoking in the room. 'The smoke detectors don't lie,' the woman says. We are lying naked and are arguing with her through the door. We don't want to get dressed. We don't want to get up. But eventually we get up and go to the police station.

We don't have any expectations that they will find the people who smashed our car, but the night they damaged it we wrote a crime report, and that means we now need to go to the police to answer questions.

– How did we end up here?
– I don't know, owl, but I'm scared!

We're laughing in the police station corridor, playing with our petrol station toys. It took twenty minutes to persuade the cop to write 'free woman' in the box for my 'family status'. 'That doesn't exist as a family status!' he tries to protest, but I manage to persuade him that it really does.

And then the motel administrator says that she loves Pussy Riot. She takes a photo with us and the next day the car mechanics who are installing the windscreen invite us to go to a hockey match together. The indoor stadium is full, a grey wolf – a mascot – takes the hand of a boy who smiles at him in response. And everything seems to be fine. Everything is fine. The deadly virus remains only in detention centres and courts to forbid family and friends from visiting. But it's not here.

warm ice rink

The car is ready, all we have to do is wait for Marina and go back home. We wait, check out local bars, try Chepetskoye beer, the best I have ever drunk in the country. We play table football, buy glittery dresses.

The day before Marina's release, we go to the ice rink. Twilight. We are the only ones skating. Around the rink – a garland of warm lamps. In its centre – an illuminated fir tree. We whirl around it, circle by circle, circle by circle, my head is spinning a bit; Lucy refuses to kiss me because it is 'too romantic'. Olya has red cheeks from the cold, and Keller is wearing the warmest down coat. We laugh like children.

Andrei Keller will not live to see twenty. He will die not far from the village of Marinka in Ukraine. On my birthday – 6 June 2023. A drone operator. An occupier. Possibly a murderer. I won't see him like this. He will remain the one who asked me to take a picture of him with the ginger cat in the shop opposite the ice rink, where we went for cigarettes, the one who had funny phrases that he never repeated for the camera, a child who grew up without a mother, who called Olya 'Aunt Olya' because for him she was a grown-up. I don't know how to forgive 'grown-ups' who send children to war to occupy other countries. There's probably no way to forgive. And they haven't asked for forgiveness. They don't need it.

saucepan for spice

They don't release Marina from the detention centre. They open a criminal case against her and take her to jail in Izhevsk.

We learn this as we are taking off our skates. We decide to go to Izhevsk, the capital of Udmurtia, the birthplace of the Kalashnikov rifle.

The criminal case is for an old theft of a saucepan from a shop. She had been stealing everything possible, selling it and getting drugs. Did she have a chance for a different life in this village? Perhaps, but a very small one. What did Marina's son, Danya, have to live through? Apart from a children's home, his mother's letters from prison, his mother herself for a little time, and then letters from prison again? And the sweets she sent him for half her prison wages. Danya played on the computer because life outside of it didn't look like life. And then he turns eighteen, he goes to Moscow, war starts and he is drafted into the army. Is there a chance that he will not sign a contract to fight in Ukraine? There is, but a very small one.

We stay in Izhevsk so we can bring another food parcel to Marina, we write her a letter and meet with the coordinator of Navalny's headquarters – Ivan. He shows us messages on local Udmurt chats confirming our car was smashed by the cops. Marina tells a lawyer who visits her in the detention centre that a woman has been planted in her cell to ask constantly what action Pussy Riot are planning in Udmurtia.

She will not be coming out anytime soon, we have to go back. Rita will get out of her Moscow detention centre the next day. What a trip. We didn't save our friend, and what's more they jailed her. I don't know if they would have opened a criminal case against Marina if they hadn't suspected us of planning some action. But that's how it turned out. We take two of the kittens from Marina's flat to give them good homes in Moscow. Leathery, grey, screaming lumps with ears. They travel in a cardboard box on the front passenger seat and sometimes in our arms.

'I'm so sorry that it turned out like that. I'm scared for you!
I'm so ashamed for our motherland. Although, knowing you, I
don't know who to fear the most. But you seriously frightened
everyone. Giving you a big clap!! Thank you for everything!
Thank you for my son! For the kittens too. The celebrations are
ahead. New Year and, most important, I will be forty-five! A
celebration! And I am back in here. It's the same as IK-2. Again,
they demanded that I turn my back on you. We've been here
before. I told the lawyer everything! Hugs! Happy New Year!'

– Marina

kind heart

'Why are people with a kind heart in prison?' Danya writes to
me, asking about his mum.

It takes twenty hours to reach Moscow. They will be releasing Rita from detention that night. I am worried that I'll be
late and not be there to meet her. I don't know how to answer
Danya. I start drinking wine. It's not even clear where it came
from. And the more I drink, the more painful it becomes. Olya
tells the story of how we met in the penal colony. I don't want
to listen to it, but Lucy listens. Because she doesn't want to
hear one more time that we are late. Everyone feels pain and
everyone deals with it in their own way.

'Why are people with a kind heart in prison?'

I can't handle that I'm in pain. I just can't do it. I show them
Danya's message and start to cry. I can't calm myself down,
and no one is going to calm me down. It is just unfair. People
shouldn't live like that. Children shouldn't live like that. Poverty, prisons, children's homes, I don't know how to say that
the snow lies beautifully on the pine trees and the road is also

very beautiful, but among this beauty there is us. I don't know why people with a kind heart are in prison, and more to the point, I don't know how to answer a child so that they can still have some kind of hope.

'Why are people with a kind heart in prison?'

We've arrived in Moscow in time to meet Rita. Olya kicks a chair out from underneath me. With her foot. Because she's driven the car hundreds of kilometres so I can get to the detention centre. And I'm screaming and crying. And I don't stop drinking. She closes the door and leaves. Shame and embarrassment in the apartment on Arbat. I can't find my way out, I punch the door and leave for the detention centre.

don't give up, soul of mine

Morning. The first broken bone I've had. Before the X-ray and diagnosis, I go to the court where Yulia Galyamina is being sentenced – she is one of the organizers of the protest against the constitutional amendments. My arm is hurting so much that I can barely take a photo. The accused arrives in a red dress as if she is going to a ball. Rita drives me from there to the hospital. The doctor puts on a plaster. New Year is approaching.

Parties, guests, parents, my rats, bars, coffee in the morning and cheese on laminated panels left over from the renovation. Navalny publicizes the names of his poisoners and I read out their extensive investigation to Lucy in the kitchen. Indian lamp and light bulbs. The sound of bells for Christmas. Rewatching all of *Harry Potter*.

It's snowing, we're eating hot popcorn, it's a little bit like a fairy tale, but we're not in a fairy tale and sometimes we argue; she's afraid that they will jail me if I do more actions, she wants to hug me and be by my side. Behind her not always kind jokes there is a lot of warmth and tenderness. No one knows what will happen later on, neither of us, nor our guests who come and go.

Then Navalny says, 'To be in Germany was not my choice; it is a great country, but I am not here of my own free will.' He stands on a hill with a view of a German suburb behind him. In a blue jacket with a seriously thin face. 'But I have bought a ticket home! I return to Moscow on 17 January on the Pobeda flight. Come and meet me!'

tickets home

The flight from Berlin to Moscow is sold out to journalists. Navalny boards the plane to the sound of applause. Cameras, telephones, questions, surgical masks. 'Hello, everyone!' says Navalny, and even through the mask it is clear that he is smiling.

'Alexei! Are you not scared?'

'Alexei! Are you not afraid of being arrested when you land?'

'Alexei! How are you feeling?'

'I feel that I am a citizen of Russia who has the absolute right to return home,' Navalny says, pushing through the crowd of journalists.

We go to meet him. Lucy and I are in our lawyer's car, it is old and broken down, with no back seat; we go slowly through traffic jams, we don't want to be late, but many people do want this. At Vnukovo airport – a crowd. An excited one, with everyone's eyes moving from their phones to the doors and back again. Two thousand people. Some have come with flowers, some with placards: 'We are proud of you!' The police begin to push people away from the airport building. The detentions begin. Those who came to meet Navalny are dragged into avtozaks. Centre E cops mix with the crowd.

At a height of 10,000 metres, Navalny and his wife, Yuliya, watch the series *Rick and Morty* on a laptop. Yuliya understands everything. She understands that this is his last two hours of freedom. Their last two hours of freedom. She knows that as soon as the plane lands, they will take him away. For a long time. But she doesn't know yet that it will be for ever. They laugh, look back and share one set of earphones between them.

The pilot announces that due to technical reasons they won't be landing in Vnukovo airport. The plane changes course. A change in route that thousands of people are following. We won't get to the other airport in time. Our lawyer pulls a person out from the group of detainees. I drink sweet coffee from a vending machine and look at my phone. And then I look around. Opposite me there's a shop with an advert for sportswear – a sponsor of the Olympics, where the Cossacks beat us up.

to love the motherland

'Why did you come back?
In answering this question I already feel annoyed, for two
reasons. The first – at myself, for not being able to find the right
words so that everyone can understand why and stop asking
me. The second – at Russian politics over the last decade, which
has instilled a cynicism and love of conspiracy in society to the
extent that people simply don't trust your motives. Like, if you
came back, it means you must have done a deal with someone.
But it hasn't worked out. Or it hasn't worked out – yet. There's
some kind of cunning plan, in which the towers of the Kremlin

have a part to play. In any case, there must be some SECRET underlying reason. After all, in politics all is not as it seems.

But there are no secrets or schemes. It's actually very simple. I have my country and my convictions. And I don't want to turn my back on my country or my convictions. And I cannot betray either the first or the second. If your convictions are worth anything, then you have to stand by them. And if necessary be prepared to pay the price.
And if you're not prepared to, then you don't have any convictions. You just think you do. But they aren't convictions or principles – just thoughts in your head.

There is a different expectation placed on me. I travelled the country and announced from the stage, "I promise that I will not let you down, I will not deceive you, I will not abandon you." By returning, I fulfilled my promise to my voters. After all, there must come a time when they are not lied to.'

– Alexei Navalny

They detain him at passport control. The plane needed to be diverted so the crowd of people who love him are left in a different corner of the city. Admiration and bewilderment, the front covers of the world's newspapers, and behind the scenes, negotiations. Navalny's action is an action with a capital 'A' – a return to your motherland that will kill you. But he doesn't know that yet, and neither do we. We watch his team's investigation about Putin's palace, we read the announcement of an unsanctioned protest. He's worth coming out for. A criminal case awaits us. Awaits many of us, but among the many, it awaits the two of us – Lucy and me, sitting on different benches in a deserted night-time airport.

House Arrest

The day before the protest, cops compiled lists, distributed them to other cops, saying, 'These people on the lists, lock them up for a day, by any means possible, so that tomorrow they don't make it to the squares.' And they lock them up. They detain people on the streets, at train stations, at the doors of apartments, in the apartments themselves, take them straight from their homes. According to the lists. But others will come out. They will also be put on the list, and then more will come out. And even if not tomorrow but at some point, it will no longer be possible to list everyone. Activists will write lists of thugs in uniform, lists of the real criminals.

day before the protest

'They've arrived at ours! Lucy's apartment is surrounded by the cops and they cut off the electricity. So I want to say, comrade major, go fuck yourself, we have candles 🔥. Let's meet tomorrow in the city centre. For our freedom and yours!'

– me on Instagram

'To joke is cool, but all the same we must go out on the streets tomorrow and send the grandad and his friends to hell. (Even though I no longer believe in anything and don't expect anything, but I can't stay at home.)'

– Lucy Shtein's Twitter

We have no light all evening. Not just light – no electricity at all. A grey car is parked opposite the entrance. At the end of the street, by the red church – an avtozak.

this is our everything

Lucy says, 'Let's go to bed, and not go anywhere tonight,' although this night – the night before the protest – is the only time when we can slip past the Centre E cops who are sleeping in their car. She doesn't want to stay in another apartment, she wants to stay at home. She wants me by her side. On a wooden board – tea lights.

The first friend was detained leaving our lift – he had tried to reconnect our electricity. The second friend was detained on the doorstep of our apartment – he slipped a power bank under the door.

Both received fifteen detention days for disobeying the legitimate demands of the police. That's what they call it these days.

Cops are in the archway, cops are round the corner from our building, ready steady go, wake up, it's time. We sprint outside, we jump in the back seat of a red car, we shout, 'Put your foot down! Let's go!' We laugh, we take a video, we laugh again. We are on the way to the protest.

The third friend, Lucy's close friend, the owner of the red car, they arrest after a few days. He will receive a year's conditional sentence for a crime that he didn't commit. They will fake the charge: 'Attack on a policeman'.

> 'Two members of Pussy Riot, Maria Alyokhina and
> Lucy Shtein, under detention, hit a policeman with a car in
> central Moscow.'

Armoured avtozaks along the main street. Islands of people. Rows of cosmonauts. War of people with people. And each time – terrible screams. Each time it is someone's first time. And screams.

one for all and all for one

Snowballs fly at riot police helmets and armoured cars, batons, batons, blows, screams: 'For Navalny!' 'Putin is a thief!' 'That's enough!', batons and more blows. The crowd chants, 'I'm not afraid! We are not afraid!' An unequal battle which we've lost before it started. Against the background of New Year's Eve lights and snowflake decorations. The crowd chants, 'We have no weapons.' That is possibly the problem. We have no weapons. Surgical masks with drops of blood lie in the dirty snow.

It's as if they forgot to spread salt to melt the avenue's ice and everyone who runs down it constantly falls, both we and the cops all fall, get up and run again. People run from the cops to avoid being detained, cops run to detain the people.

When in 2012 I hid in that same avenue from the cops, knowing that they had opened a criminal case against us, it wasn't funny, it was a bit scary, and now? Now – it already isn't.

bolshoi theatre

They detain us near the Bolshoi Theatre, almost near the Kremlin. A Centre E cop, a Michelin man in a Valentino jacket, is leading a small handful of young, uniformed sergeants. A stocky, boorish person, small in height, with a belly and red hair.

– Are we going to bicker and like yesterday shout, 'Cops are fags?'

– What fags? I said: 'Cops – shame of Russia.'
– Let's go.

In the avtozak a two-metre-tall cop hangs over Lucy and whispers, 'What are you staring at? I will fuck you up right here.' She calmly answers, 'Well, go on, fuck me up.'

cops – shame of russia

They drive us to the Arbat police station. Cops run up to me. Two of them twist my arms behind my back, the third one reaches into my pocket and takes my phone. With twisted arms they lead me to the body check. We are kept in the station overnight before the court.

A large cage in the Arbat police station. Three walls, bars, bars in squares, dull, dusty, transparent plastic bars. If you look closely, you can see that someone has drawn hearts in the dust. Many of them, in almost every square, even in the highest ones, which are difficult to reach.

They don't put us together – 'Due to the pandemic, a distance of one and a half metres must be maintained.' It's Lucy's first overnight stay at a police station, so I ask for her to be put in the cage with hearts. And I go to a small dark cell, with a bench and a dim light. These places don't scare me. I try not to think about how the cops twisted my arms, bending them backwards to lead me down the corridor. Long ago I learned that it's better just to fall asleep in the cell.

On the way to the court in the morning, Lucy says that she and the others had pounded all morning on their cage walls asking when they would be finally taken out, and so she was surprised I had simply asked the cops, when they came to take me, for 'five minutes more sleep'.

hearts in the dust

'Your child is turning fourteen soon? Soon it won't be just fines.' The judge leafs through my case.

It's a fairly well-fed case – with detentions, fines, new detentions. I say, 'You behave terribly even for a Russian judge.' She imposes the maximum possible fine.

Lucy gets ten detention days. These are her first ever days in detention and I return to the apartment to pack things for her, to make lists of people who will visit her, lists of things to give her tomorrow, after queuing for four hours – hundreds of other people have received detention days. The detention centre is overflowing – we stand in the queue to hand over food, and the cops stand in a queue to hand over the accused. One activist has already spent a day 'serving his sentence' in a police car, the cops are 'serving' together with the activist. They can't leave until they hand him over to the detention centre, but there's no room there.

no room

Detained: 4,002 people in 125 cities – the highest for 9 years.

Any protest in Russia ends in queues with parcels at a prison. This protest is no exception. For many, this has been their first ever protest.

Ahead is a series of criminal cases, united under the name 'Palace Case'. One hundred and eighty-eight defendants all over Russia.

I am in touch with Lucy's friends and relatives. I tell them that the detention centre is not in another realm, you will return, that it's only ten days, that it can be fun in prison. My head fills up with the passport numbers of friends and relatives who want to visit. We stand near the dark blue gates of the detention centre with relatives of other activists, we're cold, we joke and stamp our feet. We didn't know each other and don't get to know each other well. None of us has noticed how quickly our different lives have ended up in one place, in that queue at the metal gates.

One day = one visit. I give way to her friends. I think, 'It's only ten days.' We believe that we will see each other soon, fall asleep side by side like before. But we won't for a long time.

arrests record-high

'We've stalled!' A white minivan with a blue 'police' stripe has stopped at the corner of the court building.

Four detainees press their faces to the window. Two of them had tried to give us a power bank and turn our electricity back on. The other two are theatre director Vika, detained with us at the protest, and Lucy. They shout, 'We've arrived, comrade major; we will take it from here.' The door opens. All four leave and go into the court, for an appeal that will make no difference, apart from the chance for us to see each other in the smoking gazebo of the Moscow City Court. Navalny's team announces the next unsanctioned protest to be held in the coming days.

– Mash, you're here again, mumbles the guard who is escorting them. You're not arrested. He nods towards the other four. These ones are.

He means that the arrested and the 'free' don't walk together and don't communicate.

- I'll always be here! I'll be in your dreams, I answer the escort guard.
- That's all we need, he sighs.

i'll be in your dreams

It is cold. We hug under the round hat of the smoking gazebo. Lucy jumps into my arms. She says, 'Don't go to the protest, they'll jail you.' She says, 'What's going on in the news? Let me read it!' She says, 'I've missed you! Missed you!' I've also missed her, but instead of saying that, I say, 'Of course I'm going to the protest.'

- You're a revolutionary! The escort guard comes to life. Just like a century ago, in 1917.

He and I are left standing in the smoking gazebo.

- I don't want it to be like a century ago. Then they built the Gulags and shot each other.
- Soon we'll be shooting each other again.
- I don't want to shoot you. Do you want to shoot me?
- Can it be any other way in a revolution?

shades of grey

When everyone is taken to court, I leave the smoking gazebo for a coffee. At the court's metal gates, two men run up from behind. In plain clothes. In dark grey.

- Wait.
- Who are you?
- Criminal Investigation Department.

Two red ID cards flash before my eyes.

- And?
- And . . . The first speaks slowly. We need someone as a witness.
- I can't come with you. I'm called as a witness in the court.
- Ummm . . . We've received a call, slowly and awkwardly continues the second, that a bomb has been planted in the court!
- Seriously? I grin. An actual bomb?

They take me under the arms and lead me to the road. On the side of the road there is a car – also grey. They force me into it.

- Why is there no trust in officers? the first one begins.
- Have you seen yourself in the mirror? No uniforms, no names, pushing me into a car with no official markings. Do you know who you look like?
- Who? The second turns his head from the driver's seat. Gangsters?
- I've always wondered, says the first, how many people there are now in your Pussy Riot . . .
- You'll get enough of just me! I scream.
- Calm down, the transport will be arriving any time now! they scream back.
- What transport?
- One with official markings, says the first.
- Which ones?
- Ones that identify it, says the second.

the system is activated

The 'GLONASS' system allows you to monitor an object moving along a route, the object must pass control points according to a prearranged timetable.

'The GLONASS system is activated,' a metallic voice announces. The video recorder with a speaker is attached to the chest of a large, body-armoured cop. The grey pair of plainclothes cops give me over to the cops in uniform. The door to the avtozak cage closes.

– How long till we get there?
– Fifty minutes.
– Where are we going?
– To our destination.

'The GLONASS system is deactivated.' I squeeze my legs together; I squeeze into a corner. I'm desperate to pee. How long till we get there? Forty minutes. We've already driven for half an hour. Traffic jams! So where are we going? To our destination! Is it difficult to say where? After a couple of seconds of staring at me, the body-armoured cop says the address. Lucy's address. Why are we going there? When can I go to the toilet? Why there? When is the toilet stop?

The avtozak parks. 'The GLONASS system is deactivated.' Body-armoured No. 1 takes out the ringing phone from his pocket. 'Do you have the tools? We don't have any. No. No! Everyone is on the road today – we don't have any!' It's a search. I should have guessed right away. I don't say a word and squeeze my legs together.

moving objects

The body-armoured ones switch over. 'The system is activated.'

- What's the time?
- 7 p.m.
- When can I go to the toilet?
- Soon.

Switch over. 'The system is deactivated.'

- What's the time?
- 8 p.m.
- When can I go to the toilet?
- Soon.

I desperately want to pee. It's cold. No. 1 says to No. 2, 'It'll be Friday soon. I'm going to Auchan with mine, and you?' 'I'm knackered.' 'I can see that. I'm wondering what to buy, we need to do a food shop.' No. 1 lowers his head, scrolling through his messages. 'I love you,' says a female voice.

'I'm going to piss in your avtozak,' I say.

'The system is activated.' Yes, I'll do it here under your camera. I will just take off my trousers and piss right here. After a short conference, the door of the avtozak opens. Hardly moving my legs, I walk with the escort to the nearest doors. The doors of a private clinic. The body-armoured cop says to the receptionist, 'The girl needs the toilet, can we?' The nurse agrees. She doesn't have many options.

'We also went,' says the armoured man as we walk back to the avtozak. 'We work overtime, and don't get paid for it. So we don't have any rights either!'

I look at him and want to say, 'You can at least pee without an escort,' but I say, 'Are you serious?'

my first search

I'm sitting on a chair in the middle of the room. Around me, seven strangers. Behind me, a broken-down door. To Lucy's apartment. This is a search as part of a criminal case. A new criminal case – a 'sanitary' case, as they soon will call it.

– You, Maria Vladimirovna, are a witness, says the girl-
   investigator. And you have rights.

She takes out a well-thumbed law book and starts reading out from it.

This isn't like what I've seen online – the cops, sledgehammers, an apartment turned inside out. It seems polite. They have opened a criminal case against us but we don't know it yet. The investigator's thin fingers turn the pages, she's worried and wants this to be over. She's tired. She's new to the job, you can hear it in her voice, which is not used to giving orders.

Three witnesses, a guy, a girl and an old man, stand further away. They've been taken off the street to verify that I'm not being tortured and to sign the search protocol.

Three cops: an ever-obliging district cop (a child two-metre high) and two Centre E cops. They stand behind my shoulders, like the opposite of bodyguards.

– You have the right to a lawyer, the investigator reads.
– So I can call my lawyer?

– No, you can't. The investigative process has already started.
– But you just read that I can?

The voice continues to read. Beyond the window it's evening. I repeat, under my breath, that this isn't even my apartment. I ask, 'Is any apartment where I have spent time liable to be searched?' Zero reaction. And the voice continues to read. A dark, calm winter's evening. I can hear myself saying, 'I hate you' – 'I hate you. You are descendants of the Chekists, who took people from this building in the 1930s in Black Ravens. This house was a Last Address.'

And just recently there were renovations. Under five layers of wallpaper – under a green layer with flowers – newspaper clippings. We saved the news about Stalin's death. Edith Piaf played from the old lady neighbour's apartment. Everything could be heard through the thin wall. Mattresses in the kitchen. Breakfast on a laminated board. Harry Potter for Christmas. Two packets of popcorn. Three packets of popcorn. Come on, fairy tale, stop this fucking shit!

riddikulus

One Centre E cop inspects the collection of Alla Pugacheva CDs, opens each red box. The second Centre E cop crawls under the bed. He crawls out with a small object. 'What's this?' he asks out loud, realizing that if he just quietly turned it in his hands no one would answer. The witness-guy says, 'Sticks from an e-cigarette.' 'What?' 'Not drugs.' The witness-guy grins.

The old man-witness turns up the volume on his phone and it begins to ring loudly, the old man answers the call, the

Centre E cop interrupts: 'Investigative activities are in process, it is forbidden to talk!' The old man stares at the Centre E cop and says, 'I'm working.'

A Last Address is the name given to a building where people were arrested and never returned. A graffiti of a revolver on the wall – the barrel is pointing at the onlooker.

last address

A lawyer suddenly enters the room. He tells me, 'I'm one of you.' Looking at his name, I realize that he is. I just can't understand how he found me. 'This search is all over the news, and Masha, you can use your phone. It is not forbidden.' The faces of the Centre E cops fall.

My mum messages, 'How's it going? They've searched here. Everything went calmly. They took your passport and left. You should have hidden it better.'

An hour later I find out that my Instagram post calling people to go to the protest is the basis of this criminal case. The seized laptop and flash drives of photographs have been turned into 'evidence' and have been sealed in a plastic bag.

They take me to a night-time interrogation, where in the space of a few minutes I switch from being the 'witness' to the 'accused', and this means that I will not be released from the station. This is an arrest for forty-eight hours and while they select my preventative measures. This is a criminal case and that means it is serious.

sanitary case

A series of criminal cases opened after the Navalny protest, involving 188 defendants across Russia. The human rights defenders call it 'the Palace Case' – in honour of Navalny team's investigation into Putin's palace, released after his return home and arrest. A golden palace on Gelendzhik Bay with toilet brushes for 700 euros, vineyards, a hookah bar, complete with a striptease dancing pole and aqua disco.

Officially the court cases are initiated on non-political charges. The last attempt to play with the West. What political prisoners? They're basic criminals.

But in Russia, the pandemic was also used as an excuse to introduce a new article in the criminal code that at first does not seem repressive: *violation of sanitary and epidemiological rules.*

This is the very article that forms the basis of the Sanitary Case. Its defendants are: Navalny's key lawyer, Navalny's brother, Navalny's press secretary and the chief of Navalny's Moscow HQ. And us.

> *'According to the investigators, the defendants published public calls to join a protest, which created a threat of mass infection from Covid.'*
> – Sanitary Case file

petrovka 38

– I will not take off my underwear, and I will not squat naked. Also, there'll be no spreading apart my bum cheeks, I announce from the threshold.

Body search. Like ten years ago. I am in a cage, a cage in a room, with a bright light and a girl in uniform.

- You've already been with us before, so you know yourself what the rules are.
- Of course, I know. It took me two years to discover that it isn't legal.
- It is legal. There's an order . . .
- A confidential one?
- A confidential one.
- So, if it's confidential that means there's no way I can read it
- Oh, I don't know, take off your underpants and enough already!
- I won't take them off.
- But you might have a mobile up there! the girl remonstrates.
- You really think I would have a mobile UP THERE?

It takes five minutes to work out that a mobile would not fit UP THERE. The next day, human rights defenders come to see me in my cell. They ask, 'Has anything changed over the years?' I think of answering, 'In prison – no; within me – yes. It's somehow become not scary,' but I say sleepily, 'Yeah it's changed.' The surprised human rights defender asks, 'Really – how exactly?' And I reply, 'They've painted the walls a light blue.'

closed trials

'Russia will be free!' laughs the chunky escort guard. 'Only a bit later!' he adds, and closes the door of the avtozak's cell. In the avtozak everyone is a political. We left in the morning. We sit in the holding cell of the court's basement for five hours. We already know that we will be put under house arrest – it is not difficult to work out. The strictest possible measure under our criminal article.

The Mayor of Moscow announces that Covid restrictions will be lifted, bars and cafés will open, but there is a pandemic in the courts as before. Friends and journalists freeze on the street. They take me to an empty courtroom. Handcuffs. Aquarium. Judge. Just like before. But this time in silence.

house arrest

'The Court rules during the period of house arrest that the suspect be prohibited:
– to leave place of residence without the written permission of the investigator
– to use any means of communication or the Internet
– to send or receive items in the post or via telegram.'

– court document

A boy in uniform puts a black ankle bracelet on my right leg. He twists the two tiny metal threads. I go down to the basement. I get into a white car with a green stripe.

'I'm Vlad. I'm going to be your inspector. I have to monitor that you comply with your house arrest,' says the boy, and sits behind the wheel.

'I am not the enemy,' he adds, then he starts the engine and takes off his fur hat. Blond hair, light blue eyes.

inspector vlad

We drive across snowy Moscow. Evening. From the camera flashes at the court, we drive to the building where I was born. To the forest with birch trees and a ravine.

Inspector Vlad feels a bit awkward. The first thing he tells my mum is that he is not the enemy.

He plugs in the black telephone with a receiver – a fsinphone – in the middle of the apartment. Then I need to place my leg with the ankle bracelet near it and wait for a signal, then I need to walk around the apartment so that the phone understands where it's possible to go. Twice it has not understood.

where it's possible to go

> *Masha!*
> *Fucking bastards!*
> *I really miss and think about you.*
> *It's not that bad here, but I don't know when I will see you*
> *again. I am really frustrated at my total helplessness. Today*
> *they jammed our radio. We don't know anything and we can't*
> *find out anything.*
> *In any case, we will get through this! I have terrible*
> *handwriting, I know.*
> *What on earth!*
> *THE FUCKERS!!!*
> – Lucy, Detention Centre No. 2

I'm writing a letter to Lucy at the detention centre, and our miracle lawyer, who has already become overnight her lawyer, is walking around the kitchen and is arguing with me. He won't simply say, 'Masha, just write that you love her and that you'll wait.' He has tried for several hours to prove to me that if Lucy gives evidence, then they will free her and not put her under house arrest like me. A month from now, he will shower her with flowers while I sit with an ankle bracelet on my leg like a collar around my neck not knowing what to do. I haven't been on a course about 'love under house arrest'. Dissidents don't write about that. Jealousy, meanness, personal rage – these things aren't in Soviet memoirs. About how to survive if the system breaks you, perhaps – but what if it's not actually the system that's breaking you?

write that you love

'Lucy! I also miss you very much! But we need to be prepared – they could keep us apart for a long time. Maybe up to a year or two. We are accused of 'a minor crime', so they can only give a maximum detention period of six months. I think that if I am in pre-trial detention (SIZO)* it will spur them on to investigate faster. I'm thinking about leaving the apartment. House arrest is a short leash. I don't like it. I don't want it. Come out soon while I am not in jail! Think up a nickname you are going to use to write to jail, otherwise the censor will not let it through.'

– Masha, 30 January 2021

I wake up from a ring on the door. I open up. Two Centre E cops in Covid masks stand on the doorstep, asking, 'Can we

---

* A SIZO is a pre-trial detention centre.

take a picture of you?' It's the day of the protest that I was intending to go to just a few days ago. The one I'll now be watching from home. Now I'm going to have to watch everything from home. My childhood home turned into a prison.

- No! You can't 'take a picture', just leave. I am
  forbidden to talk to you, according to the court! I
  answer.

They've sent the Centre E cops to take photographic evidence that I really haven't gone to the protest rally.

People are gathering near the prison, Matrosskaya Tishina (Sailor's Silence), where Navalny is jailed. They are beaten up, dragged through the snow, pulled from a crowd. They are beaten up in other towns too.

'I can't breathe,' shouts a guy from Chelyabinsk while three cosmonaut riot police press his face into the snow.

The fsinphone rings – a check – the ankle bracelet made a mistake and thinks I've run off the balcony. I lift the receiver and say, 'I'm in position' – although what kind of position I am in is not clear.

Tasers, batons, cold avtozaks, confiscated passports, confiscated apartment keys, threats of planted drugs, broken ribs and chipped teeth – 5,754 people are detained across Russia.

sailor's silence

Masha! Please don't do this! I need you. I was crying reading this. SIZO is not even a short leash. You will be with them. We can be in contact under house arrest. That way there will be many more opportunities. No one needs to make a sacrifice. They will probably free us after two

months. It's already hard enough that we can't see each
other. Wait for my court hearing, I'll be out, we can talk
and discuss everything then. I'm not afraid of the court
and know that we are in the right. We will be able to
communicate. They can't control that.
The maximum they can keep you under house arrest for
a minor crime is half a year, not two! I know that you can
handle everything, but I need you. I realize that you don't like
control and do everything your own way, but I'm just asking
because I love you, actually.
Please no impulsive moves, or my heart will fucking explode.
Or I'll follow you into jail.

– Lucy, Detention Centre No. 2, 1 February 2021

i'll be out soon!

A crowd of journalists surround the cage-aquarium. In it, behind brown metal frames, behind bulletproof glass, is the man who returned home. The man who dared. Here he stands, smiling and joking, here he draws a heart on the glass for his wife, Yuliya, as if there is no crowd, no fear, no court.

The old criminal case against the Navalny brothers, the Yves Rocher Case. Back in 2014 they didn't dare give Alexei a proper jail sentence but gave him a conditional one. They did jail his brother, Oleg, for three and a half years, taking him hostage. The old, trumped-up lawsuit has found new life.

With a conditional sentence, you are obliged every month to visit the FSIN inspector and report – here you are, you haven't escaped anywhere and are 'behaving well'. When they poisoned Alexei with military-grade poison and his family took him to Berlin to be treated, according to FSIN logic, while he was connected up to tubes and wired up to hospital equipment, he was meant to immediately regain consciousness and fly to the inspector to sign a piece of paper. Simply because he hadn't done this, the Moscow City Court exchanged his conditional sentence for a real one. They sentenced him to two years and eight months in jail, and his brother Oleg became a defendant in a second criminal case, becoming our accomplice.

But there is an alternate reality where none of these court cases exist, none of the thousands of fake cases, a reality where there is truth and love, a reality that we have not seen in Russia.

how are you country?

The court placed municipal deputy Lucy Stein under
house arrest.
The same decision was made using the same charges for:
Anti-Corruption Foundation lawyer Lyubov Sobol,
the brother of the opposition leader Alexei Navalny, Oleg,
the coordinator of Navalny's Moscow headquarters,
Oleg Stepanov,
the head of the 'Alliance of Doctors', Anastasia Vasilyeva,
and a member of the Pussy Riot group, Maria Alyokhina.
– 3 February 2021

Inspector Vlad comes at ten in the morning. I take a long time to get ready.

Moscow is cold and grey. How are the people who are waiting in freezing buses, in worsening queues, to start their detention time? The detention centres are overflowing; they are taking people over sixty kilometres into the countryside. How are the people who fell under batons when they went to the square after

Navalny's trial? How is the girl who they suffocated with a plastic bag in the police station to extract her password from her, so they could look at her social media? How are you, country?

ginger tea

Fourth floor. There's a sign on the metal door – Criminal Investigations. The investigator is late. A cop from criminal investigations brings me ginger tea and a Mars bar. Then a man wearing a tie comes into the office, a major; he gives me documents.

> 'Alyokhina M. V. incited the violation of sanitary and
> epidemiological rules, causing a threat of mass disease to
> people, influencing others to commit a crime through her
> appeals and persuasion.'
>
> – court document

- Why have I suddenly moved from being a simple offender to being an instigator?
- To be honest, I don't know, the major with the tie quietly says.
- Did you even read these documents you've given me?
- To be honest, NO.
- Bear in mind that the investigation team was only put together on Saturday!

The Quiet One suddenly raises his head.

- You mean at the weekend, I clarify.
- Yes! he responds, happy to be understood. At the weekend they called everyone into work!

An investigation team – fourteen investigators from all over

Russia. They investigate Instagram posts. They even brought people from Siberia to do this work.

'I don't understand the accusation,' I write on the protocol, and hear an echo of my voice from 2012. These were the words I spoke in the Pussy Riot trial.

mama

Today my son rang on my new number. He rang and immediately hung up. He probably rang to ask something and then realized that he shouldn't call on this number because it is new and the cops don't know about it. That they've put a wiretap on my relatives' numbers is highly likely, just to identify my new number and then be able to put a wiretap on me. Like on my old phone. It takes him a couple of rings to remember this simple fact. Filipp is thirteen. And his mother is not a criminal. But he remembered.

When they put me in jail, Filipp was five years old. 'Mum sang a loud song against Putin,' he would explain to other kids to explain why I wasn't around. One visit every three months, a room with a kitchen where you could make your own food. The thing that doesn't exist in a colony and that you miss very much – home-cooked food. You can read to your child at night, you can play board games and pretend during those three days of the visit that you are at home. On the window – bars. Behind them – the orange lights of the zone. There is one thought that you can't contemplate. The thought that you are 'a bad mother'. Otherwise you simply can't fight with these prison guards. I can't imagine what his life was like without me during those less than two years. My mother tells me one story as we go out to the covered balcony. My favourite balcony, which is becoming my new prison.

'We were walking along the street, and I said to him,
"Well, when mum comes out . . ." and he suddenly said to
me, "I don't think Mum will ever come out . . ." I felt kind of
sick. I said in a very confident voice, "Fil, don't ever dream of
thinking that. Mum will definitely come out, I just can't tell
you exactly when." That was in the autumn, and I knew that
you were due to come out in March. I said that I knew you
would come out, absolutely-absolutely, but I couldn't tell him
exactly when. Well, I don't know if he believed me or not, but
he didn't bother me with it anymore, he seemed to calm down,
but I felt really bad when he suddenly said it so sadly.'

shovel and solitude

Five in the morning. You can hear a metal shovel scraping the asphalt under the window. They are removing the snow. Removing the snow in the dark. The worker is clearing the road for people going to work later.

In the penal colony, wrapped in a down shawl and coat, I also cleared the snow with a shovel – I left the solitary confinement cell for the solitary confinement yard at about six in the morning. I took the shovel and cleared the yard and path to it. I cleared the yard, where no one would come, where they weren't going to walk or go to work. I cleared it for myself. To properly wake up.

If there is a sound of solitude, then for me it is this sound – the sound of a shovel on asphalt in the dark.

'And this thing about solitude is very important. It is
an important goal of the authorities. One of the greatest
philosophers, Luna Lovegood, said something about this . . .
Remember her in Harry Potter? And talking to Harry
in some difficult time or other, she said, "Well, if I were

*Voldemort . . . I'd want you to feel cut off from everyone
else . . ." There can be no doubt that our own Voldemort in
his palace also wants that.'*
– Alexei Navalny's closing statement at court, 20 February 2021

cogs

House arrest is not a simple thing. Everything is mixed
up: sometimes friends don't act like friends – firstly, you've
pissed them off over the years; secondly, your preventative
measures for them are nothing more than self-isolation,
which 'we all had to go through during the pandemic'.
Then there's a man in uniform who doesn't behave like a
pig – he says, sitting next to you, 'I also hitchhiked when I
was younger to my home in Ryazan from the penal colony
where I worked and back. I had no money, so I hitchhiked.
My uniform into a backpack, a cover story about "going
home to my aunt in a Mordovian village" to the driver, and
then I'd arrived.'

You hate the Investigative Committee who lead the criminal case – but here is the quiet major standing in the court
and mumbling, 'I ask you to leave the preventative measures
as before.' He mumbles as if he is ashamed and lazy to be
involved in such a thing. It could be that he really is ashamed
and lazy – you will never know.

You hate FSIN – the descendant of the Soviet prison camp
system. But hey! This isn't a prison camp; after all, no one is
torturing you, are they? This inspector is simply escorting you
from court to court, criticizing the system on the way. He is
not a sadist – also he takes beautiful photos, he showed them
to you on Instagram.

You know that neither the Quiet One nor Inspector Vlad made the decision to criminally prosecute you, and neither did the judge. These people are simply following orders. These people simply don't want to lose their job. And now their work is to keep you under house arrest. And they do their job. Without any excitement. If they are told to do another job, they will do another.

why?

I go down the stairs. I'm forbidden to cross the threshold of the apartment. I go down the stairs. Six-twenty in the morning. When crossing the threshold border – the border that the bracelet remembers – the fsinphone receives a signal about the violation and transmits it to the station on duty. I leave the building. The ankle bracelet doesn't know where I'm going. I get into a taxi and say urgently, 'Please, hurry, go as fast as you can!' The driver replies, 'Okay, okay. But there are potholes in the road.' Once we've cleared the rough bit of road, he asks, 'What's going on?' I tell him, 'I've escaped house arrest.'

A friend's calm voice comes over my phone's speaker: 'Maybe you should turn around?' I'm in the car and watching the dawn. Blue, cold, just wow. Of course I won't turn around.

dawn – violation

You're not thinking. They won't understand you. You're not a mother who has broken her arrest to go to a sick child. You drank a bottle of white and then went to the girl who you fell in love with and who the system made your accomplice. Your lawyer grabbed your hands and asked you not to. Nikita gave you a cat – maybe a cat will calm her. Although the point is not being calm. The point is that they set the parameters of the game where we are criminals and should sit at home. And look, don't leave. It will be worse if you do. There – in jail, in the SIZO – it will be worse. Be afraid. And if you won't be afraid, they will take even this freedom from you. And everyone believed this. But is that really freedom?

communicating with an accomplice – violation

'I call everyone – her mother, her son's father, her lawyer –
will you contain her? But then again, a bulldozer couldn't
hold her back.
I have fifteen minutes. The telephone is ringing non-stop:
'Don't open the door.' They are scared that I will commit a
violation and end up in jail. Four letters are flashing in their
heads: JAIL. I don't pick up, put on my trousers and go to
pencil my eyebrows. The station on duty has already received
a signal about the escape. The cops will be here soon, our
amazing lawyers and friends are racing here. I pencil my
eyebrows – how can my girl see me without eyebrows?'
– Lucy, house arrest apartment, March

I manage to enter the apartment, I manage to hug her. Everything, of course, is not as we'd planned it many times on the chat. Planned but didn't dare. Planned and didn't tell anyone. Not only because no one, or almost no one, would understand, but because we really did believe it would be worst of all if they forbade us even to message.

open the door – a violation

*'A nice prison camp with kind inspectors and soft sofas,
where people are forced to fear going and to fear hugging one
another, although they are innocent and everyone absolutely
knows it.'*

– Lucy

hug – a violation

Our messages don't transmit heartbeats. For now.

I manage to hug her, feel a few of those heartbeats, strong
ones. And time runs out.

Rescuers come to the rescue. Our lovelorn lawyer, who has
showered Lucy's kitchen with flowers. Her ex, who repeats,
'Does anyone know what to do?' Do what? My lawyer. In shock.
I call the inspector and say, 'I want you to leave.' He thinks I'm
talking about the apartment where I am not.

– I haven't gone there yet.
– I want you to leave.
– I have a protocol I need to write.
– I want you to leave the system that is imprisoning us!

And then they carry me out. They can bear you. But no one
can bear me in there. Many people cannot bear me at all. This
is a play on words in Russian. It doesn't properly translate. This
whole situation cannot be translated because it could only
happen here. In Russia. Two girls knocking on the door from
different sides. What is this?

a bottle of white

'With force, they drag us to each side of the door, so that the accomplices aren't found together. My lawyer sits on the floor and holds the door with his back – he is very big. I can't move him even an inch. He's in love with me, and he sees danger not just in the four letters of JAIL, but in the four letters of M-a-sh-a. He thinks she wants to put me in jail. I think I'm giving up my lawyer, and I'm yelling and swearing about it. I almost never yell, but she is crying and banging on the door.'

– Lucy, house arrest apartment, March

I'm sitting on the windowsill in the hallway. It is obvious that the entire chain of the system has reacted and the cops are about to exit the lift. I'm crying on the windowsill. The head of the investigation team says about my escape, 'This is completely inopportune now.' To conduct a case against corpses – that would be opportune. So they don't have to deal with such unexpected escapes.

I have no regrets. I'm going to the police station. The cops are silent and are wondering, 'Why the fuck did she have to leave her building?' I am silent and wonder, 'Why the fuck did you put this bracelet on me?' And in this silence, we understand each other. 'This is Masha,' says the duty guard. And no one else says anything. And it's dawn again. 'When you pick a girl up from a club in the early morning,' jokes Inspector Vlad, and he drives me home. After all, this is not a fully-fledged escape attempt. And everyone turns a blind eye.

four letters

In a remote school in the Urals, a girl called Lesya makes a wall of newspaper clippings for 8 March – International Women's Day. Lesya is eleven years old. 'Strong and Brave' is the title – and underneath it are women Lesya has decided are strong and brave: Rosa Luxemburg, Simone de Beauvoir, Sofia Kovalevskaya, and among these women there are several defendants in the Sanitary Case, including me.

I look at the photo of the newspaper wall while I sit on the balcony with the bracelet. I found it online and am looking at it. It is so cute that I'm about to cry.

When they first caught us after 'Punk Prayer', on 8 March 2012, Navalny came to the prison at Petrovka to support us. And now I'm sitting here with this ankle bracelet because of a post in his support.

strong and brave

> *'In Moscow, a drunken probation officer barely able to stand on his feet scattered important documents containing personal data in the metro subway. About five metres away, around the corner from him, his car keys. In another couple of metres, a judge's request. Signed, sealed and containing personal data.'*
> – Ren-TV propaganda channel video, 16 March 2021

The fsinmobile is taking me to court. The court will extend my house arrest by two more months. On the way, Vlad shows me the video of his drunken colleague in the metro and asks, 'What do you think?'

- The guy got drunk; it happens.
- He disgraced us, don't you think?
- The people who torture prisoners to death in penal colonies are disgracing you. This guy just got drunk.
- Ah, seems that the inspector is one of yours.
- Well, in which case, all is not lost then. At least someone still has a heart.

'Mama – anarchy; Papa – a glass of port wine.' The guard opens the court gates. 'It will be an epic arrival,' says Vlad as we approach the back entrance and the speakers of the fsinmobile are screaming out a protest song from my parents' generation.

epic arrival

Friends wave to me from the other side of the court gates. If you turn your head to the left, the angle is the same as back then. Back then there were many people behind the gates supporting us at the trial, but I didn't know any of them . . . and now there are only five, but they are all like family. I still haven't fully understood what I feel, because now I am one of many. Many thousands of political prisoners in this country.

Putin has packed a whole stadium to 'celebrate the annexation of Crimea', but no one is allowed into our court hearing.

'Accused, put on your masks,' says the judge, sitting there without a mask.

Judge Dudar – Putin's judge, who gave sentences to innocent people in the Bolotnaya and Moscow cases, who gave the green light to the criminal case against Alexei and Oleg Navalny – looks at the list of artists who have demanded our release and with a smirk gives it to the investigator. 'Take a look.'

'Among the signatories are film directors Pedro Almódovar and Spike Jonze, actors Whoopi Goldberg, Gillian Anderson and Mia Farrow, artist Marina Abramovich, and the European Film Academy.'

– Mediazona, 17 March 2021

The head of the investigation team – a senior investigator of particularly important cases, Spesivtsev – a grey man with dim eyes, looks down at the table, and says, 'The investigation needs more time.'

My house arrest is extended by two months.

particularly important cases

After the trial, the investigator hands me a 'permission to visit a doctor', signed an hour after my lawyer's statement that if they don't let me go anywhere, I'll go out by myself.

The metro. The train leaves a tunnel into the city. I look at the sky – a light blue sunset with clouds. It's as if I haven't looked at everything through glass these last months. That I can leave home without being afraid and I can travel on the metro without panicking. As if. But I am going to see the doctor with an inspector as an escort.

– Do you have a sex life? asks the gynaecologist. How about contraception?
– In general, I do have a life, but I live, I mean, I sleep, with a woman.
– That can also happen! the doctor cheerfully responds. It's also a kind of contraception.

The polyclinic is a few kilometres from Lucy's home, and I'm not even allowed to message her. Only from the toilet.

'Wear this mask,' says the nurse, and gives me a mask. Crowds in the metro don't have masks, crowds in bars don't have masks, the 100,000 people in Putin's stadium don't have masks, but I have this criminal case and a bloody ankle bracelet.

When we leave, it's dark. 'We are so close to her home,' I say to Vlad. 'Just one metro stop away.'

close

– Sorry again, how long have you been a . . .?
– What? Bisexual? I interrupt as I realize he is
  embarrassed by the word. Since I was about fifteen.

An old man is playing the accordion, people are throwing coins into his bag. Arbat – I ran away from home to here as a teenager, it has the same life of street musicians and hippies as fifteen years ago.

– Look, how big the moon is, says Vlad.
– Yep, I reply.
– It's great that we went out on the street. You needed
  to be taken for a little walk.

I want things to be called by their proper names. If the state wants to put me in jail for an Instagram post, I'm not afraid – let them put me in prison. But don't say that I am arrested at home. I'm not arrested at home. It can't be a home if the state has made it into a prison. This is not a street but a monitored route from point A to point B. And this is not a little walk under the light of the moon, it is an escort by an inspector who, although he isn't wearing a uniform right now, is still an inspector.

a route under the moon

'Once a woman I was in charge of died. She called an ambulance, the ambulance took her to hospital where she died, and they sent me to the morgue to take off her ankle bracelet.'

– What was it like?
– I had never been in a morgue before. As soon as you go in, you can smell it.
– What?
– It's impossible to describe. The smell of carcasses. And you get dizzy. It's freezing in there and the cold delays the smell. But for the first few minutes I couldn't stand up.
– And then?
– And then the pathologist came out, smiled and said, 'Come through.' I went through, and the corpses were lying almost on top of each other, and mine was at the very end, so I had to cross the entire room. I said, 'I can't, I won't go. Here's the device, I'll explain how to take off the ankle bracelet.' Then I realize that the doctor can't handle it and I go to him. I just walk and imagine that these are not real people.
– And who are they, in that case?
– Well, they're like mutilated dolls. There's a man's head that is all cut and stitched back together. So, as I cross the room, I think about puppets and how everyone is like puppets in the theatre.

– Did you manage to remove the ankle bracelet?
– I did.
– And what did you do with it after that?
– What did I do with it? Well, I put it on you, Mash!

ankle bracelet on a corpse

A couple of days later Vlad gives me a tracker. The tracker replaces the inspector. Now I need to take it with me to the polyclinic and charge it when I get back. I try to put it on charge, but the cable falls out, the cradle is loose.

On our chats, we start affectionately calling the tracker 'mashinka'. A black bar with flashing lights, which under no circumstances should be forgotten.

Inside the 'mashinka' – a SIM and Russian GPS – GLONASS. If you forget it a long way from the ankle bracelet, this means 'an escape attempt'. Your route is transmitted to your inspector's computer. You can get to the clinic via any route and any means of transport, but only via the shortest way, without stopping or shopping.

But you can trick the 'mashinka'. You can buy a jammer on the black market illegally. Some drivers jam their meters with them so their bosses can't see where they are. We get one. Next, we need to check it.

the flight of the valkyrie

After turning on the jammer, I have to disappear from the map on the FSIN computer and then suddenly appear in a new place. The route should be displayed as a straight line from

279

point A to point B, as if it had been drawn by a ruler. Or as if the car I'm travelling in had flown over rooftops and rivers. If you jam the tracker for a bit, it will look like a simple coincidence. When Putin and his officials travel to the Kremlin, it's hard to get a signal in the centre.

After the first 'flights', they note to the inspector that I have a 'faulty tracker'. It's true the tracker doesn't seem very correct: when I leave the house and walk for a kilometre, the tracker 'doesn't notice'. 'Made in Russia'.

> *'Russian troops are on the border with Ukraine. Should we*
> *expect a new war?*
> *After being on exercise, Russian troops are in no hurry to*
> *leave the border regions with Ukraine, confirms* The New
> York Times, *citing American military sources. At the same*
> *time, hundreds of posts on Russian social media have appeared*
> *about the transfer of military equipment closer to the Russian-*
> *Ukrainian border and to Crimea, annexed by Russia in 2021.'*
>
> – BBC report, 1 April 2021

made in russia

You get used to not leaving home alone, not going on the metro alone. A bunch of silly jokes about the nineteenth century are in my head. From when we women needed to be chaperoned. But this isn't the nineteenth century. It is paranoia. Near my home – there could be surveillance; in the metro – there could be surveillance. I have a phone full of our nudes, and I really don't want them to be seized.

I seem like a normal person, I'm not wearing prison uniform, but I look around me on the metro when I'm sitting down and I look back when I walk. My right leg has an ankle bracelet, but you probably wouldn't notice.

polyclinic.ru

This is our mega plan to meet up. It took a couple of weeks to develop. Choose one clinic. Register with different doctors but book an appointment at the same time. Keep your fingers crossed for the investigator to give permission and not notice anything. I go with the tracker, you – with your inspector.

I am very nervous when I walk there and very nervous when I see you. Your inspector is sitting on a bench by the entrance. You walk up the steps, I – also but only after a few minutes. So that we don't arouse any suspicion.

We go down another staircase to the lower ground floor. We joke that this is a date in the X-ray basement.

x-ray date

The nurses pass by.

- Are you being a problem, girls? Watch out, they'll put you on YouTube and then what will you do?

The physiotherapist waves his hand.

- Do you have an appointment?
- No, we just have some . . . problems!
- We're just taking some photos!

We're just. Sitting on a bench under a tree. A tree in a pot. A bench in the basement of the polyclinic. Opposite us, the word 'conscience' on the wall. You say, 'Look, there's the word "conscience".' I say, 'It's an advert for a credit card.' You say, 'Our investigator needs to apply for a credit card of conscience.'

And we laugh. We kiss. We take selfies with the tracker. And laugh again. After all, this black 'mashinka' from the major is supposed to be controlling something somehow.

conscience on credit

This is the first time I don't think about the fact that I'm following a route. I'm just going home. For the first time in all this time, the music doesn't irritate me. And then my son comes home with a trophy for first place, won by his team at a paintball game.

You message: 'On the way back I couldn't stop smiling. Live music played on the Arbat. I smiled and thought how the inspector didn't catch on.'

'That means that it was a good day?'

'The best.'

two teams

The defendants in our case are divided into two teams, they don't want to judge eight defendants all at once – we simply wouldn't all fit in the courtroom. So they judge us in fours. I am in a separate group to Lucy, and the court hearings are a rare opportunity for us to see each other, and we think about it all the time.

It is an appeal of our house arrest. Our four will be brought to court first, and the day after tomorrow they will bring Lucy's four. We don't have any expectations of the hearing, just like we don't have any expectations of Russian courts in general.

But this time something strange happens. The judge with a short haircut like the Quidditch instructor, Madam Hooch, sits on the bench, asks the defendants for their names, and then suddenly discovers that the investigator hasn't sent us copies of the complaints – neither to us nor to the lawyers, so officially the participants do not know why they are in the courtroom. Including the prosecutor. The judge asks everyone their opinion: is it possible to conduct a hearing if no one has the complaint documents?

madam hooch

- Investigator, your opinion.
- I consider it possible to review, the bald lieutenant colonel says, looking at the table.
- Review what? the judge asks sternly.
- The complaints.

The lieutenant is stressed.

- Prosecutor, your opinion.
- I consider it possible to review.
- And do you have copies of the complaints, have you read them?

The prosecutor laughs, fiddles with his sleeves, laughs again and says, 'No, I don't have them, I haven't read them.'

'They can put a person in jail for lawlessness, but they can't hold a trial without documents – no way,' my lawyer notes with a bitter smile. The hearing is postponed to the day after tomorrow, the same day as Lucy's, just a few hours earlier.

the very same day

When I return home, we decide to drag out our hearings as much as possible: we come up with endless challenges to the judge, we come up with reasons to object to the court's personnel, we come up with our lawyer being late, we come up with filming the hearing, after all the court is closed. A video would provoke them to take me out of the courtroom to the corridor. Where Lucy will already be waiting for me.

sounds like a plan

The night before our hearings we – Lucy and I – don't sleep, we make T-shirts for the court and write on them:

Article 123, Russian Constitution:
Open trials are one of the most important principles of
justice in the Russian Federation.

The next day when my hearing is underway, my lawyer warns that Lucy has almost arrived, and that means it's time. I get the camera, put it on the table and turn it on.

The court bailiff approaches and says, 'Stop filming!'

I answer, 'According to the constitution we have the right to an open trial.'

– This is an open trial.
– Then why is the courtroom empty?
– You are not obeying the lawful demand of a bailiff.
– Which is more important: the constitution or the demand of a bailiff?

remains of the constitution

There's a phone ringing in the judge's deliberation room. She gets up suddenly and leaves the bench. Our plan was that the bailiff was supposed to take just me out of the courtroom, but he takes everyone out. There's been a call to say there's a bomb threat; they make an announcement to evacuate.

We see each other in the corridor. 'Separate them, break them up!' the bald lieutenant colonel yells, and we are so happy that we can't tear ourselves away from each other. 'Don't you see that they are communicating?' he shouts at our inspectors. 'It's forbidden!' They both turn to him and say, 'Well, yes, here everyone communicates with each other.' 'And recently my eyesight has got worse,' says Vlad.

We stand on the street, hugging one another. 'Why did they take you out?'

because we are bombs

We kiss each other, the cameras click. Friends, lawyers, passers-by move like free particles or atoms. And then we go to a café. To a Georgian khinkali one. Like normal people on a normal day. We are in a café like normal people but with one difference – we can't order food. Because what kind of food are we talking about? We have a countdown of minutes before the evacuation is over. And it isn't a normal day, we have an appeal against our preventative measures, interrupted by a telephone call about a bomb.

Our inspectors and lawyers are sitting on the table behind. On the neighbouring one – a cop. Oleg Navalny is sitting opposite and asks:

- Mash, tell me, how many reports did you have in the colony?
- Four.
- Ha! That's chicken feed! I had no less than forty!

chicken feed

When it's time to return to the court, we ask for the bill and run to the basement. We shut ourselves in the toilet. I've never kissed anyone so hard in a khinkali café toilet before. And then we return to the court. They lead Lucy into the courtroom. Our team waits in the corridor. It is late evening; we have, it seems, already spent an eternity in this court with brown doors.

Vlad says, 'I'm going for some food.' My inspector shouldn't leave me on my own, but he goes to the shop for food. He returns with two large plastic bags: pizza, juice, cheese. The lawyers try to clarify how much money he's owed. He says, 'Have you gone mad? This is a hundred points of karma for me, you don't owe me anything.'

a hundred points

When Lucy comes out of the courtroom, she says a three-letter word – ZOD. They've changed her group's preventative measures. Everyone is so tired that no one believes it.

ZOD is a prohibition of specific activities, a curfew; now Lucy only has to be at home from 8 p.m. until 6 a.m. We are still forbidden to communicate. We run to the toilet again, smoke on the windowsill. There's a blue pattern on the tiles. As if we were now by the ocean.

specific activities

The court carries our group's hearing over to the next day – it is too late to start now. It is raining. Pouring rain and it's dark. The fsinmobile is parked in the same place where the criminal investigators pushed me into the police car. Vlad stops the car and says, 'Don't look.'

   – At what?
   – What you are about to see will be very weird!!

He opens the glove compartment, gets out some medical masks, cuts off their string and ties them together. In the torrential rain he opens the bonnet and attaches the string to the broken windscreen wiper. Otherwise we wouldn't get to our destination. He is mending a broken windscreen wiper in the pouring rain and comes back to the fsinmobile. He says, 'And I now will say something else.'

a bonus from me

Vlad says, 'The court bailiffs took me to one side and asked "man to man" that I bring you tomorrow to the back entrance half an hour early, so that they can serve you with a protocol for filming in the courtroom without a lawyer being present. They asked me to "cooperate".' He says to me, "Tell your lawyer to come earlier and I won't take you to any back door." What are they thinking, arseholes? Like right now we're driving about as normal, and tomorrow, I'll suddenly throw you out of the back door, like, "Sorry, Mash." No way.'

We go home in the dark, Vlad stands in the lift in the corner and suddenly says, 'Go fuck yourself, major.' I say, 'Look, don't post this on social media. As you know yourself, it means house arrest and all that goes with it.'

cooperation

Snow in April, it snows all morning. The court bailiffs catch me at the entrance, push me into a small room and write a report. They drag me into a small room, and behind me, in the hallway, a statue of Themis looks on. My house arrest remains in force.

'Damn, and I'd already prepared the documents!' says Vlad. He hoped that my preventative measures would be changed to be more lenient, just like Lucy's.

> *'Western leaders, one by one, express concern over the concentration of Russian troops at the Ukrainian border. There's a lot of motorized rifle equipment, airborne equipment, artillery. Very powerful weapons, like "Grad" or "Uragan", are in evidence. Enough for a full-scale war.'*
>
> – Radio Svoboda, 7 April 2021

curfew

I've been living on the covered balcony for three months now. It's beautiful and wooden; it has a heated floor and a floor lamp from Ikea. It has windows, behind them are trees and on their branches now, instead of snow, mini leaves. Spring.

People usually ask, 'What about sex in prison?' What about sex under house arrest in an apartment full of relatives?

Two people separated by ankle bracelets, and one of us – Lucy – has suddenly received 'a relaxation of preventative measures'. After our first meeting, the meeting the day after my hearing, a meeting for a couple of hours when we were both so happy that I forgot to take the 'mashinka' with me to the doctor, and Lucy was late for the start of her curfew, the question pops up: what now?

sex on schedule

Another thing: it's funny how when you're fifteen you wait for your parents to leave. Not only is she forbidden to come to me, we are forbidden to communicate, but there is also a house full of people here.

To come and see me, she gets into a car somewhere on the street where there's no CCTV. She changes into a green cloak and black mask in the car, adds rave-style red glasses, leaves the taxi at the same place where there's no CCTV, but already in disguise, and then I open the door.

I say, 'You look like a soldier or a special agent in that green cloak.' I say, 'A curfew is something from wartime.' And for a long time now I have been thinking that there is actually a war going on in our country; it is just not very visible from the outside. And in this war between the system and the human, such days are memorable.

special agent's cloak

We often joke about the cops: 'Are you listening to us, guys? How do you like the sounds? Did you miss us?' Or what a violation report would look like: 13 April, 14.39, they were lying naked on the balcony, laughing, taking photos – in the photo it is possible to see the face of one of the violators flooded with a strange light.'

A couple of weeks later, Lucy forgets to put on her agent's cloak for the first time and leaves as she is, in denim. They immediately issue me with a report, this time a real one, 'for communicating with an accomplice' and attach a photo taken by CCTV at my building's entrance.

In the evening Vlad arrives and says that 'the mashinka is glitching'. He tinkers with it a long time, and then appears on the balcony and asks, 'Mash, if you get a phone call and you hear an echo of your voice or of the person you're talking to on the line – what is that?'

it is a wiretap

I smile and answer, 'Well, it's either something up with your phone or it's them.' The acceptance stage takes about five minutes, then he repeats at least ten times, 'I don't want this!' I say, 'Well, look at me, you think that I wanted this? You think that any of us wanted this?'

> *Searches are conducted of the headquarters of Navalny in Irkutsk, Pskov, Penza and Krasnodar*
>
> – News from 15 April 2021

Vlad calls me the next day.

– Tomorrow we will go to the doctors together.
Without the mashinka. I will explain everything to
you later.
– You've also started to call the tracker mashinka!

He comes to pick me up in the morning in jeans, a jacket,
trainers – he doesn't look at all like an inspector. He says hello
to my mother.

At the polyclinic we go out to smoke. I say, 'You know that
if someone is listening to your phone, it can work as a microphone, even if you're not talking on it.'

'So where do you put it?'

'In the other room! Or in the washing machine. Or even in
the fridge.'

you think that anyone wanted this?

A café. Between my visits to the doctor it's a break and we go to
have lunch in a café. Vlad takes his phone further away – to the
till: 'I put it there to charge for a bit.' He returns to the table and
says that yesterday a cop came to his office. The cop looked at my
case for three hours and asked about 'strange gaps in the tracker's route'. Vlad says that the cop said it like he suspected him of
some kind of crime: 'He even looked in my filing cabinet, started
digging around. It was awful, I felt very dirty, I wanted to go for
a shower.' He said, 'The cop asked, "How many reported violations does she have? And how many should she actually have?"'

– And what did you say?
– One.

- They were angry because you hadn't written a report about our kiss near the court.
- Write a report!
- I don't want to.

show me love

A few days later, we go to the Investigative Committee. In the car Vlad asks, 'Mash, what's happened?'

> *'The organizers of the charity evening "Show Me Love" in support of LGBTQ people said their event was disrupted by the police. Activists of the pro-government movements, NOD and SERB, came there dressed as "emergency psychiatric care" – "Everyone here is our patient," one of them said.'*
> – Meduza, 17 April

- Why has it upset you so much?
- The guys spent two months preparing this charity event in support of us. Moscow is a large metropolis, 13 million people, they barely found a venue, wrote 'secret place', but pro-Putin groups found it and broke it up.
- I think I saw those people near the Belarus embassy at the protests, Vlad manages to say. I'm trying to read the news less. All I want to do is take photos and move closer towards my dream of making art.
- And before that, do you know where they went? To the cemetery. Someone I know is a municipal deputy, he takes excursions round the cemetery and explains who is buried there. He talks about how, in Soviet

times, they ceremonially cremated people by day for money, and by night brought corpses from prisons and burnt them. The pro-Putin people sprayed pepper gas in the eyes of women who were on his excursion and screamed at him that he was a foreign agent. And all of this next to gravestones of people who were killed in Soviet times for nothing. You talk about protests at the Belarus embassy, but in Belarus itself they shoot protesting people.

this is for you

At the entrance of the Investigative Committee there is an exhibition of children's drawings on the theme of corruption. An angel doesn't extend his hand to a cop, who takes a bribe. Tsar Peter threatens to hang anyone on a rope who steals from the treasury. At the same time, Navalny, who is fighting corruption in prison on hunger strike, is requesting to see a doctor, and the activities of his anti-corruption fund are equated to extremism.

children's drawings

One of my eyes becomes a red ball after we leave. Vlad jokes that I have developed an allergy to the Investigative Committee.

– What was that all about?
– They have developed a new expertise – 'portrait': experts will compare our passport photos with avatars on Instagram and Twitter.

portrait expertise

– Tell me about Lucy, says Vlad on our way back home.

We are stuck in traffic.

– I don't know what to say, I reply out of habit,
  although of course I know.

When I saw her for the first time, she sat in the centre of the
apartment on a chair. Guests milled around her and she seemed
to be sad. Seemed to be. A thousand years ago. I had turned up
at that apartment by chance and quickly left. I had seen her in
the news – she had put a clown's nose on a stone Stalin, she
had become a municipal deputy, she had made headlines about
the rising generation of young politicians. A girl with big black
eyes and a tattoo of a Picasso angel on her wrist.

– It is like a comedy, I say to Vlad. We hung rainbow
  flags around the city and fell in love.
– She is a . . . too? Vlad asks uncertainly.
– No, she hasn't been with a woman before. I think she
  surprised herself.

There are things which are difficult to tell friends and which
you definitely won't tell a FSIN inspector, whatever he's like.
In the end you are not going to say why you are sad, who you
are jealous of. You don't say how you are tired of constant self-
censorship, of impotence, of your room. I don't know what
would have happened if we didn't go to the rally, what would
have happened if Navalny hadn't returned, I don't know what
would have happened and I don't know what will happen.

putin – a murderer

'A prison ceases to be a prison when there is support and open-ness. If you think that house arrest = self-censorship – no. You know the time and place,' I tweet on Twitter. I sit on the balcony in tears. Three months since Navalny's return. He has kept up his hunger strike. His comrades announce a protest. I think that I can escape with the ankle bracelet. Just for a short time. I've already succeeded once before. Even if only for a few minutes. But the rally is soon, and I'm scared to go there alone. Sasha Sofeev is in detention – we need to find him a lawyer. His case is in the evening and I watch the protest like I did the last one – on my phone.

Someone wrote on their jacket 'Russia will be happy', Navalny's words from court. A woman in a down jacket with pink fur stands with the placard 'Alexei, thank you for everything!' Hard hats and boots, helmets and batons. Tasers. Cries. People shout in unison, 'Putin is a murderer, Putin is a murderer, Putin is a murderer, Putin is a murderer.'

Avtozaks are huge metal animals, tall, grey, the ultimate vehicles of evil. On the central post office there is an illuminated screen with the inscription 'And this is also Russia.'

1,984 people are detained.

1,984

Pokrov city, a barracks with blacked-out windows. Sometimes I feel I live in a shoe box, loop stiches, I'm a seamstress, just like in the text book, hunger strike, square snowdrifts, I don't have any methods of communication with the outside world.

I am against this war, I ask to finish this, the switch of general regime to a strict regime, Melekhovo, prisoners' union, unbuttoned a button, fifteen days in solitary confinement, didn't put his hands behind his back, quoted the decision of the ECHR, quoted it again, quoted it once more, autumn in solitary confinement, refused to clean the fence, didn't clean the yard well, did not put on a jacket, said the word fuck, washed half an hour earlier than was supposed to, cough and fever, new year with the homeless and the psychotic, one screams, the second is sad, screams for fourteen hours, a roaring uterine wail, I washed the homeless – and it's better to call him a tractor driver, you sent me lots of Christmas trees and Father Christmases in letters, I hung them around the cell, an hour later, during the search, they took everything down, but the mood remained, and don't think I'm crazy, after all, in quantum physics there is an amazing incomprehensible link between particles that works instantly at any distance, two years ago I returned to Russia, our miserable and tortured motherland needs to be saved, it's been robbed, wounded, dragged into an aggressive war and turned into a prison, threads-strings-wires, to my wife, to my children, to my parents, to my brother, to all my loved ones, incorrectly announced himself, lost seven kilogrammes, stay strong my love, again incorrectly announced himself, we are deeply concerned, incorrectly announced himself, received an Oscar, what was the reason is not clarified, refused to work, 180 days in solitary confinement, incorrectly announced himself, I don't incite hatred, a person has two legs: a conscience and an intellect, an extremist case, Russia, with broken bones, is now floundering in a puddle of either mud or blood, 207 days in solitary confinement, in horror and a cold sweat I jump up on my bunk at night, when it seems to me that we again had a chance, but we again went down the same road, as in the nineties, incorrectly presented form with court's permission for phone calls and visits, insulted the dignity of the warrant officer, refused to leave his cell in protest against the confiscation of writing materials, didn't respond to the reformative training, did not reform as expected, disappeared from the colony, where is Navalny, snowy nothingness, Harp, low sky, the polar night, a church behind barbed wire, February, improperly announced himself, a zone of permafrost, I laugh at least three times a day, radio receiving station in the cell, extremely gloomy and sounds like a funeral march, what was the reason is not clarified, food through the hatch in the door, bread on top of a mug like bread on top of a vodka shot, kutia rice – like at a wake, 308 days in solitary confinement, emergency doctors confirmed the death of the convicted, convicted Navalny felt unwell after his walk, what was the reason is not clarified, goodbye Alexei Anatolyevich says the judge.*

and this is also russia

- So I posted a letter to Navalny.
- Why are you telling me this.
- 'cause I'm already near home and everything is okay.
- You, what, left the house?
- Yes, I already told you, I went out to post a letter.
- Oh nooooooo! I'm coming over straight away!

* After returning to Russia, his arrest at the airport, detention and transportation to the penal colony, Alexey Navalny was placed in solitary confinement 27 times. The last time was February 14, 2024. After 1.5 days they found him dead. This text is in his memory. Alexei's words sound through the 27 ludicrous reasons for violations given in reports by the prison guards, including quotations from his letters and statements to the courts.

'I left home to post a letter to political prisoner
Alexei Navalny as he is on hunger strike
and I consider it my civic duty to support him.
I took the monitoring mashinka with me, so that no one
would lose me and think that this was an escape.'

– explanatory note to FSIN, 22 April 2021

discredited employee

I say to Vlad, 'Why are you looking at me like I am a pain in the ass? This is just the beginning.' He smiles and replies, 'No, it's not.' He is sitting opposite me at the kitchen table; on the side table there's a stack of my diaries from the three months of this arrest. He takes a pen, a clean sheet of paper and writes. He doesn't talk aloud but writes – for two reasons: firstly, he's aware the phone is tapped; secondly – it is, I realize later, a gesture of solidarity – he's showing me that I'm not alone, that we're all sitting here under surveillance.

I am now – a discredited employee
They don't believe me about anything
Yesterday they came again to inspect me
I won't be your inspector anymore
I'm being transferred to another place
I hope everything turns out okay, maybe we'll see each other some day
P.S. Do you remember the dude from the video? It seems they have
made him your inspector :)

discipline and punishment

A curfew cuts life into segments. In one visit you don't have time to do much, and the ankle bracelet doesn't give you an extension. And if before you used to sleep together, wake up, cut up tomatoes for breakfast, watch a film in the evening, now all these activities are cut up by the days – we do not have time to love and sleep and eat in the twelve hours allotted to us. It's true that not long ago I didn't have any of this with her – only notes. When it all started, she didn't fall asleep next to me, she'd leave mine to go and rest and sleep alone, she'd leave in the early morning – and now she comes in the morning so we can fall asleep together. If your shared life becomes cut up in pieces by arrest and a criminal case, can it be put back together? 'Everything will be fine!' says Lucy. 'People often wait for each other to come out of jail.' I can't understand why suddenly she loves me so much. And why we lie on the floor again.

segments

I keep wondering when the tipping point will be and I decide to pack my suitcase and leave.

- When? says Lucy.
- Well, if they kill Navalny.
- If they kill Navalny, you're going to leave me here?

I think that all my life has turned into one major violation. And not because I am 'a bad girl', but you can see for yourself: the rules are shit.

For the first time the investigator didn't let me go to the dentist, but I just went. It was good that Lucy was with me.

be queer – do crime

A turn on the highway, a traffic cop slowly approaches the taxi, lightly playing with his regulation baton.

– That's creepy, right? laughs the taxi driver.
– Yes! we chorus.

The taxi driver isn't aware that, for him, this traffic cop is just a check of his driving licence, but for us it is a potential detention.

– We are wearing ankle bracelets, says Lucy.
– What? Really? What for?
– For calls to go to a protest rally!
– What protest was that, how much did they pay you?
– They didn't pay us!
– So why did you go?
– To make this country better! I say.

make the country better

– Fucking hell, girls!
– I am extremely late, please could you drive as quickly as possible? If the dentist doesn't treat my tooth today and write a report about it, then it won't be good! I am under house arrest after all!
– How do you see a dentist under house arrest?

– The investigator gives permission!
– How much time has he given you?
– He hasn't given any!
– Fucking hell, girls!
– We're also not allowed to communicate with one
  another because we are accomplices! says Lucy.
– Fucking bubble-gum!
– Can't you go any faster?
– I don't have a propeller, we'd have to break the speed
  limit. We'll get there, but if not at least we'll wear
  ankle bracelets together!

russia will be happy

*'In order for a new person to come into the world, two
people must agree in advance that they will make some
sacrifices. This new person will be agony to give birth to, and
then you have to spend sleepless nights with them, and then
you will have to get a dog for them. Then walk that dog.
Likewise, in order for a new, free, rich country to be born, it
has to have parents. Those who want it. Those who expect it
and are willing to make some sacrifices for its birth, knowing
that it will be worth it.'*

– Alexei Navalny (04.06.1976–16.02.2024)

12.
Arrest Carousels

Seven square metres is the standard size of an apartment's balcony in the former USSR. This is the size of my mother's covered balcony where I spend my house arrest. In a fourteen-storey panel building. Built in 1974. This is one of hundreds of thousands of panel buildings. One entrance. A green bench and a lilac bush.

My mother's cocker spaniel, Nicole, lives here too. My mum raised me alone, worked from morning till night. She is a computer programmer. In the USSR it was a new cool profession. And she dedicated her life to it. She worked for an American company. In 2021, after an attack by Russian hackers on the US government, the Russian office was closed. The entire department, including my mother, was laid off.

seven square metres

As a child, I left this apartment, took the bus and visited her at work. They had the Internet. I would find things online that they didn't tell me about at school – hippies, punks, counter-culture communities. I watched the film *Earthlings* and became a vegetarian. At fifteen.

When I was imprisoned, Mum took a break from work so that she could visit me in the colony. She travelled with bags from this apartment and returned to it. When I left the colony – after all the tours and protests – I also returned here.

And now, when a case was opened against me again, they put me under house arrest. From this balcony, from this apartment, I go out to meet the new inspector.

inspector ilya

It's very funny, but it's really him – the drunken inspector from the news who lost his documents and car keys in the metro. My new inspector. Ilya. Angular, shy, like a forester. On the first day he doesn't come into the flat, he is embarrassed – 'I'd rather stay in the car.' With pride he shows me he's rigged up a stereo to the dashboard and is playing a flash drive of Russian songs from the 90s.

The song 'Filthy Whores Will Be Punished' plays. He turns red, skips to the next one – 'That's not my kind of music, I don't listen to that sort!'

It's already May, but it's still cold.

- I wonder how many fsinmobiles there are in Moscow.
- Twenty-eight branches, one car per branch.
- Twenty-eight fsinmobiles for a city of 13 million people?
- Yes, ma'am!
- So it's only us that are driven everywhere in fsinmobiles? That's a VIP service!
- There are different levels of control – first, second, third – and you and your band are the highest. They need to report your every step to the very top.

vip-control

'The police have detained Pussy Riot member Veronika Nikulshina. Four cops had been waiting for the young woman

near the entrance to her home since the morning. They explained the detention with the phrase: "If the boss says so, it must be for a reason." '

– Mediazona, 7 May

'The police detained Pussy Riot member Alexander Sofeev at the concert of a rapper. Centre E stated that Sofeev is suspected of minor hooliganism.'

– Novaya Gazeta, 8 May

My hearing for filming in court is scheduled for 9 a.m. Ilya comes for me early. Very early. At 6.30. 'So, who is a fine young man and won't be late today?' Ilya smiles and answers himself, 'I'm the fine young man!'

The same terrible music plays from the flash drive. Neither of us has slept enough, but we leave on time. Nothing special, but we are trying to behave properly.

Before the unfortunate video on the TV channel, Ilya was a senior inspector, he knew his city district like the back of his hand. Ten years in the system, a year until his pension and then – bam! Demotion, transfer to another branch and me. Apparently, as special punishment.

behave properly

'I missed the fucking turn again.' He doesn't know the area where I grew up at all and hopes that after our case he'll be transferred back to his home branch. But for now, he has to drive me to pointless hearings and doesn't quite trust me.

– Damn, on Thursday we have a uniform review, Ilya suddenly says.

– What's that?
– A line-up in front of the boss, a mandatory
  procedure – to see if any of our shit is torn, like an
  epaulette, or that our uniform isn't creased.
– Is the General checking it out?
– Yes, that dick who screamed more than anyone else
  that I should be fired after the damned video.
– Let me make a doctor's appointment on Thursday,
  and you will be obliged to accompany me there via
  VIP service and will miss the General. What time will
  he be there?
– At twelve.
– Let's try! I had a chat with Vlad about you. I said to
  him, 'Don't blame him.' I know that you disgraced
  some people, disgraced the people who torture
  prisoners in penal colonies, and that you transport
  political prisoners. You got drunk once – that means
  you've still got a heart.

He was glowing. I didn't think that such a trifle could make a
man so happy. A few minutes later, when I go into the store to
buy cigarettes and the cashier says, 'I won't sell them without a
passport,' Ilya comes up, looks him directly in the eye and says,
'She's with me.' The cigarettes are immediately handed over.

– So they could have taken me to the police station and
  called my relatives, but instead the assholes decided
  to make a video of me and sell it to a TV channel.
  When Navalny flew back, they ordered me to wash
  the car. 'Do it faster, it might be needed' – I washed it
  with my own money; the boss returned half, also out
  of his own pocket. That car is like the state. Cracked
  glass, broken headlights, a battery which the previous

inspector changed with his own cash. But in front of
the bosses everything needs to shine.

fourteen candles

– What is that on your leg? a boy asks.

Filya's friends are here. Up near the ceiling – balloons from
Lucy; on the plate – slices of cake from mum.
 On the cake – fourteen candles.
 Filipp is fourteen years old.
 My son is fourteen. I don't know what wish he made.

– An ankle bracelet, I answer the boy. I'm under house
 arrest and am not allowed to leave home.

I find board games and we play the shortest ones – it's already
evening. I feel awkward, but I try. I'm often ashamed and now I am
too. We played board games during long visits in the penal colony.
Long visits lasting three days; visits with close relatives were once
every three months. Since then, I've really loved board games.
 Filipp is fourteen, which means that from this day on they
can give me detention days instead of fines. That will happen
very soon. They will start catching us around town and jailing
us. We call this chain of detention days 'arrest carousels'.

arrest carousels

*'Usually, the Russian arrest carousel starts with a detention for
hooliganism or for censored language. For this they give a person
ten to fifteen detention days, and immediately after their release*

they pin another administrative article on them – for example,
for resisting the police. The chain of arrests can continue without
end – similar to a carousel which someone is constantly spinning.'
– diary of Sasha Sofeev

'In Moscow, for the second time in a week they detained
Pussy Riot member Nika Nikulshina.'
– Mediazona, 16 June

someone is spinning

'In Moscow they detained Pussy Riot member Alexander
Sofeev and his friend. A huge avtozak arrived with lots of cops
and Centre E cops.'
– Mediazona, 22 June

'In Moscow the police detained municipal deputy and member
of Pussy Riot Lucy Shtein, a defendant in the "Sanitary Case".'
– Mediazona, 22 June

In the morning, as she left home, they detained Lucy.

'Does anyone know that I ALREADY have an ankle bracelet?'
– Lucy Shtein's Twitter

After five months under house arrest, all the days are mixed up.

News about arrests – every day.
News about searches – every day.
News about new criminal cases.
News about new details of FSB poisonings.

every day

I don't even know what day it is. The anniversary of the begin-ning of the Great Patriotic War. The anniversary of when Hitler attacked the Soviet Union. Anna is detained in the afternoon.

> '*In Moscow they detained the film director and Pussy Riot member Anna Kuzminykh. They arrested her while leaving a beauty salon. The police declined to explain the reason for her detention.*'
>
> – Mediazona, 22 June

I'm raging on the balcony. Olya comes up and says, 'Mash, please forgive me.' Half an hour ago we had a fight because I said that the Great Patriotic War was 'just some war'. Fascism of the last century doesn't worry me as much as contempo-rary fascism, but for her there is no contemporary kind. I say, 'I want to get out. Get out and go.' She says, 'Let's go to see Lucy at the court.' This is a violation of my house arrest. Let's go.

– Take the apartment keys, says mum. I'm going to the theatre tonight.

We get in a taxi. A police car blocks the way. About ten people, some in uniform, some civilians, lead us to the avtozak. The homeless men scattered around my building turn out to be surveillance. The avtozak is parked a hundred metres from my building but round the corner, so I couldn't see it from the balcony. We just go to it.

In the report they don't write that we simply went with them. They write 'police resistance'.

police resistance

In the station three well-built men twist Olya's arms, twist her
and cut off the cross from her neck, 'so you don't hang yourself'. We stay for the night.

There are cells along the corridor with blacked-out windows and the stink of the homeless. Metal brown doors with
peepholes and open feeding hatches. You can hang your head
out of them like in a guillotine and chat. The cell corridor leads
to the toilet, so the smell of the homeless mixes with the smell
of pee. It's a toilet used by everyone, both us and the duty cops.

– And where's the one they cut the cross off? asks the
  district cop as he passes my cell.
– She's signing a protocol.
– Because I looked through the peephole of her cell
  and it was empty. I thought that it was like in a movie,
  when one minute she was there and the next she
  wasn't – that she had flown up and was hanging from
  the ceiling
– That's my department.
– And you are?
– I'm from Pussy Riot.
– Ah, it's your building that we are always stuck at!
  Maybe you can move somewhere else?

*'On 23 June, the Moscow courts arrested three members of
Pussy Riot and detained four of their friends for fifteen days.
Formally the arrested admitted to being guilty of resisting
police or of petty hooliganism.
According to police reports, they were arrested as the*

security forces suspected them of planning an action on the
anniversary of the start of the Great Patriotic War.'

– Meduza, 25 June

just some war

Fifteen detention days.

Seven people received fifteen detention days.

Sasha Four Eyes does not believe until the very end that he will be detained. He looks at the wall and repeats, 'Maybe they'll only give a fine?' The brown doors and brown stripes of the court corridor walls say clearly with their appearance, 'No, there will be nothing out of the ordinary here.'

An obese, indifferent judge in glasses reads us identical court decisions.

House arrest is so devastating that I am afraid to put my feelings into words. It's a summer street, evening. It's a summer evening. It's the cops – one with a long, beautiful nose. It's the walls of the avtozak and the light of the streetlights. It is as if my inside was napalmed over these five months. It's poplar fluff. June fluff. Poplar fluff flies everywhere. This fluff has been on everyone's Insta stories, but now it's here – on my cell floor. I'm in a cell.

poplar fluff

Lucy's and Anna's cells are opposite. It's Anna's birthday tomorrow. In the cell. And it's the first time I'm not seeing the detention centre just from the outside. Sasha and his friend are here too – it's all ours. 'Pussy Riot have captured Detention

Centre No. 2,' Tim jokes in a message. This is the last thing I see on my phone before they confiscate it.

- What's that on your leg? the guard asks me at inspection time.
- An ankle bracelet, I've been under house arrest for five months, without any walks at all.
- Ah, at least we have walks here! For an hour once a day!

Another guard comes in: 'France again – a draw, what's going on!' The European Football Championship is on the TV. Nika is in the same detention centre as us for fifteen days because she bought tickets to the match.

Summer 2018. Pussy Riot ran onto the football pitch of the World Cup with their action 'Heavenly Policeman'. A photo of a happy Nika, giving a high-five to the star of the French team, Mbappé, made the international news. From that day on, according to an unspoken rule of the Russian cops, she was forbidden to go to a football match.

- Who are you rooting for? I ask the guard.
- France, of course.

special detention centre no. 2

Special Detention Centre No. 2 is like a hostel – prison style. A three-storey building behind a blue metal fence. Mustard walls, high ceilings. Round lamps in black mesh cases. There are inscriptions – notes from people who were here. In Sasha's cell, on the bunk, it says, 'Navalny was here'; in ours: 'Rita Flores – 20 days for an action near the Kremlin'. Notes from activists, politicians, artists who spent their detention days here are mixed with notes of people arrested for drunk driving or driving without a licence.

Our cell no. 3 looks out onto the exercise yard – a large concrete box with a metal mesh ceiling. Sasha and his friend are taken out for a walk, and the entire hour is like being at summer camp. We are sitting on the windowsill (the window has bars), they are 'walking in the courtyard', we talk about funny moments from our detentions, comparing avtozaks (ours had air conditioning!), we laugh. And we find out that the order to put 'our whole gang' in jail was given by the deputy chief of the Moscow police.

mustard walls

Superhot. Unusual for June: 30 degrees.

Anna's birthday. Our cell and their cell are being taken together to lunch. They don't give Anna her medicine. She has a rare disease. Fibromyalgia. A permanent hellish pain in your muscles. In Russia, almost nothing is known about this disease, medication is considered 'pills for drug addicts'. Anna goes out to lunch wearing her pale pink pyjamas inside out, with seams showing. It's as if she herself is turned inside out. She is in pain. And I say, 'I'm sorry' and hug her. I feel like it's my fault that she got these detention days. It's my fault that she's not with her loved ones on her birthday, it's my fault that she's already in pain and now it's even more painful. The paramedic gives her a black rubber bracelet with the following written on it:

from the point of no return – a beautiful view opens up

November 2019. The banner 'Stop Gulag!', ten metres, ten huge photos of political prisoners. The bridge by the Kremlin. Anna's name falls under the pen. A young director who received letters of gratitude from the 'Russian clergy' is designated as 'Pussy Riot' after this action.

- Is the borscht with meat? I ask the cook.
- With chicken.
- Is there any salad?
- With ham.
- Is this some kind of joke?
- What kind of joke – it definitely has ham! neighs the cook.
- So is there anything vegetarian?
- Vegetarian??? Ha ha! Rice!

russian privileges

This is it – the main privilege of same-sex relationships: we can be together in here. If we were a straight couple, we'd be in different cells.

Lucy brings her things into our cell. 'Don't say anything!' She puts her finger to her lips. In any case I jump for joy. We're in one cell. We will be in the same cell! With black ankle bracelets – the only ones in the whole detention centre but together.

No more of her leaving at 7 p.m. according to the schedule and spending the night alone. For a whole fifteen days. Metal bunks fixed to the floor. They don't move. But no one is giving serious thought to it. No one is giving serious thought to the round black video camera on the ceiling. We are on holiday. A holiday from house arrest, from the curfew, from disguise, from inspectors. A holiday with bars on the windows and peepholes in the metal doors.

special holiday

It's my first time in a special detention centre. The furniture is nailed to the floor, the door has a peephole and is always locked. There is no toilet; the toilet is a hole in the floor, called a parasha, behind a wooden door. The shower is once a week. You wash yourself by pouring water from a bottle over the sink under your armpits, and the rest – over the parasha.

But there are positives. Detox from endless doom scrolling of the news filled with hopelessness. And walks. After being granted the gift of walking inside a concrete box, I start to train. I put my pink rug in the middle of the exercise yard.

> *workout: yoga sun salutes – 2 full cycles*
> *squat 20 – times*
> *standing on tiptoes 50 – times*
> *push-ups – 15 times*
> *chest press – 20 times*
> *repeat three times.*
> *To the last two rounds add*
> *bottom raise – 20 times each leg*
> *leg raise – 20 times each leg*
> *For the last round – cut tiptoes.*

plank – 1 minute
stretching into splits – 5–10 minutes

Jogging – twenty rounds of the exercise yard.

Laces are forbidden. They take them at the first search. So we make new ones out of wet napkins. We twist the napkins into a rope diagonally and insert them into the top holes of our trainers. If the napkins are good, these laces can hold for the whole fifteen days, even longer.

napkin laces

No one annulled our criminal case that gave us ankle bracelets. The escort guard picks us up in the morning from the detention centre and takes us to the Investigative Committee. We are riding in the avtozak cage. You probably imagine something very scary, but we can't stop laughing. A metal avtozak, black ankle bracelets, body armour hanging on hooks.

Summer city: cafés, signs, students, street after street – they rush past, we drive and look at them through the window with bars.

'Despite everything we have romance!'

city through bars

So our case doesn't become 'high profile', they divide it into eleven cases. One for each of the ten defendants and another one – an eleventh – in reserve. 'A case against unidentified persons' enables them, in the future, to prosecute anyone who also called for the protest. Prosecute them in the same way as us. It isn't the first time. During a criminal case like this or when there's a crazy new law, people delete their previous social media posts about going to protests. 'Just in case.'

Lucy and I are not accomplices anymore and this means that our hugs become a little bit more legal than they'd been over the last few months. Each of our criminal cases is contained in six stitched books.

A dull, serious, grey-mirrored building – the Investigative Committee.

'We need to familiarize you, in three days, with the court case. Ask for whatever you want!' says investigator Spesivtsev, entering the office dancing. He is wearing a T-shirt with the inscription 'Investigative Committee'. The head of the investigative group – the investigator of particularly important cases, the colonel, the robot of the courts, the grey man of the corridors – all of a sudden, he switches on his live mode and is in a good mood. 'They're always like this when they familiarize the accused with a case,' my lawyer grins.

colonel on a leash

- I have an idea! says Lucy. Allow Masha to go for walks, then adjust my curfew schedule so I can go home later.
- I'll of course think about your schedule, but as for Maria Vladimirovna and the walks – here, you understand, it's complicated. If I give her a walk – she'll stage an action. The decision is made by . . .
- Who? we ask in chorus.
- Ummm, me! the investigator catches himself.

– You just said it wasn't you.
– I didn't say that! You write and I'll go and consult . . .
with myself!

Even to allow me an hour's walk around my building, he needs
to call 'upstairs'. The colonel is on a tight leash. I eat cherries.
He goes to make the call. Of course, we are refused. Both of us.

Each day we come here as if to work. To become familiar
with the volumes of our case. Boring. We eat cherries that
the lawyers have brought and hear stories from investigators
sent here from Siberia. Not long ago they had investigated
real crimes. Egor, one of the investigators, told us how they
had caught a maniac. He had a portrait of Hitler and a snake
terrarium.

It used to be human legs in a plastic bag. Now – girls, emojis
and Instagram.

It's raining, raining hard, Olya's doing push-ups on the
asphalt. We walk in the rain, stand under a canopy in the concrete box of the exercise yard, and then return to the cell.
There's a big bottle of hot water wrapped in two wool blankets
in the corner by the table. Kettles are forbidden here, boiling
water is given out three times a day and to keep it warm we
wrap it in blankets.

wrapped hot water

If you were to wake me up in the night and say, 'Write, here's
the pen. You have fifteen minutes, then I'll take it back. You can
remember whatever you like,' I would choose to remember
how I threw my head back on the pillow. We're lying together
on a metal bunk while, one away from us, Olya is sleeping. We

are on our thirtieth joke about 'Sanyok'. At our place – cell no. 3 – we already have our local memes. Sanyok is what we call the fictional cop who monitors the video camera in the upper corner.

'Hey, Sanyok, come here, look here!'

'Come on! Seriously, fucking hell! What are these girls doing?'

We are playing out a dialogue between fictional cops watching what's happening in the 'porn' cell.

There is also 'Tyutyunnik and Polovinka'. A major general of the Investigative Committee of the Russian Federation, Y. A. Tyutyunnik has been assigned to our case, with Major General of the Ministry of Internal Affairs A. Y. Polovinka.

Pronouncing their super-funny last names has become our favourite joke. Tyutyunnik and Polovinka are everywhere, they have even become new names for our right and left boobs.

tyutyunnik and polovinka

If you throw your head back on the pillow, through the bars you can see the shade of the sky. At three or half past three it becomes brighter, it is morning. And I say, 'It's getting light, let's sleep' or, 'It's getting light – Sanyok and the guys are probably really tired.' Apart from the hypothetical Sanyok monitoring the video camera on the ceiling, there is also a peephole. When the metal eyelid of the peephole lifts, a scraping crunch is heard. A crunch, then you can see the corridor strip light or the eye of the corridor guard.

The right angle of her shoulder along which I run my hand and the eye of the guard in the background.

I never thought that I would describe this on a bunk in a

detention centre. But it is night. And I am writing. I don't know whether to count these minutes as part of my sentence.

celebration in special detention

Lucy – twenty-five.

A round date, and a first birthday behind bars.

I make a prison cake on a small plastic plate – out of biscuits and condensed milk.

I'm extremely worried that this 'prison birthday', one I find so romantic, does not make her at all happy, but I try not to show it. Doesn't work. She gave me so many presents for my birthday – a phone, a banner, a video where she and all our friends take turns wishing me a happy birthday, and she said that she loved me so that I wouldn't forget.

She loves old Soviet furniture and Soviet food, potato purée, vermicelli like the ones in soup but without the soup, the kind they dished up in Soviet canteens and schools and which most people can't stand – they give her a very warm feeling. She is even afraid to hit a pillow, because it would hurt it, all her things are loved by her and none of them is considered useless.

We are both stubborn and love Rot-Front bars – ones from childhood, which used to be better but are still quite tasty, bars that you can't find in America or Europe.

When Lucy goes to meet a visitor, Olya writes in coffee grounds over the entire cell wall 'Happy Birthday, Lucy!'

When we quarrel a few days later, she will lie on the bunk, look at the message and choose letters from it to make new words. It's a game she loves.

dream
nudes
poison
forest

*'Pussy Riot member Veronika Nikulshina, who has just
served fifteen days, has been detained for another fifteen days.'*

– Current Time TV, 2 July

*'We were taken in a car, not clear where to, and the terrifying
men with glassy eyes who had kidnapped us wouldn't answer
any of our questions. Every time we stopped by the side of the
road near the forest, I tried to figure out whose knee would be
shot first, mine or Roman's. During these stops, they threw our
phones into the river, so that our lawyers could not track our
geolocation. All these people, the entire department, spent 24
hours tracking our payments, looking at road cams, asking for
car-sharing routes so that they could take us down to the police
station and WRITE A FAKE REPORT ABOUT RESISTING
THE POLICE and lock us up again for 15 days.'*

– Nika Nikulshina's Instagram

i tried to understand

The first day I laugh, the second day I cry. I cry all day. And I
want to throw up. The radio is on. Song after song. I learn to
smile when I want to cry. Now I can't.

They stand in the exercise yard and laugh. The sun is very
bright. They are discussing how soon they will pack and leave.
They discuss where they will go – for example, to Georgia.

And how they will hang out there. All together. Sasha, Nika, Anya. Lucy also wants to leave. I take the mat and go to the other end of the yard to do push-ups. I'm scared that I'll be alone. Olya does not want to leave, I am afraid that I'll be left with my fascist friend. Anxious, scary, painful. I want to stay and continue to fight for this country's freedom no matter how elusive it might seem, and to leave for me is to give up, hold up my hands. I can't believe that my close people want to do this. I can't forgive them and I can't forgive myself for being angry with them, but I'm angry. And with that bracelet too.

> *'Masha has exploded – cries, shouts, "What do you know about what I want?"*
> *Fifteen days beyond time – phones are confiscated. Fifteen days without a reflection of yourself – no mirrors anywhere.'*
> – diary of Anna Kuzminykh

no mirrors

They take me out into the corridor and lead me to the doctor's office. All that's left of my face is one red blob. It didn't even hurt to pound on the door with my fist. The doctor's office is on the third floor.

- What's happened? You've only got one day left. Tomorrow you're going home.
- This happened! I point to my ankle bracelet. I'm not going home, I'm going to house arrest and I'm not even allowed to go for a walk.
- For what?
- For calling for a protest.
- Hmmm!

The toad-like doctor, who no one likes in here, a man with a big belly, intensely existing under his orange shirt with palm trees, takes a glass and pours himself a hawthorn tincture.

He says, 'I couldn't do that. No walks at all?' He says, 'This regime is too old and can't last much longer.' The doctor takes me downstairs.

Downstairs is the head of the detention centre. Small, with a dry body and big, attentive eyes.

– Masha, what's happened?
– I can't take any more.

He pauses, stares at me and says, 'You're a hero, you're a legend, everyone here knows you. Don't even think about cracking up, okay? If you need a walk, we will give you a walk. Then we will take everyone to the shower. And remember, you're strong, I know it and you know it.'

how do you know?

The last minutes in the cell drag on terribly long. It seems like you've done everything: packed your things, washed your hair – but the door still won't open. They show a woman into our cell. She has a clock with her, a normal alarm clock like one from Ikea. We don't take our eyes off it.

I sit on the windowsill imagining how the inspector is going to take me away. My large chequered bags are by the door.

'Do you have keys? I'm going to the theatre this evening,' my mum messages.

The blue metal gate of the detention centre opens.

i'm going to the theatre today

*'A person's human and civil rights and freedoms are of
utmost value. The acceptance, adherence and protection of
human rights and freedoms is the duty of the state.'*
— Article 2, Russian Constitution

There's a grey minivan parked at the blue gates of the detention centre. Three men in the uniform of the 2nd Riot Police
Unit push me into this grey minivan and another one from
behind, not in uniform, throws my bags onto the seat after me.
Where are we going? Silence. To my home? Silence. I'm under
house arrest, where's the inspector? Silence. I want to call a
lawyer. Violence. If you try to get your phone out of your bag,
we will twist your arm.

We draw up to my building – there is another grey minivan.
It is a lighter shade. They throw me and my bags into it. I see
the route on the sat nav – a police station – that means they are
taking me to issue another fifteen detention days. But I haven't
fully understood this yet, so I'm screaming. I'm screaming at
the hulks in the 2nd Riot Police Unit, who are trying to take
away my things. I scream at the entire police station from the
small room that they've shoved me into. I scream at the top of
my voice, loudly, as loudly as they taught me in the theatre.
Everything that has mounted up in me over the first fifteen
detention days, with a head start on the second fifteen, rolls
into one phrase: 'I have the right to a lawyer.'

In the doorway I can see Ilya – my inspector. He is standing
in his uniform, in his uniform and in horror. In one hand a cap,
in the other a form for the defendant's explanation. The hulks
do not let him into the room.

without explanation

*'Pussy Riot member Alexander Sofeev once again detained
on the day of his exit from the detention centre.'*
– Novaya Gazeta, 7 July

'Call my lawyer, Ilya! Don't you see what's going on?' I manage
to shout before the door closes. Turning my head from the
door, I catch sight of a quote from the constitution, which says
that my rights and freedoms are of the highest value. Fuck it!
I still have a long wait. I take out my pink rug and begin to do
some yoga. And then they bring me food, a huge bag of it – it
means my friends have found me. I realize that I haven't eaten
for two days, but the hulks won't let me near the bag. They will
only let me when the lawyer appears. I don't know what cheers
me up most – the cheese in the lavash he brings or his kind eyes.

They once again accuse me of resisting the police. My resistance of the police is based on the fact that – I walk. My resistance
of the police is based on the fact that – I simply live here in Russia
right now. And once again I spend the night at the police station.

– And what was Kevin Spacey like?
– What?
– You saw him in person, right?

house of cards

I go to the entrance and the exit, through the metal detector,
into the lift and along the corridors with my chequered bags.
Like a market trader, like a shuttle – that's what they called
people in my childhood who carried goods from abroad in the

same chequered bags. They brought them to sell in metro sub-ways and at the Cherkizovsky market. Only a few years will pass and Russia will get hooked on oil, there will be fewer 'shuttles', life will appear to get more satisfying, people will be frightened by scenes from the 'Wild 90s', gradually learning that 'we have never lived better than we do now.'

The 'court hearing' has started, the 'witness' enters.

– We were patrolling the district in a service vehicle. We saw a female citizen standing and using censored language. We detained her, but she resisted.
– And how did I resist?
– People have different ways of resisting: sometimes actively, sometimes passively.
– What, you want to say that I passively resisted?
– You??? No! You – actively!
– Okay, so if you were patrolling in an official vehicle, what was its number?
– I don't remember.
– Was the bodycam 'Dozor' working?
– I don't remember.
– What did the building look like, where I supposedly stood and used censored language?
– I don't remember.
– Let's release the witness, says the judge. And gives me fifteen detention days.

cell no. 5

Evening. I wait for the escort guard to the detention centre. Twenty-four hours have passed since I left it.

With the same three bags, I go to the car. This time, instead of an avtozak, it is an ordinary district police car. At the gates one of the cops says seriously, 'Good luck, Masha. You will definitely win.' The other two get ready to move through the gates. They don't confiscate my phone. I sit in the passenger seat and record the evening beyond the window. Like in a taxi.

There is no one in the cage where they usually lock up the detained.

This time my cell is cell no. 5. The door opens and I see Nika. She sits on the bed in the corner next to the door. We go to smoke out of the window and joke that this is like a summer camp. And they have sent us here on the second shift.

second shift

Here there are only two female cells. Not just for the special detention centre, two for the whole of Moscow. Women are rarely given detention days. So how do girls usually end up here?

Dasha, the daughter of a military official and a bank director, drank beer, caught a taxi and asked the taxi driver to let her drive, and the taxi driver agreed. It's not known what happened to the taxi driver, but Dasha received ten detention days. She tells great stories about the webcam industry, can twerk, and teaches us a little. To twerk, of course. Alla had refused to wear a Covid mask and told the cop to go fuck himself. She and her friends are Rodnovers – Russian neo-pagans. Instead of signing the call log she writes 'woman Alla'; she doesn't just say, 'thank you', but 'thank you, kind person'.

woman alla

On her last day, Alla told us her wishes. She wished for me to have more 'feminine energy', since I have lots of masculine already. When I asked what she meant by feminine and masculine, she replied that feminine is acceptance, but that I resist a lot of things. Why Alla didn't agree to wear a mask, I didn't bother to ask.

> – Masha, get ready for the shower, says the guard, opening the cell door.
> – Just me? What about an extra shower for the rest?
> – Get ready! They have taken Anna there. You're going together.

> *'Pussy Riot member Anna Kuzminykh has been detained again in Moscow. The young woman was arrested as she was leaving her home with a suitcase. After fifteen days in the special detention centre, she was going to see her parents in Nizhny Novgorod to celebrate her birthday with family. The charge is police resistance. The court has arrested Kuzminykh for ten detention days.'*
>
> *– 9 July*

There is no hot water, which is okay for me, but each icy drop is a shock to Anna's body. Between laughter and tears she says, 'Imagine, this guard takes me to the shower and is repeating over and over, "I caved in, I caved in, I gave Alyokhina an extra shower."' But does he understand what he actually gave us?'

Things from her suitcase have been poured into a big black sack. It is behind the shower door. I carry it to the cell.

between laughter and tears

For breakfast, lunch and dinner we go to the canteen. A small room. Two long tables. Metal bowls and metal spoons. No metal forks – they're dangerous. Plastic ones from Chinese noodle soups – a rarity – are also forbidden. I eat only with those; I don't like spoons.

They bring food in large military green urns with the supplier's name on. It is called 'Cruise Tour'. Volunteers, not the detained, usually serve our food. Today is Sunday and there are no volunteers. So Nika and I are serving up. We are ladling rice soup into metal bowls, spooning out mashed potatoes and kotleti* that have lost their shape. We leave some salad for ourselves.

'Are you from Pussy Riot?' the guys from the first cell ask. 'Can we get your autograph?'

I put down the ladle and Nika puts down the tongs for the kotleti. We give our autographs to each of them. It seems they didn't ask as a joke.

cruise tour

'Detentions, fines, arrests, threats, assaults, and abductions from home seemed like just scary fairground rides. You could fall off one of them and get hurt, but you couldn't stop riding. After all, freedom doesn't exist unless you fight for it every day.'
– Sasha Sofeev

* Meat patties.

Nika has a panic attack. She cries and repeats 'door', probably because the door is closed.

It's very stuffy; we hang wet sheets on the open sash of the window. Anna is in pain all day from her illness that isn't considered an illness in Russia. In the next-door cell there are arguments and shouts, I can only catch 'Allah is the only' and 'there are many Lenin streets.'

smoking gazebo

Every court decision can be appealed. That's why we always end up in the Moscow City Court, where appeals are made. Appeals that almost never change anything.

A smoking gazebo and an avtozak parked nearby. It brought us here to appeal our detention days. Now Lucy comes to me. July. And not a single snowflake. It seems like a lifetime ago since she jumped into my arms and said, 'Don't go to the rally, they'll put you in jail.' I didn't go to that rally and they jailed me anyway. And they jailed her. They jailed everyone. Opposite the court's entrance is an ice-cream van and everyone is running to it. They are buying Plombir and Eskimo. Next to the gazebo – an apple tree. And there are small green apples on it. We kiss all the time.

plombir and eskimo

The judge listens attentively. Tall, grey, with alert eyes, Judge Grishin, says, 'Let's watch a movie.' He plays the video of my detention. He doesn't have a secretary, he types his own decisions and refuses calling the people who witnessed me being detained to give evidence. He sits behind a computer like a secretary, then he goes up to the podium and sits in the armchair like a judge, he studies me closely, resting his hand on his chin.

'The police love you, we can say that at least,' he says.

'For a long time already,' I reply.

I look him directly in the eye and say, 'I know what your decision will be and it is never too late to change your mind.'

He says, 'Here, of course, there are no final words, but perhaps you would like to add something?'

I say, 'Russia will be free.'

And he replies, 'That is certain,' and then quietly adds, 'But from whom?'

judge with alert eyes

'What's all the excitement about?' asks Nika. Evening, detention centre exercise yard. Sasha's cell is above the yard. Sasha also likes this judge, he says so, smiling through the barred window.

'Why are you going crazy over a judge? Just because he was "sweet and interesting"?' Nika continues, 'He would have been interesting if he had changed something, but he changed nothing.'

I say, 'You just haven't seen sadists. There are sadists, there are half-robots, and there are those who understand that they are wrong, locking us up as best they can, and who ask forgiveness for what they're doing. The difference is in the detail. And sometimes the detail means a lot.'

Nika says, 'I still don't get it.'

I stand and look at her, at the sky through the metal mesh, at the poplar tree beyond the exercise yard wall, and think, 'Have we really learned to be happy at least when somebody in epaulettes or a robe understands their mistakes?'

and the light shines in the darkness

Nika has another panic attack. Breathing rapidly, holding on to the corridor wall, looking at the illuminated sign saying 'Exit' and realizing that there is no exit beyond it. Lying curled up and not wanting anything – this is an honest response. This, I think, is how you should react to this cycle of fucking hell, detention days, captivity. Because it is wrong and abnormal. This is something to scream about.

I worry a lot, worry, grieve; there are times when pain overwhelms me and I can't understand what I want. Nika comes to me. She takes a pen, sits on the bed, draws a heart on my leg and underneath it writes, 'And the light shines in the darkness. And the darkness has not overcome it.'

These words say that there is light before death, and this light is greater than death – these lines. Nika gets out. I trace her inscription every day with a pen and shortly after Lucy will come to my balcony with a tattoo artist who will trace the words with their ink.

'Pussy Riot member Veronika Nikulshina and artist Roman Durov have left Russia. They abandoned the country straight after Nikulshina was let out of the detention centre, where she had spent her second detention of fifteen days in a row.'
– OVD-Info, 18 July

and the darkness has not overcome it

The windows of Sasha's cell no. 2 look out onto the exercise yard. We talk about how he will also fly out in a day's time. For a while. Is it painful to see everyone flying out? Yes. But I don't admit it to myself. I hug as much as I can. Anna stands next to me in a pink T-shirt. Anna is like a fresco, with white skin, huge eyes and an Orthodox faith in a kind heart. It is raining. Rain is better than stuffiness.

> *'Director Anna Kuzminykh has decided to leave Russia. She spent two periods of detention days in a row.'*
>
> – MBK Media, 19 July

Anna got out. I am the only political left in our cell. I roll out my pink rug in the exercise yard and do my exercises. Out of habit I look up. Sasha is not at the window. I lie on the rug. Rare drops of rain fall on my face. Rare tears flow down and mix with the drops on the rug.

> *'A member of Pussy Riot, Sasha Sofeev, has left Russia.'*
>
> – OVD-Info, 20 July

a whole eternity

'One day the bars on the cell windows became too thick, and it became increasingly difficult for the elusive light to penetrate through. I didn't want the light to go out completely. On one of the last days of my fourth detention, I was sitting in the visitors' room and slowly listed out loud: my laptop, two portable hard drives.

I asked to pack everything in one bag, to buy tickets, and to be taken to the airport immediately after my release. As a farewell, my country solemnly escorts me out with a cortège of blacked-out cars and with silent strangers following me to the departure zone.

When my passport was stamped and I boarded the plane, it seemed that we waited a whole eternity to take off. And now it feels

*as if all that happened an eternity ago. Now I don't know where
the rest of my things are, and I can't remember exactly which
things I left behind. But I know I've been able to take something
more with me – and it will definitely stay with me for ever.'*

– Sasha Sofeev

will definitely stay

- Mash, hi! Sasha's no. 2 cellmate shouts from the
  window. You're doing great! You're training!
- If I don't train, I'll go mad.
- Are you writing a book? shouts the cellmate. Sasha
  left my first book as a present for him.
- I'll try.
- You'll write a second one?
- I'll try.

It's hard to talk. I do squats, looking at the concrete wall that
separates me from the poplar tree, I do press-ups, looking at
the metal mesh separating us, me and the sky. I don't know
what will happen next, I try not to listen to the conversations
of my cellmates. They are mostly about spice. Or about guys.
A lot about guys. Sometimes it seems to me that half the country is hooked on spice. Maybe more. Or drink vodka. Many
that aren't hooked on drugs and don't drink vodka take anti-
depressants. A scary picture. And it's as if there is no other.

- I just have one question, says the girl in a pink skirt
  and green top with crimson hair and a face like
  Princess Fiona from *Shrek*. And it's not about fucking
  politics. Is it true that Madonna wanted to buy the
  rights to your story?

daggers to the heart

A day before my release, I'm in tears. News about the guys leaving the country are like daggers to the heart. I know that it is probably not for ever. But it is 'just all at once'.

The level of nonsense in the cell is somewhere between 'microchipped vaccinations' and the 'prison romance' of spice-addict Tanya and some prisoner from cell no. 8. I start to shout at Spice Tanya. I shout at her for walking around the cell and singing a song where two men tie a girl up and rape her. I shout, 'How can you sing such a song when you yourself were also beaten up?' She replies, 'You don't like anything. I just wanted to take my mind off the fact that I'm in jail.' She was beaten up by a Chechen for the whole four years they lived together and then he took away their child. Or rather he didn't take the child away – on divorce in Chechnya children always stay with the man and the divorced woman is considered disgraced. I dreamed of fighting for women's rights in Chechnya. And I yelled at a victim. She was only being unbearable.

– I'm a bad feminist, I tell my lawyer, when leaving our meeting, and when I return to the cell I see that she is smoking my cigarettes.

bad feminist

Princess Fiona is about to be let out in an hour. When she sees me crying, she stops drawing a green lawn in her notebook, comes up and says, 'I know what to write at the end of your new book.'

- What?
- Count all the days, all the hours, that you have spent in captivity, all the hours that you have spent with a psychologist, all the pills you've taken when you haven't slept because of this fucked-up mess. Count everything. And write these numbers at the end of the book. You really believe in what you're doing, right?
- Yes, I do, I reply.
- So write down the cost of your beliefs and your actions.

what cost?

Arrest carousels have become a method of pushing activists out of the country. You don't know when they will start, when they will end. You don't know whether the carousel will be followed by a criminal case with a much longer term than fifteen days. Go to jail, leave the country or shut up and pray that this prison agony passes you by – these are three options that have become the only possible reality for those who care. And we have only just begun to understand this.

> '*Pussy Riot member Rita Flores has been arrested for resisting police and given fifteen detention days. Flores was detained near her home without an explanation. A police report stated that Flores bore a resemblance to a woman suspect who they are looking for in connection with the theft of a purse from a "Halal" shop.*'

I had run out of food and Rita had gone to the shop for me. At the door of our cell there's a white plastic bag. In it, carrots, cigarettes and popcorn, and also some tortilla chips. 'They detained Rita' is written in blue pen on their yellow packet. In Olya's handwriting.

- So, Masha, today you're going home. As soon as you get there, pack your things and go join the others in warmer countries, says the kind guard.
- No, I answer, half asleep. I won't be going to any warmer countries.
- Okay, then! Stay at home, and we will remember you and will be proud that we had such a person here with us.

such a person

Ilya arrives at the blue gates of Special Detention Centre No. 2. He takes my chequered bags and carries them to the boot. I get into the fsinmobile. We set off from one arrest to another. The last cigarette. I open the window, put my hand out and the wind blows on my hand and face. The sun is shining.

- Mash, sorry for what happened at the police station, says Ilya. The boss told me: 'You didn't see anything, your phone was switched off, and all of tomorrow your phone will be switched off.'

13.

Nazi Propaganda

- Mash, get up. It's time to go to court!
- Give me another five minutes!
- Masha, come on! Get out of bed, otherwise I'll climb
  in there with you!

This is not harassment, this is a morning conversation with an inspector. Ilya has arrived and stands by the door. This is my first court appearance. It is called 'provisional'. A useless process, where the 'court' decides to keep me under house arrest.

Olya, still here after the party to celebrate me leaving the detention centre, has opened the door to the inspector and asks him, 'Do you want coffee?' Inspector Ilya feels comfortable answering, 'Why coffee, when you have some champagne left over?' In one gulp he drinks 'one for the road' and we drive away. We drive to the court, which arrests me for another half year.

one for the road

The next day Lucy arrives and from the threshold says, 'Let's go for a walk.' I haven't woken up fully and don't understand. I answer, 'Are you out of your mind?' and then say almost immediately, 'Of course, let's go.' Let's go violate.

I dress, she eats gooseberries, I take my pink yoga rug, we go to the shop. I buy a lavash and water, she buys a 'Rainbow' ice cream. She eats it in the playground and photographs me doing sun salutations. It is after midday, but under arrest you can salute the sun at that time of day too.

rainbow ice cream

Two people in plain clothes appear after fifteen minutes.

'On 3 July the head of the Russian Women's Union, Ekaterina Lakhova, complained to Vladimir Putin about the growing number of rainbows in adverts. She claimed that children could become accustomed to the LGBT flag. Lakhova referred in particular to the ice cream "Rainbow" – a multicoloured lolly. If such images on labels promote LGBT, Putin responded, then this needs to be controlled, "just not aggressively".'

Lucy is eating a 'Rainbow' ice cream, I'm doing my exercises, two FSB officers are sitting on a nearby bench in the playground; one is pretending to talk on FaceTime, but he's taking photos of me.

Then we go home. I get my first ever tattoo, the one with Nika's inscription from the detention centre, and watch *Why Women Kill*. The next day we find out we have Covid.

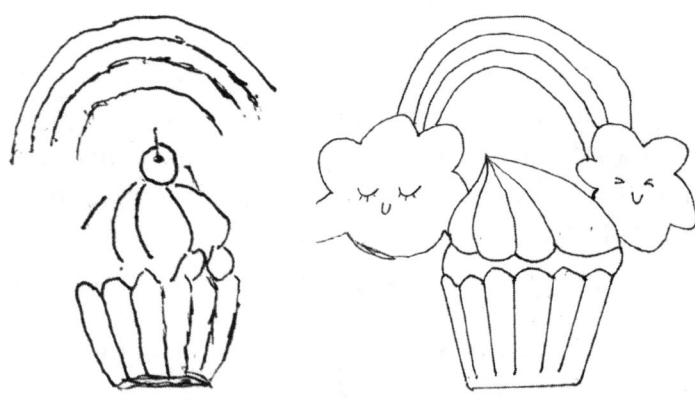

white and grey

One of Filipp's two rats – the white one – dies in the night. Mum buries him behind our building. The second one starts to leave its cage and come to me. I have a fever, with a temperature of almost 40, my chest feels like it's filled with broken glass.

'My heart feels as if it has been rubbed with a pumice stone,' Lucy messages. She was infected when taking me on the illegal walk. And I got it in the detention centre.

As soon as you enter the world of detention days, your life means nothing to the state.

crime against health

The first day 'on the merits' in court, the judge yells at my inspector and throws him out of the courtroom, although I am under house arrest and the FSIN inspector is required to stay with me if I am not at home.

- I'm feeling much worse, messages Lucy. If I die, do you think we'd have spirit sex?
- Like in that episode of *Black Mirror*, 'San Junipero'?

With a temperature and a negative test result, I continue to go to court.

black mirror

The witnesses are two cops. The one with grey hair and experience answers honestly, 'I saw people in masks at the rally.' The other, a prepared servant of the regime, confirms the basis of the accusation. He nods with conviction that our social media posts could have killed someone. The only witnesses to our 'crime' are the cops who beat people at each rally. They are at a loss over the lawyer's questions.

- Was social distancing observed in the 'official transport'?
- I can't remember.

But I remember. In one avtozak, which is after all 'official transport', the cops packed twenty to thirty people into a tiny cage. They dragged them over the ground, twisted their arms, beat them with Tasers and batons.

social distancing

'Citizens of the Russian Federation shall have the right to assemble peacefully, without weapons, to hold rallies, meetings and demonstrations, marches and pickets.'
– Article 31, Russian Constitution

- How does a permitted rally differ from an unsanctioned one?
- Objection.
- Have you read Article 31 of the constitution?
- Objection.

I can't remember the moment when everyone got used to it. And stopped caring. I can't remember the moment when everyone got tired. The West is only interested in Russia as an actor on the international stage. Doping scandals, invasions of foreign territory – fine, they'll read about that, they'll still worry about that. But they are only worried enough to say, 'We are concerned.' And what's happening inside Russia has long been unimportant. Everyone is tired of reading about arrests, sentences, poisonings. They've ticked the 'dictatorship' box for our country. And now it is all considered the Russian norm.

> *'The Tverskoy District Court in Moscow has detained a member of Pussy Riot, Rita Flores, for fifteen days for her Instagram post of Tokio Hotel's lead singer. She photoshopped a photo of a man in SS uniform with a swastika armband, with the caption "Don't let glamour overwhelm you" underneath. They detained Flores leaving the Moscow detention centre where she'd spent fifteen days for resisting the police.'*
>
> – Mediazona, 13 August

russian norm

We know that they won't give us a real sentence. The legal background behind the Sanitary Case means that the sentence will carry certain conditions or will be a limitation of freedoms. Limitation of freedoms is the same curfew with an ankle bracelet. Most likely that is what it will be. Lucy and I have a plan for us to end up in the same flat – but I need to be made officially homeless.

By default, the court orders you to be under house arrest at the address where you are officially registered. You are not allowed to change your address or move. You have to be removed from the register, in other words become homeless. If I'm officially made homeless, then when the sentence comes into force and they put a bracelet on me, the only address they can assign will be the one I choose. Lucy's.

operation homeless

When Lucy tests positive, she has to go into self-isolation. She's very sick. But she's doing all the paperwork to get me removed from the registry.

We are both worried, worried and arguing. The thought of her leaving the country as soon as they take off her bracelet is poisoning me. She wants us to stop being constantly detained, but I can't imagine a life where there are no cops and no resistance.

ass in a sling

Since the white rat died, the second – the grey one – has been coming to me more often. He sleeps with his tail curled up by my pillow. I didn't know that rats could make friends, find you, stay close and give support.

Ilya is supposed to pick me up. It's the latest pointless appeal. August.

The rat jumps from the bed and twists his leg. I'm worried about going to the court; what if it is paralysis?

Lucy's court proceedings have already started, she has waited for a break to come to see me. Ilya is hurrying me up to get into the fsinmobile.

– But we aren't accomplices anymore, so we can talk, I object.

- They're watching us, there's a cop in a white car. You are messing with my head, Ilya laments.

And we hug.

- Get in the car, I've got 'Fear' playing. Let's go, let's go!

He returns me home to the balcony. And just in case, writes a violation report.

anti-tank ditch

There's not much time left before the verdict. The judge gives me permission to leave the house to go to the clinic, without dates, without times, without restrictions. I go every day. There and back. Today I'm going with Lucy.

We talk about prisons. This time about prisons in Norway. I talk about the island of Bastøy, where prisoners feed cows and perform rock music.

We walk through the forest, we walk to the ravine, where I used to run around as a little girl, slide down the snow on a sledge, where I pushed my son in a pushchair. I take a picture of Lucy with a birch tree. Everything is a little blurry; although the flash is working, nothing seems normal.

I want to show her this ravine because it's a place that's dear to me. My place. The place that springs to mind when anyone says 'home'. On one side of the ravine is the shop where we used to go for ice cream; on the other, the way to the metro.

We don't talk much. Over the months that we spent under arrest and couldn't see each other, over the weeks that we spent in the detention centre, we talked a lot; so now we just look at the leaves – they are green.

The real name of this place, nicknamed the ravine by the

locals, is the Kuntsev Anti-Tank Ditch. It was dug in 1941, when the Red Army was defending Moscow from Hitler's troops, who were approaching the city.

drop in the ocean

'It is obvious to everyone that there is no real trial going on now, that we have to play this game both on the defence and the prosecution sides.
My case is not special. Although this sentence will naturally be unfair, but against the backdrop of the monstrous terms that people are given for nothing, this is already seen as a piece of cake. By supporting this act of injustice, which may seem insignificant to you, you are supporting a whole system of political persecution, a system of torture, poisoning, murder. You enable, in the name of supporting the authorities, the ruining of lives in penal colonies, the separation of parents from their children, theft and electoral fraud. My case is a drop in the ocean, but the destruction of human rights in Russia is made up of such drops. Even if not this time, it is never too late to act differently.'

– from Lucy's final statement

it is never too late to act differently

'Municipal deputy and Pussy Riot member Lucy Shtein has been given a year of restriction of freedom in the "Sanitary Case".'

– Mediazona, 25 August

The defendants in our case, Navalny's key people, are abandoning Russia one by one after receiving their sentences. His brother Oleg is also going. We lie on my wooden bed and read the news.

When you receive a sentence, your ankle bracelet is taken off; when the sentence comes into force, the bracelet is put back on. The period between the day of sentencing and the day it takes effect (after an appeal process) is at least a month. People leave the country on the first or next day after their sentencing.

Lucy's ankle bracelet has been removed. I know how much she wants to leave, and that I'm the one thing holding her back. She lies on the bed and strokes the rat. The rat, whom we named Mr Rat, still limps. We are learning how to treat him. He falls asleep near the pillow.

– Will Mr Rat be in the book? she asks.
– Of course he will, I answer.

We eat sushi in a shopping mall. Lucy buys my mum flowers for her birthday. I'm writing my final statement for the court. A criminal sentence has become something mundane, something that you can receive between your morning coffee and lunch.

of course he will

'I don't know which is the bigger restriction on my freedom, an ankle bracelet or Putin's order to appoint a judge. As a judge, you will handle as many political cases as you are told to, you will write documents and call them judgements, knowing that nothing in them was your decision, and all this just to keep the chair you sit in. You say that slavery was abolished over a century ago, but who are you then? You follow the prison camp mantra: "You die today, I'll die

tomorrow." You think, "It's better if I act unfairly now but keep my job, let someone else suffer. Better someone else than me." Everyone knows that anyone can be imprisoned. Just no one knows how to stop this.
The answer is simple. You need to forget the phrase: "It's not up to me" and take responsibility. That is freedom, if, of course, anyone needs it.
Stay in the prison camp and live according to camp rules or get out of it – it's up to each one of us. I made my choice. Now it's your turn.'

– from my final statement

your turn

'Pussy Riot member Maria Alyokhina has been given a year of restriction of freedom in the "Sanitary Case".'

– Mediazona, 10 September

Ilya crouches on one knee in the court corridor, takes out a screwdriver and unscrews the bracelet, takes it off and, without saying goodbye, disappears.

'Let's go for a smoke!' I say to my lawyer while the sentence is being printed. We run to the staircase. I smoke under the 'Smoking is Forbidden' sign, my lawyer laughs.

Tonight is the first evening in eight months I've been able to go out. Lucy is ill and I demand that my friend Aya takes me to a bar. A bar or a club. We arrive, music is playing, people are dancing, I don't know anyone. After a couple of drinks, I feel sad that my friends have left the country. I go out for a smoke and see two girls arguing near the entrance. Some kind of domestic, totally stupid argument; they are in a relationship. I can hear everything,

I listen. Night. I chain smoke and after a while say, 'Girls, you love each other. Don't waste your time fighting, it's so stupid. I've been under house arrest for more than six months now and I haven't had any of these carefree nights where you can just be together and dance. You have no idea how amazing it is to just be able to do that!' One of the girls turns to me and says, 'Fuck off!'

I begin to cry. 'Let's go!' I say to Aya. As we are leaving, the other girl runs up to us and says, 'Thank you for everything.'

smoking is forbidden

We pack a chequered bag and go to the Arbat. To Lucy's building with a black cat on the wall. It was from here that we went to the rally eight months ago and we haven't been back together since.

The feeling that just staying in Russia and not leaving is already an act of heroism, because 'well, you understand, there is a purge going on', the feeling that you can't go to a therapist with a problem, because your story will be impossible to understand without the words 'cops', 'twenty-four hours', 'house arrest', 'prohibition of actions', 'pre-trial detention centre', 'restriction of freedom'. Sometimes we were jealous, offended, wanted attention, got lost; sometimes we didn't know how to express our feelings; sometimes we were too demanding or too angry.

But we won't talk about it without special words, and people are afraid of such words, they close themselves off from such words, they try not to think about such things, but I still want you to know that I am alive, we are alive, and we are not going through this hell as heroes as always; sometimes we don't know what to do; not sometimes – often. We just don't talk about it into the microphone.

The first few nights seem strange. As if we have grown used to living under house arrest and to not going out, but now we do it in the same apartment.

we are alive

British journalist Sarah stands in front of the Bolshoi Theatre. We are standing opposite her. She wants to film the place where we were detained. Autumn.

- We came out of the lane and the cops were here. Yes, here.
- Can you come out again? asks the journalist, and points the camera at us.

We do it. She asks us to repeat it. We do it. She asks us to come out again. And again. And again. The square near the Bolshoi Theatre is a crescent. On the opposite side of the crescent is a *Russia Today* propaganda camera. They're filming a story. Episode after episode flashes through my head of how I should run up and smash their camera. Just stop all this.

for whom the bell tolls

'It's naive to think that all of this is the private problems
of private individuals, and your house is on the outskirts,
your shirt is closer to your body, and it doesn't concern you
personally at all. It will overtake everyone, and therefore never
ask for whom the bell tolls – it tolls for you.'
– Rapper Face

Artists who dare to speak out against the authorities have their concerts cancelled, and they are blacklisted. It doesn't matter how large the stadiums they fill are, how many followers they have, or how famous they are. There are no more protest rallies, but the steamroller of repression is being rolled so hard that you don't need a reason to ban someone or put them in jail. Ordinary activists and stars are placed in the same category: censorship.

Every Friday, the Ministry of Justice publishes its list of foreign agents. Once on the list, residents of Russia must label each of their posts with the phrase 'Material created by a foreign agent'. A stigma created to humiliate, intimidate and self-censor. People refuse to work with foreign agents, they are afraid to be paid even for teaching a foreign agent's child. If you live in Russia and you don't give a fuck about the stigma, a criminal case is brought against you and you go to jail.

tear your hair out

At first, out of habit, you sit at home and read the news, but then you go out for cigarettes, and see how people are going about their daily lives. They live their lives as if nothing terrible is happening around them, as if no one was jailed today, as if another person was not forced out of the country, not put on the wanted list, no relatives dragged to the FSB for questioning. They walk around, laugh, take photos. I feel alienated, it's as if an invisible gap is growing between me and what is happening around me. People ask me, 'Why should I tear my hair out?' And I answer, 'Well, it might be good if you did.'

the abyss grows

I'm starting to drink more often. It's like I want to get back to the fun times when we had just met. But I feel like times are changing. I don't know, I don't understand, I don't see how to live together. I just don't know how to do it. I want to do new things together, but when I start doing them, I feel like I'm failing. Lucy is getting out of bed less and less. She realizes that she won't have a job or a future in this country. But she doesn't want a one-way ticket out. She puts up with it. She's still in the grip of the virus. The virus that the authorities used to put us in jail. She wants to watch a movie. We choose *The Handmaid's Tale*.

nolite te bastardes carborundorum

Drive to the woods – Rublevsky forest – walk into a swamp of autumn leaves and scream. Out of helplessness. Put on a balaclava and scream, take it off, let my hair down and scream – as much as you can, alone in the forest. The forest is painted red, orange and green – bright, deep colours – and no one is around. Only the girl who is filming me. I want that scream to stay with me.

A scream in the trees, a scream on a forest path, at the crossing of forest paths, a scream on a wooden bench, at a wooden table with an empty bullet casing on it for some reason.

> *'Russian troop movements near Ukraine border prompt concern in US, Europe.'*

The court loses my sentence documents. They're turning a year of restriction into a year and a half. It's unclear when the sentence will take effect, when they'll put the bracelet back on and the rest of the sentence will start. The sooner it starts, the sooner it'll be over.

'The artist Farhad Israfilli-Gelman has been detained in Moscow for fifteen days for "resisting police." Exactly a year ago he was in an action with Pussy Riot.'

this is limbo

The friend who lent us her car for the trip to Udmurtia steps out of a window. From a window on the seventh floor – she's lucky as she falls on a canopy two floors below and not onto the ground. A leg amputation and a wheelchair. 'Do you want to be like me?' her anti-war placard. Diana is mixing cocktails in Mutabor, a nightclub. A naked party, the disgraced elite of Russian pop culture, exiled to occupied cities in Ukraine to praise the army.

'Masha, I can't get out of bed,' says Aya. 'I'm dreaming of explosions, aeroplanes, bombs.' 'Masha, why have you abandoned me,' shouts Sasha in a voice note from Georgia. I feel bad, we all feel bad, bad, bad. Hot air.

'Putin declared Russia to be a peace-loving country.'
– Lenta.ru, 18 November

'US warns allies of possible Russian incursion as troops amass near Ukraine.'
– The New York Times, 19 November

'Russia will expand not because it's good and not because it's bad, but because it's physics.'
– Vladislav Surkov, 20 November

'At any moment, there's potential for tensions to rise so high that millions of Ukrainians will flee and seek refuge in other places.'

— Nikolai Patrushev, 23 November

check-check

- Check-check. Are you in Moscow? I want to invite you somewhere, my friend messages – Misha, a photographer from New York.
- Of course, I'm in Moscow – where else would I be during a conditional sentence? I would like to answer, but instead I ask, Where?
- GES-2.
- What is GES-2?
- A House of Culture next to your cathedral.

The centre of Moscow, Scandinavian style, white walls and huge windows. GES-2 is a trendy new gallery in a former power station that I know nothing about. Overlooking the Cathedral of Christ the Saviour. Putin's oligarch, Leonid Mikhelson, spent 470 million dollars on it. To be fashionable, to appeal to hipsters, and so that the people who steal in Russia and spend it in the West can tell that the place has status. At the entrance is a fashionable sculpture by a fashionable Swiss artist, a piece of clay. Maximally like a mound of shit.

hello! i'm an artist!

I get out of the taxi and walk to the entrance. Misha and the Icelandic artist Ragnar Kjartansson, who is staging the exhibition, are there to meet me. 'Hello! I'm an artist!' he says in Russian, 'and this is Santa Barbara!' The soap opera *Santa Barbara* was watched endlessly in Russia during the 1990s, a window onto the Western world for a young Russia being formed on the site of the Soviet Union. The phrase 'It's all gone a bit Santa Barbara' became a catchphrase for messy relationships. I laugh and answer, 'Your Santa Barbara is nowhere near ours.' It's a good thing that he doesn't know what I mean.

– For me your 'Punk Prayer' is one of the greatest performances in the history of art, says Ragnar. I'm staying in an apartment with a view onto the Pussy Riot church!

He is giving me a princess's welcome. 'Your visit is as important as one from Putin!' Ragnar jokes.

I want to shout that this is all a façade. It just seems that this city looks like a normal city, but here they are constantly imprisoning and torturing. This is the hardest year, I want to scream, but I say this with a suppressed grin. No one will understand if you start yelling, and it wouldn't look like a performance. It would look like plain hysteria.

santa barbara

A day later I return with Lucy. I introduce her to Ragnar. We've had enough of Santa Barbara. We go to the second floor – to a dark room. To watch a film.

A six-hour concert, where against a pink backdrop, dressed in a tuxedo, Ragnar sings the same words over again – 'sorrow conquers happiness'. Behind him, an orchestra, musicians in black tie, black evening dresses, a piano, trombones, violins, double basses, a golden harp. There's a video projection in a dark room. Visitors to the exhibition enter and exit the room.

We sit on a bench. This is all that I want to show her – this song without a beginning or an end – sorrow conquers happiness.

As if this was the film *Mulholland Drive*'s Club Silencio. And what has been and what will be – a dream and an illusion. Sorrow conquers happiness.

At the entrance to the room, a sign with the performance's title. In Russian and in English. In English – the original name of the work. It's called 'God'. In Russian, it's 'untitled'. 'Have you seen it?' I ask Ragnar, 'Instead of "God", they've written "untitled".' He replies, 'They said you can't say that word in Russian.' 'Are you joking?'

sorrow conquers happiness

- They detained me, pushed me into a car, people in plainclothes. They're saying Alyokhina should come with her lawyer to the station.
- Tell them I'll have a coffee and then come.

In 2018, Lucy shared a link on social media to a Ukrainian army group's page. The ultra-patriots got angry and released a clip titled 'Lucy Shtein – Deputy Fascist', drawing a Nazi cap on the front. She found it funny and posted a screenshot on her Facebook page, with 'Attention! A person with the surname Shtein is accused of Nazism' and then a quote from the singer Monetochka, 'Mama, I'm not Nazi saluting.' Three years later, she's facing a Nazi-style prosecution.

mama, i'm not nazi saluting

Two empty chequered bags – bags for the detention centre, which had been kept in the corner of the room since the summer. I bring them into the middle. I pack things, medicine and books. I give one bag to my friend to give to Lucy and take the other myself.

- Do you know what will happen when you leave here? the lawyer asks me as I get into the lift.
- Of course I know, I'll go to jail for fifteen days.

If there's an arrest protocol for 'Nazi propaganda' for Deputy Shtein, that means I have one too. A grey car is parked near the entrance. I exit, the door of the car opens, the lawyer and I get in, he sits in the front seat, I get in the back, there's a cop on either side of us.

- Check the chat, they're asking if we'll be there soon, I say to my lawyer.
- Add me to your chat, says the cop driver jokingly.

I raise my head and reply, 'Do you know the New Greatness Case? It's a case based on a chat set up by teenagers. They gave the main guy seven years, and when he was arrested, on his birthday, they broke the door down to his flat and raped him in the kitchen.'
A pause hangs in the air.

- You probably hate us all, says the cop driver.
- Not everyone, I answer, and not always. But you do know what you're doing right now, don't you?
- What? What am I doing right now? I'm just making a delivery. Imagine you're a pizza.

A minute later, he misses the turning and we arrive at the wrong police station.

'If I'm a pizza, then you should be fired for this delivery.'

what are you doing?

The first ever cell I can't fall asleep in. A sealed cell with no windows or feeding hatch in the door. Blue walls. A cold bright white spotlight instead of a light bulb. A brown platform for a mattress.

It's impossible to sleep. Too bright and too stuffy. And this is December, with snow and cold beyond the wall.

'Hey, I blindfolded myself with my black T-shirt,' Lucy says cheerfully in the morning. 'It seemed to work.'

nazi trial

In the morning, we are both brought to court. Aya, having heard about our Nazi-court, asks the lawyers to call her as witness.

– How long have you known Maria Alyokhina?
– More than ten years.
– Do you often visit her home?
– Yes, regularly.
– Have you seen a portrait of Hitler or a bust of Goebbels or anything like that there?
– Are you crazy? You know, I'm used to her being arrested for insulting the feelings of some believers or other, for being LGBT, or for protesting against Putin. But this is totally surreal.
– No more questions.

*'The evidence is a photographic image of the President
of the Republic of Belarus A. G. Lukashenko, surrounded
by a decorative frame. In the lower part of the frame
there is a regular equilateral cross with "broken" ends
at right angles ("a swastika") of a golden colour on
a red background with dots of a golden colour closer
to its centre.'*

– my detention protocol

The judge doesn't make eye contact, because her gaze is constantly lowered to the table and it seems like she's asleep. It all seems like a dream. An ordinary Russian dream – a cocktail of absurdity mixed with absurdity. I am on trial for displaying Nazi symbols. We're accused of essentially promoting Nazism. Nazism, Karl! How is that even possible? If the arrest carousel needs to be continued, why not the usual police resistance? Why Nazism?

After being in my courtroom, Aya goes 'to bear witness' in Lucy's.

– Have you known Ludmila Shtein for a long time?
– For a couple of years.
– Did she display sympathy for Nazi beliefs?
– Are you mad? How can Ludmila SHTEIN possibly be a Nazi?

why nazism?

*'In Moscow Pussy Riot members Alyokhina and Shtein
were detained for fifteen and fourteen days for pictures with
swastikas.'*

– Mediazona, 17 December

357

After the trial, they return us to the police station. We sit in the corridor, waiting for the transfer to the detention centre; we scrutinize the cops. The years go by, but there is one thing that is timeless – a cop and his clothes. A down jacket, a kit bag, pointy-toed shoes, and here I come, unremarkable. I'm coming to detain you.

– Come on, for fuck's sake? To Sakharovo??? An indignant chubby cop is on the phone.
– Sakharovo??? we yell with the same intonation a second later. How long does it take to get there?
– Two hours! The cop looks around, and trying to cheer himself and us up, he adds, We'll turn on the blue light, we'll race there.

world of invisible people

The Sakharovo Migration Centre is outside the city, a journey of more than two hours to where detained migrants subject to deportation are held; at the beginning of the year, all the protesters who could not fit into the overcrowded special detention centres were brought here. And now here – to the world of invisible people – they will bring us.

Three chubby cop-donuts all the way talking about how America wants to conquer us and how we Russians should fight this. Halfway down the road I say to one of them, 'Imagine there is no America, no enemies, and no one wants to conquer us.' And he answers, 'What then is there?' I say, 'Russia with poverty, corruption, lack of elections and no independent court.' The donut crumples and concedes, 'Well, okay, I agree there are problems, yes, there are problems! But ask your parents, they'll say it was great in the USSR!'

- What about the Great Terror?
- That was under Stalin.
- And what about after, when they jailed people for books? All my favourite dissidents of the 70s were jailed for samizdat!
- What dissidents? They were hippies! We don't need those boiled jeans and fashion trainers!

donuts against america

Abba's 'Happy New Year' plays on the radio, Lucy says, 'Turn it up.' We are driving out of Moscow, the donuts continue to criticize America.

- All these protesters – just puppets of the USA!
- So you think we also work for the USA?
- Yes, and you don't even know it!

The bald driver turns the radio down and says:

- You girls are so brainwashed.
- We're brainwashed? Lucy asks wryly. You've been driving people for three hours out of the city, who you know are being sent to jail for nothing, and we're the ones who are brainwashed?
- Well, we aren't the ones who jailed them, we're just driving!
- And others 'just write a report', and yet others 'just stamp the court decision', while all of them 'simply have nothing to do with it'.

359

white houses of sakharovo

We finally arrive. 'At fucking last, the gates of hell, hahaha,' the bald donut driver says. 'Open up! I've got some administrative detentions here!' He nods to the man who has come out of the booth at the gate. 'It's not this way,' the cop replies. 'It's over there, turn around and go to the other gate.'

- I told you! laughs the donut on the right.
- What did you tell me? snarls the bald one. Last time we came to this one!
- I told you it wasn't here, insists the one on the right.
- You told me what exactly???? yells the bald one behind the wheel.
- Stop fucking arguing! interjects the third, sitting next to us.

Behind the barbed wire – white houses. New white houses in a row. And white streetlights. Identical shiny plastic houses that are no different except for the numbers above each porch. We drive along them – past the white empty shiny porches. We stop at the last one, the only one with a person standing outside.

- Hi there! The boy in the uniform with tattoos is waving at us. It is Seryozha from Detention Centre No. 2.
- Hi there! Lucy and I shout back through the back-seat window.
- Stop! Detained! the bald man shouts at us automatically. Oh, I mean, don't shout out of the window! I'll open the door. Then come out one by one.

one by one

I take the chequered bag and go into the white house. 'Separate your things from Lucy's straight away,' says Seryozha. 'You'll be in different cells. Upstairs have said so. And don't ask me about it. I've had my phone cut off all day.'

- That's fucked up.
- That's right. Fucked up.
- And there's no way to be in the same one?
- No way! You have no idea what's been going on here all day. Everybody's been on high alert. Waiting for you all day. They've been ringing all day.

The phone rings. 'Yes, hello, senior duty officer. Yes, they've been brought in. Yes. Yes. YES.'

When Lucy is led into the room for examinations, I only manage to tell her, 'We're forbidden to be together.' And I manage to hug her too. They take me to the cell. I look back: she is standing very sadly in my grey sweatshirt that says 'your torture will not kill our ideas'.

plastic world has won

It feels like you are in a video game or a photoshop mock-up, a soulless plastic box. I'm in white plastic box No. 13. On the plastic ceiling are eight bright white lights and three brand-new video cameras. Ten white metal bunks nailed to the floor. The same number of white bedside tables. Disposable synthetic bed linen with the added bonus of shocks from static electricity.

– Oh, there's a shower in the cell! I say.
– It only works on Sundays! the guard solemnly announces and closes the door.

It looks like a mental hospital. But it's not a mental hospital: the white huts are a Covid isolation centre for detained migrants, which isn't needed and so has been handed over to the cops as a detention centre. Goodbye high ceilings and walls drawn on by opposition members, hello plastic world!

ward no. 13

In a cell meant for ten people, there's one girl, a Kirghiz, Adilya.

– I was in here on my own and I cried. I didn't want to be alone. I knocked on the door, said, 'Why have you transferred me? I don't want to be alone.' And they told me, 'A good girl will be here soon, you'll share with her.' And so, you're the good girl?
– Well, apparently.

For the next few hours she walks around the cell, knocks on the door, walks around again. She comes up to me and asks, 'Are you sure it's not possible to get out of here early?' I say, 'No'; then after ten minutes she says, 'I can't take it, my heart can't take it.' I say, 'Yes it can.' And again, she asks, 'Don't you have a watch?' No. I really don't. There's only one watch – the watch on her T-shirt. Half of the dial is always at five to twelve, the other half has turned into a butterfly.

good girl

There is no canteen here; the food, or as they call it in prison, balanda, is delivered on trolleys by detained guys. Balanders. They pass notes, cigarettes and food from cell to cell. This informal bonus works for everyone but of course not for us – the cops yell at anyone who tries to take my and Lucy's correspondence.

> 'At night, I thought that it's very offensive that they called us fascists. Don't like it.
> In the fifth cell there are two more boys, they were brought in from pickets protesting against the construction of some road. The rest of their cell are all "balanders", who I hope will take these letters.
> They gave me a great welcome yesterday! They shook hands, brought me food, and today they handed me some kind of drawing (! :)). It's of a castle. Very strange! If we can, we should read about fascism during these detention days.
> I read Brave New World overnight.'
> – Masha, 17 December

brave new world

The exercise yard is big – it stretches along all the cells of the white house. I am in ward 13, Lucy is in ward 3; the wards are at opposite ends of the house. We are under special control.

During a walk, I go up to her window. A cop with a video camera, who was sent to film how I walk for an hour inside the mesh box, yells, 'Move away'; another cop at the same time goes into her cell and locks the window. The windows have removable handles – like in a psychiatric hospital; all the cops have video cameras. They make films about us every day and send them to bosses at Petrovka HQ.

We write notes on each side of the forbidden window and show them to each other like they are placards at solitary pickets. 'It is forbidden to communicate!' yells the duty officer. 'Why is everyone else allowed to, and we aren't allowed to?' 'No one is allowed.' 'But you don't lock anyone else's windows!'

The detention days in this sterile, wintry, far-from-the-city detention centre should feel as different as possible from a special holiday in a country mansion. The cops were ordered from above to do everything this time so that it didn't feel like a summer camp. If you haven't left the country yet, you will be made to see and feel where the country is going.

After a walk in the cell, Adilya says:

– Your girlfriend is very beautiful. Is she also an artist?
– Something like that.
– And where do you perform? In the circus? In the circus, right?

circus under special control

A couple of days later we realize that all the white houses except ours are empty. In addition to the usual cops, the 2nd Riot Police Unit have been assigned to guard ours. The 2nd Special Regiment are big body-armoured guys who are mostly sent to catch activists and disperse protests. Now they are occupied with no less important business – they walk along the corridor with a video camera and film how the balanders deliver lunch to the cells. They climb up onto the windowsill to lock Lucy's cell window while I walk near it (and vice versa), they film how I throw snowballs at the locked window.

– Let's play, says Adilya.

We take turns squatting and rolling each other on the icy tiles of the exercise yard. Behind the bars, a member of the 2nd Riot Police Unit is shuffling from foot to foot.

beyond the fence

– What's beyond the fence? Adilya asks.
– Forest.
– Forest? What's forest? I don't know that word.
– Well, forest. Trees.
– Are there any animals?

She is twenty-five, has pink hair and is a child. Having come to Russia like hundreds of thousands of other Central Asian migrants, she doesn't understand Russian well, and this is not surprising – there are no language courses for migrants here, nor are there any courses for social adaptation or employment. There is only one course for migrants in Russia – a free course on survival.

– Is she okay? asks the guard, seeing how Adilya is staring at the mesh of the fence and crying.
– What do you think? Of course she's not okay. She feels bad and ashamed. She fell in love, lived with a guy, and he started seeing another girl. She was jealous, persuaded him to let her drive, she hit a fence, ended up here, and this asshole has never even brought her a parcel and has dumped her – of course she is not okay.

Communal rooms for ten people to sleep in and the lowest-paid jobs: cleaners, street sweepers, builders, couriers, fast-food deliverers, for two bucks an hour – all the work that 'a proud titular nation' refuses to do.

– And why are you here? the guard can't help asking.
– Me? For nothing! I'm a political.

free course on survival

'*If people don't know their rights and have no one to protect them, the authorities will do anything to them. I think while we are here, our mission is to tell them about their rights and help them. Well, you've been doing that for a long time :); they try to hide violations from politicals.*
During the night my brain was in overdrive, I couldn't sleep, my head was spinning with all sorts of plans of revenge on the cops. By morning it had gone, but sometimes I get angry, although maybe that's a good thing.
They don't deserve kindness or leniency.'

– Lucy

'*I was really upset that they called us fascists, I know it's stupid and illegal, but this time I was deeply offended. I wasn't so offended when it was "witch" and "enemy of the people".*
Talking about violations ++. Did the floor of your cell also flood? We washed, 10 minutes each, then we saw a hell of a flood. The whole cell was covered in very smelly water that spilled out from under the wall. We understood immediately why the shower only works for two hours a week.

Adilya realized after the latest walk that you and I are in love and asked if you were jealous of me. It was funny.'

— Masha, 20 December

we're in love

The heater in the avtozak is broken. We think that this will be our only meeting before the New Year, until the end of our detention days – a meeting in an icy avtozak on the way to court.

'Every time, after the lawyer's speech, I think, "How can you not change anything after such a great speech?" And then another judge says, "No change," and something dies inside me,' Lucy says.

We warm ourselves against each other in the icy vehicle – it takes three hours one way from Sakharovo to the court. We are silent, laughing, hugging each other, looking at the wall. The shadow from the bars jumps on the shadow from the bars jumps on the shadow from the bars.

In this bleak apocalypse there is only one cheerful thing on the way back to Sakharovo – a lilac iPhone in the pocket of Lucy's jacket.

- If I'm able to get this into the cell, I'll pass you a message that, 'The lawyer is coming.'
- If not, I'll say, 'No lawyer.'

We take a photo in the avtozak cell, wait until the donut-escort turns away, eat a sweet and come back to our white madhouse.

An hour later, the duty cop comes into my cell, asks for sugar for Lucy, smiles and adds, 'By the way, she says that the lawyer is coming.' I smile too. It's funny that it was him who said these words.

bleak apocalypse

Don't you want to scream? Adilya suddenly asks.

If you don't talk to her for a while, she starts to worry. Going over everything that happened to her for the hundredth time and blaming herself.

- Why?
- So that everyone in the world can hear. To be heard, you have to shout loudly.

They're taking me out of the cell to a visit. Lucy too. We sit in neighbouring rooms and knock on the wall to leave at the same time and find a cell together along the corridor. They don't let us do that either. They lead us out one by one.

What will happen if we see each other? What will happen if we walk down the corridor together?

They have been tasked with protecting Russia 'from chaos': but what is Russia, if not a huge piece of land marked by a border – difficult to say. And not only that: Russia itself does not know what it is. The best people from culture and society were driven into camps, tortured and shot at firing ranges. And now they've taken their lines and started to quote them, calling them the 'Russian Classics'.

empire must die

- You have a lot of patience, a lot, says Adilya.

After a week in the cell, she displays the full range of symptoms of an inmate: loss of appetite, insomnia, sudden outbursts of rage. There are normally only a few outlets for rage in the cell. A person just walks around, around and around; the monotonous sound of rubber flip-flops slapping the floor – that's all the rage you have.

– It's just that this isn't my first time in jail, I say.
– Not your first time here? Do you make the same mistake over and over again?
– Not my first time because I am involved in politics.
– Politics – what is it? I've forgotten this word.
– I'm against this state, against Putin, and that's not a mistake.
– Putin's a good man.
– He's a thief and a murderer.
– He lets us come here to work.
– You work for a pittance, live in terrible conditions and you don't know Russian well.
– Who then, if not Putin?
– Whoever, whoever wants to. Whoever will be elected.

It's surprising that the question that is indelibly stamped into the heads of the guards I hear from a half-legal migrant. 'If not him, then who?' This is so fucking fucked up! Adilya interrupts my silence. She's just got an electric shock from a disposable sheet.

sound of rubber flip-flops

'My cellmates are leaving tomorrow. If they don't send anyone else here, I'll go on hunger strike until they transfer me to you. Being alone in a 13-bed

cell, when two girls are already in a 10-bed cell – I'm pissed off.
They told me the order to exert pressure
and separate us comes from "very high, higher than Petrovka".
Let them go fuck themselves. If they try
to transfer Adilya over to me, tell them you're not going to be
alone either and will do the same.
I haven't got your answer yet, maybe they'll give it to me
at breakfast (and I will hand this note over). Was it inside the
Zygar book? I don't understand, did the cops take it or perhaps
it was never in the book?
It was very funny yesterday. The cop gave me the book with
the words: "You, what, you read Zygar? He's a fag!" I said,
"Ha, well, I am too." He got confused and closed the door.
Miss you. I hope this lil' skeleton doesn't crack up. I love
you. Let's go on hunger strike, so they unite our cells and stop
isolating us from each other! Freedom doesn't exist unless you
fight for it every day :)'

– Lucy

missed you

'Detained for pictures with swastikas, Pussy Riot members
Shtein and Alyokhina have declared a hunger strike in the
migrant centre in Sakharovo.'

– Mediazona, 25 December

This is Lucy's first ever hunger strike, a hunger strike demanding that we not be separated. Of course I agree. But I'm worried about her health. There is no doctor in this detention centre because the state has no money for doctors for detained people.

By law, people on hunger strike have their blood pressure, their temperature and their blood sugar monitored every day. So, from the first day of the strike, and for every day after that an ambulance comes to us.

- There are only two things that are a pity to lose: freedom and health, says the ambulance doctor, measuring my blood pressure. Although actually, there is a third thing – honour.
- Well, that's what we're trying to fight for.
- By undermining your health?

The doctor says, 'I would immediately put you in the same cell together and remove everyone else.' I reply, 'Those who have jailed us should be put in the cell.'

fanny revolt

'I talked to a surprisingly nice dude from the special regiment on the walk. He asked me last time how to translate Pussy Riot. I said, "Fanny revolt." In the morning, he asked me, "When is the next Pussy Riot?" I said, "TODAY!" I've finished reading the memoirs and started Empire! *I can give you* The Rise and Fall of the Third Reich *(I need to learn what we're in jail for). The staff is trying to talk me out of the hunger strike, food keeps being brought in. I still have serious shakes and am weak. Do you want a pillowcase and an eye mask? Love you.'*

– Lucy, 25 December

'*I'll take the pillowcase and the book about the Third Reich! I also had a debate with Adilya and yesterday's guard. He said that nothing would change this way (before he said that he had worked at the protests in January and that not many people came out for change, it sounded like more were needed:)).*
With Adilya – I'm already used to her understanding everything after about three days.
She's already understood that I don't need a guy, she's understood that we are politicals, that a protest against corruption is cool ("we also need one in our country"), and I hope she will also understand about the hunger strike (so far she is actively offering me food).
She also said, "For there to be change, you need a lot of people, and are there lots of you? Or only you and Lucy?" I said, "There are, but they are afraid." She said, "If everyone is afraid, there won't be change."'

–♥Masha

pillowcase and the third reich

On a walk, I think about food, remembering the vegetarian sha-warma from the Mexican grandma we had ordered not long ago. In the evening, the ambulance arrives again. After taking my temperature, blood pressure, oxygen levels, the medic asks:

– Why the hunger strike?
– We want to be together.
– Why are you in separate cells?
– The boss said it is forbidden to put politicals together.
– And you –politicals – what do you stand for?
– For freedom.

The medic looks at me sympathetically and says:

– We abolished serfdom not that long ago, people aren't ready for your freedom yet.
– Come on. I am thirty-three years old and I am ready. You are probably about the same age as me, I think you are ready too. The girls – I nod at the female guards – are up for it, so they are ready. Why do you think others are not ready? And to use your logic, there was slavery in the United States until recently, and in Germany eighty years ago – a negligible period by the standards of history – they exterminated people in gas chambers. And now in the centre of their capital there is a memorial to the victims of repression. And people there have lives that are not super perfect but are definitely better than here. I've been there.

There's silence in the white room used for examinations. The girl-duty guards are smiling.

no bread

Although I stay on hunger strike, they don't isolate me and bring food to the cell every day. Adilya puts my untouched food in bags – one bag with bread, one with soup and porridge – and puts them by the door. When the door opens to serve supper, she asks if the bags can be put in the corridor. 'I told you tomorrow! The rubbish is taken out in the morning!' the guard barks at her, and forcefully kicks the bag with bread back to the cell. 'But some people have no bread,' says Adilya when we are alone and adds, 'I don't understand it.'

In the corridor, a guard asks me, 'What's the point?' I answer, 'Well, you may not understand my point, but when you fight for what matters to you, remember me.'

Seventy-three years ago, my favourite poet, Osip Mandelstam, died in detention of typhoid.

After the incident with the bread, Adilya is upset and remains silent for a long time. Then she pulls out a small tube, a disposable tube of blue shampoo like they have in hotels – her sister who works as a cleaner gave it to her. She hands it to me and she says, 'When I get out, and you are on your last day – the 31st – wash your hair. It is beautiful. And you are beautiful.'

what if?

'Shtein asked me to read you her statement,' a guard named Vika says as she comes in to check the cell and hands me a piece of paper. I quickly glance to see what's on it. Tears come to my eyes, but I don't show it, I just say, 'I won't do that.'

The door closes. Lucy has stopped her hunger strike.

I go to the toilet and cry.

> *I really overestimated my own strength, but I can't do it any longer. Not only starving myself, but resisting, persuading, explaining. No one around me has understood, not my cellmates, not the doctors, not the staff. One of the cops said to me something like, "Your friend is experienced, strong and principled, but you'll give up." And it has turned out to be true. I just became ill and lonely. That asshole just fucked me over again, that one who closes the window. I tried to warn you, but they wouldn't let me. It's hard to coordinate actions when notes go missing, they chase you from the window, and no chance to talk.*

I was left alone with a book about the Gulag and constant abuse in there. I just couldn't stand it + I was scared for my already shitty health + I blamed myself for using the ambulance, and it is offensive that we're suffering in here and they don't give a fuck, they're having fun.'

– Lucy

After the tears, waves of anger overwhelm me. I'd like to see each of the cops, who said our actions didn't make sense, fight for something that makes sense to them. It's easy to ridicule and devalue if you're ridiculing someone else, but what if they are just like you? What if it is actually you?

set for a catastrophe

I look at the white wall of this 'ward' of the Covid hospital, which has been handed over to the cops as a detention centre, where migrants are kept mixed with politicals. It's built like a set for a catastrophe or dystopia, like quarantine after being exposed to aliens, and wherever you look there is alienation and isolation. I look at all this and somehow I feel that I am not alone. It's like something in me is saying, 'Don't be afraid,' and something else is saying, 'I'm not afraid.' It's as if at this moment I have God with me, or the various people who have travelled a difficult path with me. And I know for sure that I won't get sick or die. Probably that's too much pathos for the fourth day of hunger strike.

The next morning the door opens. After the usual breakfast trolley, human rights defenders enter our cell. Two human rights defenders and some higher-ranking cops with large stars on their epaulettes.

I start talking. About the fact that the 'sheets' give you an electric shock, about the fact that there is no doctor and if someone gets sick, we have to call an ambulance every time, about the constant filming and locked windows, about the fact that I don't understand why Lucy and I were separated in two ten-bed cells.

The head of the detention centre wipes sweat from his forehead every ten seconds. The human rights defenders write something in a notebook. Finally, the big district colonel says:

- We'll give you and Lucy a shared walk!
- A walk is fine, I reply, but I will not stop my hunger strike.
- That's a pity, says the human rights defender, raising her head. It would have been a beautiful story . . .

Time stretches out and hangs in the air. The small curly-haired duty guard jokingly says to his colleagues, 'Attention!' as I walk down the corridor to the exercise yard. To our walk. The walk we achieved with this hunger strike.

our walk

Lucy stands alone in a huge, long, snow-covered exercise yard for our walk. Tired, wearing a child's blue hat with a pompom. She hugs me and I throw snow, it falls through the bars of the ceiling. White, glistening mini-flakes.

We laugh at how special they've made our walk. They've arranged for the yard to be guarded – two cops with video cameras. They stand behind metal mesh, at opposite ends, and stomp around. Their very important task for today is to film two girls walking together for the first time and a Kyrgyz woman freezing next to them.

– Are you leaving soon? It's cold! complains one of the
guards.
– You have a warm jacket! I answer. Do you know
where it was made?
– They used to sew them in the penal colonies.
– They still do.

The zone. Penal Colony 28, Berezniki town – that's where
my last hunger strike was. Eight years ago.

pass a test

When I return to my cell, Adilya says, 'Those people in epaulettes came. I guess you'll have problems now.' I say, 'No. They
will have problems.'
I remember how in the morning she told the human rights
defenders, 'My bedding is good! Everything is good!', although
each night I see it giving her an electric shock. I ask, 'Why did
you say that?' Although I know why – she was scared.

– This isn't real life, says Adilya. Real life only
comes after death and meeting God, and this was
just a test.
– Okay, so what does it mean to pass an inspection? To
lie, because 'otherwise there will be problems', or to
tell the truth?
– I've been watching you, she slowly answers. You
haven't eaten anything for five days, you've been
exercising, you've been writing, you've said so much
to those people who came today – how do you have
the strength to do that? If you have the strength, then
God is with you, she continued, answering her own

question. But if you keep doing this, there will be a lot of problems. a lot of problems.

I don't have the strength to explain that everyone has problems, regardless of gender, race, a relationship with God or lack of. So instead I say, 'Let's play backgammon.' I feel good that she beats me a couple times, even though I only taught her a couple of days ago. The next day, she leaves the cell and even tries to sneak in the mobile phone they give us for fifteen minutes a day, but the cop sees and tells her to give it back. If she had taken the phone in front of more detention-centre guards, she would have ended up in a worse cell and been criminally prosecuted. God protected her or that cop did, one or the other, we don't know.

sentence comes into force

Peeooo-peeooo is sounding throughout the corridor – it is the duty guard making a funny noise. Lucy has been released from the detention centre. And has come back to visit me straight away. We discuss how I will leave tomorrow. Leave to greet the New Year. Three cops shout in unison in the meeting room, 'Girls, don't vape! Please! All the bosses are watching the camera right now.'

31 December, three hours until New Year.

Escorting me out is Prince Harry – that's what we've nicknamed the redhead on duty – wearing jeans and a jacket. He's smiling. They are all smiling; the prospect of celebrating New Year's Eve while on duty is nothing in comparison to Pussy Riot finally leaving and the hassle being over.

A man in uniform is carrying my bag, and when the door opens, a firework is let off.

bosses are watching

A balloon with a unicorn – Aya and Lucy hold the string on both sides. Winnie the Pooh and Piglet. Meeting a 'fascist'. They came here in advance and are keeping warm in the car. Four police cars, following them, arrived at the same car park. 'Here we go,' says Lucy. 'Good evening! If you're here for Alyokhina, so are we,' a cop says to Aya, and leaves. Aya gets out and runs to the police car. There's a girl-cop smoking beside it. She is shivering from the cold. It's minus 25 outside.

- Have you really come for Alyokhina? asks a frightened Aya, who is already working out the logistics in her head. Lucy, with the bracelet on her leg, needs to hit her curfew in Moscow, and if they put me back on the arrest carousel, they'll have to call the lawyers and follow me wherever they're taking me.
- It's also New Year's Eve for us, I also want to be with my children and family, and we've all been sent here to see Alyokhina come out.
  So we don't have to call the lawyers?

And then, very fast: juice, carrot salad, car; we are driving very fast because Lucy has a bracelet and we have to make it by 22:00. Now we will need to make it by 22:00 every day; her sentence has come into force; soon mine will too.

Just enough time to light one Bengal firework, look at everyone and arrive into the next year.

happy new year

Every sip of the juice is like a sip of a magic elixir. A very intense flavour, as if you can feel it on your skin. It feels like you could get drunk on a few drops. I asked for cherry juice and the carrot salad that Aya used to make me in prison when we first met, every morning before my trial. My favourite salad.

carrot salad (prison version):
grated carrots
pine nuts
olive oil
salt

Plastic salad bowl in my hands in the car, salad on plates in the kitchen. The little rat is a little afraid of the guests. I feel very tired. I don't feel like celebrating at all, for some reason – I just want to take a breath. It's good that we're together and everything is fine. We'll buy the projector that Lucy wants. We'll watch a movie.

- I'm just afraid of one thing, Aya says in the empty kitchen, the first morning of the first day of January. I hope they don't start a war.
- What war? I ask.
- With Ukraine.

14.
War

The system must plant people in prison.

Like planting seeds to grow wheat for bread. The system plants people in prison to grow fear. New court cases equal new stars on epaulettes. And when there are no enemies of the people left, the system can take care of everyone else.

History repeats itself because it is not taught, history repeats itself because they want to repeat it. The bloody and tragic history of a huge Russia that never managed to do the most important thing required to move on – to ask forgiveness from all those it had destroyed.

seeds of fear

– Pussy Riot is back?
– How else would you have it?

No, I'm not asleep, I'm detained again. Opposite me – the bars of the monkey cell; around me – cops going from office to office; on my back – a rucksack with the Hogwarts emblem. A black rucksack with gold stitches. The detention protocol. Again for Nazism.

nazism again

I was detained at the exit of the inspectorate. My first scheduled check-in at FSIN. I have to check in twice a month. The sentence came into force, they put a bracelet on me, and the countdown began. There would be an end to my sentence – or so I thought.

What the hell? It's been less than two months since I left detention – why Nazism again? Is it a new trend to call us Nazis? How long will this continue?

- Why did you bring so much stuff? – the young cop is surprised to see me in the corridor with my market-trader bags. They will let you go home soon.
- No one will let me go.
- I'm sure they will, says the young guy.

> *'Maria Alyokhina is detained for fifteen days for Nazi propaganda.'*
> – Interfax, 8 February

drive you out of russia

- They want to drive you out of Russia, only what will they do when you've gone? a cop speculates on the return journey from court.

He and a colleague carry my bags, backpack and a pretty bag from Lucy (this time she packed my things) into my cell and I go into the police station to wait for transportation to the special detention centre with the same Hogwarts backpack. Inside the backpack – the FSIN tracker; on my leg – the ankle

bracelet. After a day, the lights on the tracker no longer work –
the battery died.

- The FSIN called at night, writes Lucy.
- What did they want?
- They asked why you weren't home.
- I see.
- I said you've been arrested and they asked if the
  tracker is okay.

baby

At least it's not Sakharovo. I'm returning to Special Detention
Centre No. 2, where I haven't been since summer. Everyone
comes out to greet me: the duty staff, the doctor, the director.
'We've renovated here,' he says. 'Masha, how are you? Hang on
in there!' They take me upstairs to cell no. 7. The walls are blue.
Apparently, to repaint walls blue is prison tradition. I unpack
the bags, put the food on the shelves, make the bed. Lucy has
handed over our sheets. All with little holes in them – chewed
by Mr Rat. 'Baby,' I say out loud. I want to cry. To unfold the
bedding with holes from the little rat's teeth and cry a little.

cell no. 7

If you are imprisoned for politics, they will try to make it as
apolitical as possible. 'We have no political prisoners in our
country – they are all just hooligans, just crooks, just extremists and terrorists, and now even Nazis. No politics.'

The label 'political' on their stitched-together cases won't
be shown on the news. The officer in epaulettes 'understands

everything', passing such a case to a colleague who also 'understands everything'. How far could they go 'understanding
everything' if they handed over the case from the court not
to a special detention centre but to a firing range. Would they
stop then? Uncertain.

no politics

> '*Putin should understand that body bags will come back to
> Moscow.*'
>
> – US Deputy Secretary of State, 10 February 2022

When I have put my food on the shelf, sorted my other things,
when my papers have been stacked, I've slept well, only then does
it start to hurt. 'Why Nazism again?' You even feel ashamed that
someone might have watched the news and thought it was true.

I stay up half the night, either thinking or reading by the light
of a dim bulb and the streetlights. I am reading a book I got from
an activist from a neighbouring cell in the police station – Hans
Fallada's novel *Every Man Dies Alone*. It's about an elderly couple in
Nazi Germany. Having been notified of the death of their son –
drafted to fight for Hitler – the two begin their small, 'doomed to
fail' struggle. They write anti-war postcards and leave them under
the doors of strangers' apartments and on staircases. Both will
be caught, both will be executed. A novel based on true events,
which could not have been written without the spilled blood of
principled and honest people. It made my heart beat fast.

Grisha, a medic, enters the cell during the morning rounds.
He looks like a rocker – a belt with metal studs, a USSR-1969
T-shirt. He gives me sleeping pills, and then, smiling, hands me
a notebook – 'for an autograph'. 'From Pussy Riot as a keepsake,' I write.

- So now Alyokhina is a fascist? He laughs.
- Yes, it's fucked up.

every man dies alone

'The State Department urged Americans to leave Ukraine
immediately
UK urges its citizens to leave Ukraine immediately
Norway urged its citizens to leave Ukraine
Israel began evacuating diplomat's families from Ukraine
South Korea and Japan urged their citizens to leave Ukraine
immediately
Netherlands asks its citizens to leave Ukraine as soon as
possible
North Macedonia, Montenegro and Estonia have called on
their citizens to leave Ukraine'

– Telegram channel, 11 February

Evening. Sunset. Exercise yard.

In one of the windows of a panel apartment block nearby, blue fairy lights glow. They weren't there in the summer; they were probably left over from New Year's Eve. Do the people behind this window know that someone is looking at their blue fairy lights from the exercise yard of the special detention centre? There are no fairy lights in the special detention centre, or tinsel, because they are the same as shoelaces – you could hang yourself with them.

When you're behind bars for a long time, you start to miss colour. The strawberry smell of body cream. Any bright thing: lipstick, a toy, even multicoloured crisps, are much more beautiful than just plain ones.

don't touch

'The US president suggested possible tough anti-Russian sanctions in the context of the tense situation around Ukraine.'
– Telegram channel

'Pardon my language, but we are shitting on Western sanctions.'
– Russian Ambassador to Sweden, 12 February

The door to the cell opens. There's a new face on the morning round. Major Goldobina. She's replacing the warden. Red hair pulled back into a tight ponytail. The voice of a real bitch. 'What have we got here?' she says, and starts reading my diaries stacked up on the shelf and lying on the next bunk. 'Don't touch them,' I reply, waking up. 'I'm the boss here for now and I'll touch whatever I want,' she snaps. I gather up the papers. She walks out. I feel like crying. I've completely forgotten what it's like to have hands prying without permission into something private.

I call Lucy. They allow a fifteen-minute call once a day. I miss her. We decided that it's a bad idea to be in detention at the same time, we won't end up in the same cell anyway. She was supposed to go to the inspector's office after me. When I was detained outside the inspectorate, we decided she should not leave the house and face the same fate as me.

– You shouldn't leave a little rat like that, she says over the phone. Because she also misses me.
– I can't go to sleep, she says, for a third night in a row. The whole room becomes very sad.

shouldn't leave like that

'Freedom burns with a pink flame' – writing on the wall of the exercise yard.

The guys in the first cell decided to feed the doves and threw breadcrumbs into the exercise yard. At first, I thought it was silly, there was a metal mesh over the exercise yard, but then I noticed that there were a couple of holes in the mesh. The doves immediately found them and started to peck at the crumbs. I sit and watch them. Suddenly one of the doves sets off from the grille, makes a circle above my head and sits back down.

– Hey, beautiful, how you doing? a stranger prisoner shouts to my cellmate.
– I'm fine! she replies from the exercise yard.
– Have you seen the sunset? Look at that! Ah, I'd sit with a girl now, hug her and enjoy the sunset, the prisoner says dreamily. But I'm alone here. Me and the four walls.

The sunset is actually beautiful – lilac and blue celestial veins swell on the pink sky's skin. All over the world it's Valentine's Day.

freedom burns

– How long is this going to go on? asks the boy.

The riot-police uniform he's wearing looks ridiculous on him. He's just a kid – about twenty years old. He's been asking questions the whole walk, wanting to know as much as he can about the protests.

- What?
- These detentions.
- I don't know! It's my fourth time in six months plus this – I show him my leg with the ankle bracelet.
- But you do know?
- Come on! Don't say, 'But you know you'll go to jail for a post.' It wasn't so long ago I was doing mass pickets and people like you were policing them. Then they banned protests, then pickets, then one-person pickets, then queues for one-person pickets. And only then did they start putting people in jail for posts. Follow the chain!
- Not only for posts, the boy grumbles; he wants to show that he knows something too. They gave a sentence for Minecraft.
- What's that? asks my cellmate, who had been silently listening to our 'argument'.
- Minecraft is a game, Teenagers talked about making an FSB building and blowing it up as part of their game. One got five years, the rest got conditional sentences.

not in the game

What really pisses me off is the logic that 'You're the one who's framing yourself.' Statements like 'What were you thinking when you went out on the street – you knew you'd go to jail.'

This logic has been passed down from generation to generation. This is what has taught those who survived to

survive – 'You have to stay quiet and keep your head down.'
The authorities in Russia instil in people the same idea: your
voice won't decide anything, don't open your mouth unneces-
sarily. Through torture, executions, exiles and shootings, they
kill everything bright and dissenting. Survivors of this meat
grinder of repression and poverty learned how not to act. 'We
are little people, each of us is a little person.'

I want to see the names of political prisoners everywhere.
So no one can turn away from those who have been tortured
and killed for a century. I want graffiti of the names of those
killed by Stalin on the walls of Stalin's high-rises; by Brezhnev,
on his apartment blocks; by Putin, on the White House. So it
would be impossible to say, 'I didn't know.'

little person

– Get ready for the court, Mash. You look . . . rested!
  Okay. People have survived worse. We'll make it! says
  the major, escorting me to the car.
– Is it possible sometimes not just to survive, but also to
  live?

The question remains unanswered. Two seasoned majors are
taking me through Moscow. Windows without bars. The car
is like an oven. I fantasize that these are my two bodyguards,
and I'm going to an important meeting and smoking a banana
vape, sprawled out on the back seat.

– Is there a Hyde Park in New York?
– It's in London.
– Which one is in New York?

- Central Park.
- That's the big one?
- Yes.
- The mayor is going to build a similar one in Nagatinsky Zaton.
- Half the country has no heating, no sewage system and no roads, and you're talking about Central Park in Nagatinsky Zaton! What the fuck?

The court is being evacuated – there was a bomb threat. I'm smiling. The majors don't understand why, but I enjoy watching the judges and clerks crawl out of their useless offices and fill the courtyard.

While cops with dogs search the building for a bomb, the majors and I wait in the car. My lawyer brings coffee, hands me the cup through the window.

- What's the news? I ask.
- What's there to tell? The lawyer grins. There'll be a war, they'll attack Ukraine.
- What war? What the hell do we need Ukraine for?

The major turns round from the front seat, tries to keep the conversation going: 'I personally like Holland better.'

you'll catch on

The trial starts late and makes no sense. The judge asks questions, but she doesn't need answers.

I want to say, 'Come on, Your Honour, you'll catch on. You will now stand up, laugh and cancel these detention days. And I'll go home. The ankle bracelet will break on my leg. Comrade

Major will go off to bed and the other major will go off to catch criminals. Or both will go to sleep. The Virgin Mary will banish Putin and . . .' Instead, I stand up and say, 'I won't prove to you that I'm not a Nazi. I just won't. We both know that.'

- Why are you so sad? Lucy asks. We're waiting for documents from the office and Comrade Major is ignoring that we are on a forbidden video call.
- What's the news?
- Three years in prison for the elderly father of Zhdanov – Navalny's colleague. A couple of shots fired in the direction of Ukraine.

Perhaps a cell without any news is better.

> *'Every indication is that Russia will attack Ukraine in the*
> *coming days.'*
> – Joe Biden, US President, 17 February

every indication

Lucy says, 'The rat is sick.' Comrade Major says, 'My cat died recently.' He's trying to be sympathetic.

We go outside. It's already dark. Suddenly the second major runs up and says, 'Let's take a selfie!' So we're standing on the steps. Two majors and my smiling round face between them. Is this really happening to me right now?

- Are you sure they didn't put anything in your coffee? asks the major-photographer on the way back from court.
- No! Why would they?
- I remember a long time ago, we were driving

Nemtsov. He got into the car. I think it was a cup of
tea, and then I saw that he was wasted!
– Viva la nineties! I laugh. He was a great man. Alive.

Everyone is silent. No one argues with that.

– But still, you'll abandon us, Masha, the first major
suddenly says. You are stubborn and a patriot, yes,
but you will abandon us – over there people are more
cheerful, food is tastier, in general, life is sweeter.

I want to say, 'We'll see,' but I barely hear myself say, 'I don't
want to.'

you'll abandon us

*'Wagner fighters have already arrived in the Russian-
occupied territories. With the Russian security services, they're
planning to carry out a series of terrorist acts.'*

Focus.ua – 19 February

– Mash, the war is about to start.

I hear Lucy's voice coming out of the phone.
These detention days are definitely doing their job. The city
enjoying itself at some point starts to seem like a detached
film. Like the rest of the world. If the sky is clear, it's pink. I
don't think I'll ever get out of here.
A room with a messy ceiling, a defeatist attitude and a selfie
with some majors, that's my life.

– What war? I answer jokingly. Everything is stable here
in jail.

why war?

Propaganda releases the 'news' that Ukraine is shelling Donbass. People must be saved. Russia urgently needs to 'save the people of Donbass' from Ukrainian bombs. In fact, this is preparation for the stream of information about the bombing of Kyiv, and the official annexation of two regions, Donetsk and Luhansk, which are in fact already seized – they just didn't squeeze every last drop during the 'Russian Spring'. At that point Crimea was seized and incorporated into the Russian Federation, while the Luhansk and Donetsk regions were left 'hanging'.

Years passed. During these years Putin tightened the screws inside the country, passed repressive laws, imprisoned and pressured the people out of the country who disagreed with state policy. The ground was being prepared. For what? In order to start a new war when the right moment came. Why? Because war raises popularity ratings.

Putin's popularity ratings after the pandemic are the worst they've ever been. An old corrupt man who's afraid to stick his nose out of his bunker. Negotiating at a table a kilometre long, surrounded by a crowd of FSBshniks. Things need to change. War is the perfect way to boost ratings. We need a new victory. A new victory over the new Nazis.

something unreal

Something you would've said before: 'This only happens in books.' The war is about to start. But did it ever stop? After serving two years in jail for 'Punk Prayer', we came out into another country.

Nobody prepared us for war. We didn't have lessons in school telling us what to do if your country launched an aggressive war. My country. Our country. Not me. None of us were taught what the right thing to do was. What to do when you know that your country's tanks are about to cross the border, in your name, to kill. To kill in the streets that you know, to kill those you know, to kill them and their loved ones, their relatives. That in the streets that you know where there used to be laughter, there will be tears.

where there used to be laughter, there will be tears

'Putin announced that the decision to recognize LPR and DPR will be taken today.'
'EU, UK leaders vow sanctions over Putin's recognition of breakaway Ukraine regions.'
Interfax.ru and Politico.eu – 21 February

The fifteen minutes they give on the phone is not enough. I ask for a radio – this is the first time I want to listen to the news.

The idea of a humanitarian catastrophe is being created, tens of thousands of people are being forcibly removed to Russia from the occupied eastern regions of Ukraine. On the radio they are seriously discussing whether the refugees can 'theoretically' replace migrants from Central Asia. So it's okay to take a chunk of another country; the only question is whether its refugees will successfully sweep your streets.

'If you think Putin should recognize the DPR and LPR, call (dictates the number).'

'If you think he should not, call (dictates number).'

head of the zone

'Putin ordered the Russian army to ensure "peacekeeping" in the DPR and LPR.'

– BBC, 21 February

Putin convenes a 'security council'. A pre-recording of the meeting is being passed off as a live broadcast. The only camera in the corner of the ceiling is covered with a black bag.

Everyone takes turns swearing allegiance to Putin. It's being filmed. So it can't be rewound. Now they're not just officials, they're all war criminals. The oath is about 'recognizing the sovereignty of the Luhansk and Donetsk independent republics'. Everyone understands what this means – Crimea scenario 2.0: first we recognize 'independence'; then we accept it as part of Russia. Everyone understands that this time there will be bloodshed. There will be no photos with kittens. The era of 'polite people' has passed. There will be a massacre.

Putin relaxes in his chair, as one by one they take the oath of office. It's the turn of Naryshkin, the head of the foreign intelligence service. The country's chief intelligence officer stammers like a schoolboy who has been called to the blackboard and has forgotten to do his homework. He can't say what Putin wants him to say. At first he forgets the words, then he says the wrong ones – instead of 'I support the proposal to recognize sovereignty,' he says, 'I support the decision to incorporate the republics into the Russian Federation.' Too early, Sergei.

Putin smirkingly reminds him it's 'sovereignty' that's on the agenda. And sends the humiliated spy back to his chair.

This is just like a meeting of a disciplinary commission in a penal colony. Where the heads in uniform take it in turns to scold the prisoner who has 'violated the regime'. Where they put him in the centre of the room and make him justify himself. Only, in that particular case, there's just one prisoner and several 'heads', whereas, in this one, there's only one head of the zone, and the rest – well, you get it.

virgin mary, banish putin

I have no words. I'm alone in cell no. 7. It's about to be midnight. Putin's hour-long speech ends on the radio.

Putin talks about the flight time of missiles from Kyiv to Moscow. What it really means is the flight time from Moscow to Kyiv. There'll be missiles. There'll be war.

If you looked at the camera lens in the corner of my cell, you would see a person rushing about. Walking around restlessly. Sitting on a bench. Sitting on the bed but not finding her place. The anniversary of our 'Punk Prayer' is the day the war is announced.

Ten years.

Virgin Mary, banish Putin.

Well, where are you now?

there will be war

At the blue gates, I am met by Lucy with flowers, Aya, lawyer Dima and a journalist. The bouquet is very beautiful, the bouquet is the only thing out of everything that doesn't look confused. 'War is likely; are you going to leave?' the journalist asks me. 'Let them be the ones to leave – this is my country.' I hear my voice as if from a loudspeaker. How many times will I cry listening to my answers, reading my answers, this is our country – oh, really?

The next day I walk through a shopping centre and for the first time I catch myself being ashamed, simply ashamed to walk through Moscow. There isn't one cop around, just people going about their business, going down and going up the escalator, and I can hardly even bring myself to walk. I don't have thoughts like 'Well, how can you just go about your life when the self-proclaimed president of Russia is about to start bombing another country on your behalf?' any more, I'm simply ashamed. Unspeakably and silently.

i am ashamed

At 4.58 a huge rumble woke Kramatorsk
⚡ ⚡ ⚡ *Russia launches volley fire at Ukraine with GRAD*
launcher
❗ *Odessa bombings – eyewitnesses*
❗ *In Berdyansk explosions heard*
❗ *A series of explosions near Kharkiv*
⚡ ⚡ ⚡ *Mariupol under fire*
⚡ ⚡ ⚡ *A battle has begun in Kiev*
❗ *UN calls for peace*

There are three reactions to catastrophe – fight, flight, freeze.
Freeze. In other words, play dead.
'Mash, wake up, the war has begun!'

'I have made the decision to conduct a special military
operation . . .'
– Putin, 24 February

Like in a fog. Out of which the news on Telegram pops up. Messages pop up with news about explosions. Explosions. New explosions. Cries. Fleeing people. Tears. So many tears.

Raise your head. Look out of the window – just a street. Cars go by.

Lower your head – tears. Shouts. Instagram stories of people you know and don't know. Tears.

Paralysis. Numbness. Fear. Numbness. Pain. Numbness. What are you called, you bastards? We're called words you didn't know before. We are called missile strike, we are called shelter. We are called the fucking army of the fucking Russian Federation. Shelter. Rejection. No, these aren't the same streets we used to walk down. Because if they were . . . then . . .

Numbness.

we are

fucking

fascists.

fucking fascists

Your beloved motherland is bombing my beloved motherland! – Aya's uncle calls her from Ukraine. The city of Irpin. He is standing on the balcony. Planes. Explosions. – Do something! Irpin is a small town near Kyiv.

Millions of Russians have relatives in Ukraine. The TV says we aren't bombing civilians – it's the Nazis, it's the Ukrainians who are bombing themselves. Voice recordings to Russia shouting 'Believe me' from hiding places, from down in the metro. But people don't believe the shouts, they believe the TV. Because it's easier that way.

Aya's on her way to see us. She's crying. The car has a flat

tyre. The tyre garage is round the corner. She goes in. Three
men are also there. There's a plasma TV on the wall. Putin's
address is on the screen. One of the men says, 'He's doing
the right thing! What a man! That's what they need, Khokly!'
Aya shouts, 'Why are you saying that?' He takes her by the
collar: 'Traitors. People like you should be killed.' One of the
garage people says to Aya: 'Either you shut up immediately or
you leave without a tyre.' Aya is sitting in our kitchen. A bus
full of Centre E cops is parked under our window. We don't
have even a minuscule chance of going to the square together.
None. At least one of us should make it there. 'Sit down, draw
a poster. I'll tell everyone it's from you.' I draw a poster. It says
'No to War'.

i'm drawing

My teenage son goes to a supermarket, takes a kebab and
doesn't pay for it. A few hours later the police grab him.
They take him to the police station. They say there will be a
criminal case.

'The kebab cost 100 roubles, what criminal case???'

'He pushed the guard away. Technically, it's robbery.'

'I mean, surely you can't create a criminal case for this according to the law??? Are you kidding me?' I interrogate the lawyer.

They've already held him at the police station for four hours.
I can't sleep. I'm afraid my child is going to jail; they can find
out who his mother is in a matter of seconds. The cops are
behaving strangely. The evidence has been sent off to the desk,
the decision could take up to a month. Lucy says she's leaving the country. I don't want to know this. I want to go to the
supermarket to persuade the guard to retract his statement,

I want to go to the Nemtsov Bridge with a blue and yellow bouquet – he was killed on this date at this time of night. I go out onto the balcony.

no to war

There's a procession marching under our windows. Chanting 'No to war!'

A grey car is parked under our window – surveillance. When the column approaches, we shout from the balcony: 'It's Centre E! Look out! Centre E!'

But they continue right up the avenue.

I think the coast is clear.

I hail a taxi and quickly jump in.

Police everywhere. Lots of police cars, avtozaks, fear, my hair is loose, we're driving.

At the traffic lights, my taxi is cut up by a grey car, three men leap out of it. One shoves the driver face-first onto the steering wheel. The other two come at me from the side. Rip my stuff away. They rip me like an object off the back seat and throw me out of the taxi into the grey car.

this is our country

- Why the fuck did you drag me out? I yell.
- Why the fuck did you leave? MASHA, THIS IS A POLICE STATE, WHY THE FUCK DID YOU LEAVE YOUR HOUSE??? We were parked right under your window so you could see us. Masha, why would you do that?

– I'm a free person.
– Then you'll go to jail.
– Aren't you ashamed of what you're doing? Of the hell in Ukraine, which is supported by the whole world? A brave country, a country that was our sister. People are dying, there is a war. And who is it you are fighting with? Putin is a fascist. The whole world thinks our country is a fascist occupier. Who actually supports you?
– Venezuela.
– Would you send your child to this war?
– I served myself.
– And would you send a child?

black stripes

Police station. The cell. Transparent wall with bars. No hearts. Lots of strips of black scotch tape. I see death everywhere. I'm in pain. I'm afraid. I'm ashamed. I've been against Putin for ten years. I didn't choose Putin, but he has brought in troops and I can't stop them. And people are dying. People are dying from Russian weapons. And I'm ashamed. I've protested, I've been in jail, under house arrest, in a special detention centre. I'm hysterical.

In the cell to the left: a girl with blue hair and a yellow jumper.

In the cell to the right: a girl with pale pink hair.

Tomorrow they'll both get ten detention days for this.

freeze and watch

Khamovniki Court. We're waiting in the corridor. A female lawyer says, 'Masha, why not run? I can get you through the back door. Without a passport. Out from arrest. I've got people out that way before.' I say, 'No, I don't want that.'

The male judge is listening to a story about how, who and at what time I was pulled out of the car like a terrorist. Same court. Same doors. Different courtroom. Finding myself in the same building where I received a two-year prison sentence, ten years later – I don't know how I feel.

Don't attack – it's useless. Don't run – there's nowhere to go. Freeze.

Freeze and see where we end up.

I walk up the stairs – to get detention days – then go downstairs with a suitcase – to serve them. There's a metal detector just like at the airport. I was led up the same stairs in handcuffs for the Pussy Riot verdict. Then there was no war, or endless arrests, corpses, poisonings, prison terms.

The same stairs. To get my fifteen days. For resisting the police.

The policeman drags my black suitcase. The blue fence of the special detention centre.

– Somehow your face looks familiar, jokes the guard at inspection. I'm sure I've seen you somewhere before!
– I only got out of here four days ago. Okay, fine, the joke is not brilliant, but I'll give you it.

cell no. 6

Out of seven people in the cell, five are political.

Zhenya came out with a placard: 'No to War'.

Sasha, Sveta and Ksyusha came to the square shouting 'No to War'.

And all I did was leave the house.

All day we listen to the news. The exchange rate is rising. The skies over Europe are closed to Russians. Companies are pulling out of contracts. Car dealers, aircraft and electronics companies, foreign banks are all leaving Russia because of sanctions.

I'm as ashamed as I was yesterday, but the shame is replaced by anger and rage.

For so many years we've demanded these sanctions through all the channels and parliaments. It took dead bodies to finally impose them.

Five girls sit on a windowsill, leaning against a black speaker, Chinese music playing from it.

This is the first and last time we try to find a foreign radio station.

rage

It's a strange feeling: being in prison, listening to dispatches from the front, and willing your country to lose.

My bunkmate Almaza, a Roma woman whose name means diamond in Russian, has kind, big eyes and the worst withdrawal symptoms from methadone. A baby face and a thin body. Her legs cramp up and she doesn't know where to put them, she sweats and is in pain. Something similar is happening to our country, I can feel it.

Listening to an hour of propaganda – I think how they convince people so forcefully that all is well. A bill has been passed making it illegal to say everything is wrong. Up to fifteen years in prison for 'spreading fake news' about the war.

Midnight. The Russian national anthem is playing. There are five of us and we listen to it in silence like at the cinema.

hail, country – we are proud of you

Participation in anti-war actions – a criminal offence.

Calling for sanctions against Russia – a criminal offence.

Disseminating information in disagreement with the Kremlin – a criminal offence.

I catch myself thinking I don't want to leave the special detention centre. To leave here is scary.

On the bright side, I'm not exercising alone anymore. Now I'm also training the girls. It's good to be needed. It's good when we need each other here.

But fear paralyses. I'm not afraid to go to prison, though of course I don't want to go, I'm afraid of what will happen to my family, to my mother, to my son. If I did go, I don't know if I'll ever see her again. Horror. What will be left of me, what will be left of all of us after this war?

> *'The special military operation of the Russian Armed Forces in Ukraine is proceeding strictly in accordance with the schedule, according to the plan, all the set tasks are being fulfilled.'*
> – Putin, 3 March

I go downstairs escorted by a security guard – the same one who a fortnight ago was laughing and asking about the protests. Now this twenty-year-old is scared and therefore trying to be tougher. Others aren't trying, they are walking around wide-eyed with confusion. I've never seen eyes like that before.

– This is just the beginning, man, says Grisha the medic.

scary to leave

'*Let's assume that you will get out this time. Let's sit tight, I don't think there's any point in a legal exit anymore, because re-entry under Putin's rule will only lead to prison anyway.*
Even if we don't escape from a sentence, there is nothing to prevent them from testing new and wonderful articles of the criminal code on us, so I think it's inevitable. We leave – and don't come back. We stay – and don't attract attention.
But! The important thing is that this is Putin's regime. There's a feeling that it won't last long, but the fall will be painful. There's this thing in video games: when the boss takes a heavy blow or is killed, he emits a shockwave, which doesn't hit a specific target, but all those nearby within a certain radius. It's called aoe – area of effect. People need to get out of the way in time. In this situation, it seems to me, we need to get out of the way, wait it out, and return.'

– Lucy

wait it out and return

Nikita comes to visit, hands me a letter from Lucy and says, 'So many people have become fascists in just a few days. Yogis, priests, other dudes. And everybody was amazed when it happened to Germany – how they arrived at fascism in just ten years. In just half a week, half the country has revealed themselves.'

Hundreds of companies are leaving the market.

Thousands of jobs lost.

And the number of fascists is increasing.

fascist triumph

'Children from a hospice in Kazan formed the letter Z in support of the special military operation in Ukraine.'

ins.ru – 5 March

The new symbol of war is the letter Z. 'Z' – sprayed from a paint can on Russian tanks going to kill in Ukraine. 'Z' is starting to multiply in Russian cities. Posters, stickers on cars, buses, tram stops and telegraph poles. To post 'Z' on your social media is to support the war. The Kremlin is organizing flash mobs, forcing children, including dying children, students, school children and athletes, to form that letter. The letter of war. To show the rest of the world that everyone already supports it.

letter of war

A train of refugees arrives at Berlin railway station. The Ukrainian anthem is playing, people wait with flowers, smiles, tears and signs that state how many refugees they can accommodate in their homes. Putin has made more than a million Ukrainians refugees in a week.

'Let them learn from the dump of Europe,' gurgles a propagandist on the radio. 'Ukraine doesn't need them.'

Now the only way we can find out anything about what's going on outside is by sifting the vomit of propaganda through a sieve. And we want to know.

vomit

After listening to 'regular Russian news' for just three days, one begins to wonder what is left of a person if they listen exclusively to it.

' *"Mediazona" is blocked in the Russian Federation.'*

We go out into the exercise yard. The mustard wall is covered in maroon blotches. The red-haired Major Goldobina has personally painted over our protest inscriptions. Instead of the words 'No to War', instead of 'Pussy Riot', instead of all our names – maroon stains. And the cold of March. Ice crunching under our feet. We walk in a circle. After a few minutes of silence, one of us – Sasha – takes a marker out of her pocket, goes to the wall and writes between the maroon stains, 'You can't erase us.'

– Well done! Keep fighting! shouts a man from above.

It's a voice from cell no. 2 – the one from where Sasha waved at us from the window during the summer's arrest carousels. Now Alexei Gorinov is sitting in this cell for thirty days. A municipal deputy. On the day the war started, he came out to picket.

Tech companies and clothing brands are leaving the market one by one. Cancel Culture in action – cancelling Russia the aggressor. And my Russia is in jail. But you'll be sure to hear about it.

you can't erase us

That spring, Alexei Gorinov will be sentenced to eight years in a penal colony. At a meeting of municipal deputies, he will call the war a 'war' rather than a 'special military operation' and say that holding a district competition for children's drawings while the Russian army has already killed more than a hundred Ukrainian children is a feast during the famine. He will be arrested for denunciation a week later. On the day of the verdict, standing in the court cage he will take out a piece of paper, and put it against the glass. Like a solitary picket. On the piece of paper will be written:

do you still need this war?

Of course, you can try to leave the house, try to get your passport and think things over calmly, but there are no guarantees that they will let you do that. And even if everything collapses here soon, nobody will let out political prisoners overnight. I won't abandon you, if there is a new case, I will take care of you and your family as much as I can, but I really wouldn't want that, everyone needs you to be free! It does not mean that you aren't needed behind bars, but it is still better to be free!

They beat people brutally at the protests and in police stations the cops have reached Belarusian levels. Here is a transcript of an audio recording from Brateevo police station:

Police officer: Look at her, I think she's getting kicks out of the fact that we're fucking her up.

Police officer: Look at her.

Police officer: She's fucking scum! A marginal! Putin fucking told us to fucking kill them. Motherfuckers.

Detainee: Wow.

Police officer: Putin is on our side. You are enemies of Russia. You're fucking enemies of the people. Now we'll fucking kill you here and that's it. It's a done deal. We'll get a bonus for this.

There's 13,000 detainees in Russia, there's a new series of criminal cases ahead.

The hate is overwhelming, I don't know how to live like this, there's a permanent lump in my throat, every second thought I have breaks the Criminal Code.

– Lucy

hatred overwhelms

The wall in the exercise yard has become grey. It turns out that at night Major Goldobina made the duty officer wear a protective suit left over from the pandemic and ordered him to repaint the entire courtyard grey. To paint over the maroon stains. Our beloved mustard is now also turned a shade of grey.

The first time I've dreamed about cops in years. Chasing me for a new crime. I ache at the thought of Lucy leaving, I'm scared that I won't be able to see my family – both if I go to jail for a long time and if I leave. 'You're killing yourself,' says Almaza the gypsy woman.

'Don't go to the penal colony, don't go,' she says.

A bright blue sky. More than 250 companies have suspended operations in Russia. Queues at a McDonald's. Which is also leaving. Some pharmacies are running out of insulin.

The cell door is opening.

– Alyokhina, with your things to another cell.
– Why?
– Warden's orders.
– I'm not going.
– Then the other five of you need to leave, and you'll sit in the canteen until Alyokhina moves out.
– We're not going. You'll have to take us out by force.
– You're disobeying orders!

The fog in my head clears and I see myself talking calmly to the yelling cop, I look at the girls – who, for the first time, have been threatened with new arrest days – refuse one after the other to go to the canteen, as calmly as I did. I can hardly hold back my tears, and say, 'Thank you.'

with your things

I don't know whether this is a directive from above or an 'initiative' of the red-haired major. I don't know why they want to move me to another cell. I ask questions and all I hear in reply is 'It's a direct order from a superior.'

A little later we start to think, not without reason, that there is a wiretap in the cell where they want to transfer me. We are right to think so, because everything we discuss will somehow become known to the Centre E cops.

'Kind duty guard' Seryozha opens the door of our cell and says:

- Masha, you can take one girl with you. Choose.
- I won't choose and I won't go.
- The boss said to transfer just you and I'm giving you a choice – take whoever you want.
- That's the choice in Russia. Choose your cellmate.
- So?
- I don't need that choice, thank you.

choice of cellmate

Half an hour later, the yelling guard and Seryozha enter the cell. They lift me off the bunk with the mattress. They carry me on the mattress across the corridor. To another cell. They're laughing. 'Fuck, I've been working here thirty years. I never thought I'd be doing this shit.'

- Why can't you walk yourself?
- So you can feel the shit you're being told to do.

The door slams. It slams several times. That's Sasha being transferred after me. For arguing the loudest. We make coffee. We do our evening workout. At midnight, the anthem comes on the radio again. We turn up the volume and put the radio on the window with bars.

> 'The eternal union of brothers' nations,
> Given by ancestors the people's wisdom!
> Long live our land! We are proud of you!'

It's especially bitter now. Sasha says before we sleep, 'They've forbidden people from talking about us, those of us imprisoned for opposing the war. But we are paying the price for this war, atoning for its sins by being in prison – my mother told me.'

redeem the sins

In the evening, they take me to the ground floor, to the visiting room. It's the only room with shabby walls and a toilet in the corner.

'A report will be filed on you,' says the district cop. Armageddon all around, but here everything is steady. The report 'for resisting the police' has been written by the 'kind duty guard Seryozha'. A little later he'll say he was forced to do it. The red-haired supervisor, Goldobina, made him. I don't have the strength to sympathize, but I don't feel disgust either. There's a lot of fatigue. The report means another fifteen detention days. I'm not leaving the special detention centre. The new days were arranged with the grey van of cops at the gate without show. No cameras. In silence.

i will not leave

The SIM cards I use stop working.

One SIM card is enough for only one call. No matter how much credit is on it, you can't make another call after the first one. Somehow it gets cut off. The first time, I thought it was random.

After a few SIMs died after just one call, I realized it wasn't. Lucy hands over a whole pack of SIMs. To make sure they don't run out.

News of the war, which propaganda is silent about, I get on my phone.

The rouble is depreciating, the dollar is rising, the government continues to seize the property of companies that have left Russia. I don't feel any of what is happening out there. I don't see queues at ATMs, I don't know what they're talking about in bars.

whole life under putin

A non-political woman is brought to our cell no. 7. Her name is Lisa.

- Wow, it's like a TV series in here, she says, looking around.
- Only I don't know when and what the last episode will be, I want to reply, but I catch myself wavering, staring at the wall.

Lisa is twenty-two years old and has lived her whole life under Putin. Her dad watches TV, her mum repeats what her dad says. One of her friends is a conscript fighting for the 'Russians' in Ukraine, another friend is fighting for Ukraine. She doesn't talk about politics with friends. They don't go to protests. She manages a small bar with a hookah lounge in the Moscow suburbs, she has thin arms with tattoo sleeves and a live iguana at home – she draws it on a sketchpad as she misses it. On 8 March, she drove her friends while drunk – ten detention days. And so she finds herself in a special detention centre filled with politicals.

- Pussy Riot – are they the ones who danced naked in the cathedral?
- No – I smile – we were not naked.

Propaganda has done everything so that no one hears us, propaganda has done everything so that the country does not know itself. So that people like Lisa – who have seen nothing but Putin – cannot allow themselves to think that they can change anything. There are many Lisas. But while we are in a cell together, I want to tell her what really happens.

doesn't know herself

Russia has listed Facebook and Instagram as extremist and banned them.

Bingo. Technically, now every person who has an account on Insta can go to jail for extremism.

Now, to be on these social networks you need to download a VPN. People are moving to Telegram and Russian Facebook – 'Vkontakte'. The founder of both platforms – Pavel Durov – was forced out of the country; Vkontakte was handed over to one of Putin's oligarchs. Vkontakte is controlled by the FSB, and personal correspondence becomes the basis of criminal cases.

Radio propaganda says from morning till night that hundreds of companies leaving is not a problem and repeats the word 'import substitution' like a mantra.

The news from hell comes one report after another. Their quantity exceeds all permissible limits. You get tired of asking yourself, 'Where do we go from here?' because all your experience screams that there's more where that came from. It reminds you of a dark Russian joke: 'When I thought we had hit the bottom, there was a knock from down below.' You can't believe it's real. Only the cell seems real. The cell is definitely real, the rest is not.

more hell

*'Russian people will always be able to distinguish the true
patriots from the scum and the traitors, and just to spit them
out like a midge that accidentally flew into their mouths. I am
convinced that this natural and necessary self-cleansing of
society will only strengthen our country.'*

– Putin, 16 March

In a matter of months, the country will be 'cleansed' of people like us. The loudest of those left in the country will be jailed for much longer than our two-year sentence. And everyone else? . . .

They will adapt and move on with their lives.

More than half of Russians do not have and never have had a passport; why would they need one if they have no money to go to Europe? There's no time to think about 'what country I would like to live in' – it's about survival. To believe what is happening is a 'disaster' is a privilege available to those who don't have to survive 24/7.

'Take my number, take me with you to a protest,' Lisa says.

A blue jacket hangs on a hook against the blue wall. I think I'll never get out of here. Sasha, on the other hand, did tonight. On her first free evening after fifteen detention days, she plans to read the real news, drink beer and cry.

My mum comes to visit me and tells me that a former colleague, an elderly German computer programmer, has written to her: 'Natalia, at this difficult time, I remember that you and I were friends and I hope we will continue to be, no matter what.' She tells me this on the verge of crying. A German whose parents lived under the Nazis writes to my mum, whose parents defeated the Nazis and whose president has ushered in a new era of Nazism.

no matter what

- There's a woman from Channel 1 who ran onto live TV with a 'No to War' sign!
- No way!!
- Everyone's talking about it. Her name is Marina Ovsyannikova. It's the only news that's made me happy lately.

Court. Fifteen days – resisting police. Nothing new. Everyone wants it over quickly – the judge, the prosecutor, the red-haired major.

I don't have time to go into the cell. The door opens, the duty officer informs me that I'm going to Sakharovo for the latest set of detention days. A car arrives. Two cops. We drive. At Sakharovo there's a queue of police cars. A queue of five or six hours. Inside the cars are activists who came out against the war. It's cold and it's a long wait. I persuade the cops to go for pizza. Other cops hold a place for our car in the queue. And then they take me to a search room.

- Take off your underwear and trousers.
- No, and I won't go into a room with a video camera either.
- Take them off.
- No.
- Then we won't admit you to the special detention centre today! Take her back.

The faces of my cops fall, they have waited in the queue for five hours. 'Maybe you should take them off after all,' one of them says, realizing as he says it that I won't. They lead me back to the car. In silence. All the way we drive in silence too. There's no trace of the pizza vibe left. I'll spend the night in the police station cage. In the morning, there's a second attempt.

This time they're taking me in handcuffs. This is in revenge for yesterday. All the cops come out to look at me from their police cars, I'm walking with a black suitcase on wheels, a cop is carrying my bag of strawberries. The cop nicknamed Prince Harry crosses himself at the sight of me.

There are ten people in the cell, all politicals. We sit in a circle on the floor at night after lights out. We share our thoughts. We call it a circle of support. I'm proud to see these girls. Tonight, for me, they are the best people in Russia. Cell no. 12.

ward no. 12

'*The Russians have dropped a powerful bomb on the Mariupol Theatre. Thousands of citizens, mainly mothers with children are hiding there from the shelling, and it is not known how many people have died under the rubble. Because of the constant shelling, it is impossible to remove the debris.*'

– Telegram News, 16 March

We sit down to listen to the news every hour. We gather around the radio on my bed. Radio propaganda number one, two and three. Sakharovo is far from the city. To catch even that news, you have to hold the receiver at different angles with the antenna stretched out. We twist and turn the radio, not wanting to miss any of the news hidden in the words.

We look around wide-eyed. None of us still believes this war. No one can believe it's really happening. Propagandists use phrases like 'final decision' to explain the occupation of new regions of Ukraine.

russian spring

– You shouted in your sleep again, the girls say.
– Shouted what?
– Don't touch!

For the inscription 'No to War', administrative and criminal sentences are given.

That's why only fascism growing like yeast becomes visible throughout the city. Z on car windows and windowpanes. The cops have been issued with Z patches. There are photos of children from kindergartens and even nursery groups who were given posters with Z and who formed the letter itself.

Russia has withdrawn from the Council of Europe, which means that no political prisoner, or any prisoner who has been subjected to unlawful persecution or torture, will receive compensation according to the ECHR guidelines.

During my fifteen minutes of phone time, Yana calls me; she's an eighteen-year-old girl with white curls who left our cell yesterday. She was locked up for wearing a Pussy Riot jacket from Nadya's collection.

– It's hard for me, she says. Nothing has changed. I did my detention days, I got out, and nothing has changed at all.

Each of us has come up against this thought an infinite number of times, it burns out the will to resist, suppresses the will. Nothing has changed at all. I smile only because I know I will write these words down and try very hard to make sure you, the reader, read them.

hard for me

It's harder for those on the outside. The endless doom scrolling, the panic of 'urgently leaving before the Iron Curtain comes down', the city changing before their eyes, not being clear where the train is headed – but it's clear that it's on fire.

Lucy comes to see me with Rita. The sad but determined voice of a person who is leaving. Of someone who does not know what will happen next, but does not intend to become a silent witness to a war.

18 March. On this day – eight years ago – Putin annexed Crimea. While revolution rumbled in Kyiv, the Russian army marched into Ukraine and waged war in the east. Two hundred thousand people are brought from the regions to the stadium to celebrate the 'triumph of Russian peace'. St George's ribbons are being handed out. This year is the Z edition. This year against the backdrop of a new, full-scale war, the purpose of which is to destroy Ukraine in principle.

'For a world without Nazism' – that's the name of the celebration.

Putin quotes the Bible: 'There is no greater love than this – that a man should lay down his life for his friends' (John 15:13). This is how he explains how a person ends up a Cargo 200.

train on fire

In the evening, we sit in our circle of support, discussing what needs to be done to prevent the country from turning into the Third Reich. Z banners cover squares and house façades, cities not living but surviving, observing a new round of 'greatness' thrown to them like a bone to gnaw on.

And the 'Russian world' goes on. Russian troops are advancing deep into Ukrainian Mariupol. The city on the Azov Sea, home to half a million people – green and sunny – will be turned into a skeleton within three months of war.

When the Russian army dropped a bomb on Mariupol Theatre, where entire families with children – about a thousand people – were hiding, a boy, Sasha, and his mother were near the stage. When he came round, he saw the sky instead of the ceiling. When he started calling for his mum, he realized that his mum was gone.

screams of mariupol

Eighty days of a full blockade. People in basements, melted snow instead of water, mass graves in the yards of ordinary high-rises, corpses in shopping centres, on the streets, unburied, on the roads, trying to get out, to get out of the house that is becoming a cemetery.

The last stronghold in Mariupol's defence is the Azovstal plant. The industrial giant of the Soviet Union. Eleven square kilometres. Twenty-five times the size of the Vatican. The Ukrainian military is occupying Azovstal to hold Mariupol's defences for as long as possible. The longer they hold, the longer they can draw off Russian forces. And thus save time for others. An extensive network of tunnels. People rotting alive.

Only bandages and water – when the bottled water ran out, they shot at the pipes and drank from there.

Three months of defending. Whoever survives will be taken prisoner. Azovstal defenders will be starved and tortured in Russian prisons. Almost 2,500 people. They will be taken out and locked up in the barracks of penal colony no. 120 in occupied Olenivka, which has been turned into a filtration camp.

azovstal

In a month's time, penal colony no. 120 will be hit by a Russian missile. Fifty-four defenders of Mariupol will be burnt alive, locked in prison cells. Other prisoners from Mariupol will be exchanged in the next few years and return to Ukraine emaciated, as if they'd been in a concentration camp.

The occupiers will do everything to erase the memory of their war crimes. The theatre will be covered with a false façade and then demolished. The apartments of Ukrainians who died or became refugees will be auctioned off and advertised as 'a great investment by the sea'. More than half of Mariupol's residents will become refugees. Judges and investigators will be invited from the Russian regions to work in the occupied territories for triple their salary. Russia will appoint Grozny, the capital of Russian republic Chechnya, as Mariupol's sister city.

twin city

It's out there, somewhere.
bombing again,
There's someone out there hiding their boys,

There's someone crying for a hundred days
There's someone else,
Not you,
Not you,
It's not here,
This dead house.

– Zhenya Berkovich

Today in the cell – a circle of poems. Anti-war poems will also become a crime. Evgenia Berkovich, Zhenya from cell no. 6, who came out on the first day of the war with a 'No to War' poster, who every day reads us a fairy-tale about how the Tsar was overthrown, mother of two adopted children, will be arrested for her poetry in a year's time.

The sentence is six years in prison. Officially not for anti-war poetry, which will become increasingly popular. Officially for 'justification of terrorism' in her play *Finist Yasny Sokol*. Lucy had taken me to see this play; we had kissed in the dressing room and had drunk wine, we had gone to visit friends and I had sat in the kitchen with my broken bandaged arm. And then, as if on fast-forward, Zhenya got fifteen days; a year later, Zhenya gets six years.

fairy-tale

Yana is a psychologist. Day after day, since the beginning of the war, her clients have been leaving the country. She says she began to regret that she was not allowed to cry during a session, she only felt better when she went out to picket. Tomorrow her fifteen detention days will end. 'We're all living through violence and we're told, "It's your own fault."' She quotes an anti-war letter from her community.

While we are here in the special detention centre – we feel no shame. It's as if now, in Russia, the only honest decision is to go to jail. Tell the truth and go to jail. Speak out against the war and go to jail. Not everyone wants to leave jail. Most of us just don't know what to do out there.

speak out and be in jail

When Lucy says she's leaving, it hurts.

– I don't know if I can bear to see you packing – I can't.
– You won't see it.

They write to tell me, 'Leave as soon as possible.' I am not ready to decide when and how to leave. I don't know what to get ready for. And the more I am asked, the more I am scared, the more I don't know. Dear God, please help me see which way to go. So that I will go where I haven't been yet, so that everything will work out, so that my loved ones stay alive.

That's what I say every time I go to bed. Not only that, I say other things too. To myself. Not out loud.

you won't see

Navalny, who is already in a penal colony, is given another nine years. To avoid publicity, the trial was held at the colony. The police detained the lawyers who were giving comments to journalists at the colony gates.

'I will use the war as a metaphor for your court cases – it is also built on lies, blatant lies. A few months ago, every TV report said that we would never send troops to Ukraine. Months of

lies – and then, at the click of a button, they brought troops.
The government is trying to make the entire nation become
like goldfish and not remember anything that happened
yesterday. But I am not a goldfish, I remember how in 2013
Russia opened a NATO base in the city of Ulyanovsk; everyone
was happy. And now these same people are saying that we
should arrange a bloodbath because NATO is an enemy. Brazen
lies in every word, ignoring what was said yesterday.
Of course, you will suffer a historic defeat both here and in this
stupid war that you started. It has neither purpose nor meaning.
You took forty million people and declared them Nazis. Imagine
a person living in Kharkiv, for example, a judge. He is going to
take his child to kindergarten in the morning, and one fine day, on
24 February, he is called a Nazi, and a missile kills his child.'
– Text based on Navalny's statement to the prison court on 24 May 2022

People are depressed and apathetic, nobody knows what will happen next.

I've taken two pills of Atarax. Last night I didn't sleep till morning. It's like a wooden shutter has been opened in my chest and it's slamming. It slams all the time.

short memory

Poland handed a note to the Russian ambassador and expelled all Russian diplomats from the country. The night before, smoke was billowing from the Russian embassy in Warsaw. They were burning documents.

I have never been so impatient to hear the news. There are three of us politicals left and we cling to the radio, catching one wave of propaganda after another. We swear at it, and then we tune in again. And we wait. I don't know what we're waiting for, maybe we just can't tear ourselves away, or maybe we're waiting to be told at last 'ENOUGH. IT'S ALL OVER.'

oksana

I can't sleep again until morning. A month has passed since the beginning of the war. I'm talking to Lucy on the phone:

- You didn't sleep either? Why?
- Oksana, Lucy answers in a depressed voice.
- What about Oksana? Why doesn't anyone tell me anything?
- Oksana has died.

She cared for everyone. Sincerely, from the bottom of her heart. A girl of infinite kindness – Oksana Baulina.

A journalist who left *Glamour* magazine to become part of Navalny's team. 'I can't write about underwear and make-up when my election was stolen.' When Navalny's anti-corruption fund was declared extremist, she left Russia. To avoid going to jail. To keep working.

She goes to the war immediately, in the first month. To Kyiv. To a shopping centre burned down by a Russian missile. To do a story. Without body armour. A second Russian missile hits the same place.

She urged us to leave the country, was worried, supportive. She became a friend. February – I am in the special detention centre and answer her questions about 'Punk Prayer'. March – at night in Kyiv a missile strikes. And a friend is gone.

We are silent for half a day. We can't find the words. Because there aren't any. Damn you, for driving away and killing the best.

fuck the war

An hour before leaving, the parachutist Masha, a short woman from a protest Christian community, writes 'No to War' in the snow with her boot. The guard on shift today is a loyalist. Putin saluting. In a flash, she runs to the bars in the exercise yard with a video camera. She yells, 'Walk's over!'

- What, are you afraid of writing in the snow?
- You're breaking the rules.
- What article and what rule?
- I don't know them by heart.

They take Masha away. We're covering the whole yard with the inscriptions 'No to War', 'Z is the new swastika', 'Enough lying'.

- Do you want to be detained again? It's not enough for you? yells the loyalist.
- I'll be out, but you'll be jailed for ten years.
- Why ten?
- How long till you retire?
- Seven.

After she names this figure, she shovels the snow more diligently than before. And new snow continues to fall through the bars – on her head, on our heads, on the entire exercise yard of the special detention centre.

not enough for you?

'I might not have got out today,' I say to the lawyer. Earlier the officer on duty had taken me out of my cell and told me that the colonels were demanding that another report on resisting the police be filed for me not undressing during the search.

He took me out and said, 'I'm not going to write a report. Not doing it. Period.'

And here I was, thinking, 'There was our Seryozha with tattoos, who smiled and told good jokes, and then went and signed the report for my next detention days, and here is this guy – number so-and-so – I don't even remember his badge number, not even his name. And he refused.'

And that's why we're going home now.

the one who didn't shoot

The outside of Sakharovo is painted yellow and blue – the colours of Ukraine, the colours of protest. The special detention centre is painted in the colours that they put you in a special detention centre for. I come out with shoelaces made of wet wipes and a belt made of disposable sheets. I'm met by my mum and the lawyer. And two other women holding yellow and blue balloons. One of them is the widow of a political prisoner who was beaten so badly in the penal colony that he died shortly after his release.

I get in the car and drive home. I go to Lucy's apartment, to our home. I go in and she says, 'I've just been issued a visa. I'm leaving the day after tomorrow.' I shout that I don't want to know that and I go to get cigarettes. This is my protest: to go I go to Lucy's apartment, to our home. I go in, she says, 'I'm leaving tomorrow.' She is facing the threat of a new criminal case. I shout that I won't want to know that and I go to get cigarettes. This is my protest: to go out for cigarettes, but what else can I do? She will later be sentenced to six years in absentia. I don't sleep that night, although I take sleeping pills. I am cold, although I sit in a hot bath, twice, three times, and I'm still cold. I've smoked almost all my cigarettes. I don't know how to let her go. I feel terrible and scared. Very terrible and very scared. I've never felt so terrible and so scared in any prison, and I can't say what it is that scares me, and I wake her up from her sleep by being near her, talking and just being there, and she can't answer, and then I talk louder and more, and then I realize that what I'm saying is separate from her and what I'm looking at is separate, and I'm only looking at a pair of scissors. I only stop talking when I pick them up.

I take a pair of scissors and cut off my bracelet. I've been wanting to do this for a year. That's it, I'm going to jail, I think, and I won't see her leave. That's it, they'll come and see the boxes and realize what's happening and won't let me leave, Lucy thinks.

cutting off the bracelet

An hour goes by. No one comes. We don't talk. We're hurt that neither of us cares about the other's pain. This happens so often in our country. Have we become like them? She says she needs to sleep for at least half an hour more. And despite the morning and the sun, it's as if she's tired of it all too. And then I hug her and she also starts to cry. Because I guess no one wants to leave anyone behind.

o cops. o calls to the fsinphone.

o responses.

Then: 'Hello, what happened to your bracelet?'

'I cut it off and threw it away.'

'Well, come back at 5 p.m. and we'll put a new one on.'

It's 10 a.m. You can get to another country by 5 p.m. Shock. Laughter. Shock. Red eyes from crying, both of us.

15.

Delivery Club

'Don't sell out your country, collaborator' is written on the apartment door. A large poster stuck down with superglue. The Centre E cops did it. In the middle – a photo of Lucy; on either side – Article 207 and Article 280 of the Criminal Code of the Russian Federation. Articles recently introduced.

- You are also against it? our neighbour asks in a whisper.
- Against what? I raise my head.
- Against . . . the special military operation. She lowers her head.

It's the last evening. Our neighbour gives us a scraper. I need to take down the poster from the front door. The door to the apartment that can be called ours.

in a whisper

In Russia, military censorship has begun. New criminal articles deal the final blow to free speech.

Art. 207.3 Criminal Code of the Russian Federation: 'Public dissemination of knowingly false information about the use of the Armed Forces of the Russian Federation.' Maximum jail term – up to 15 years.

Art. 280.3 Criminal Code of the Russian Federation: 'Public actions aimed at discrediting the use of the Armed Forces of the Russian Federation.' Maximum jail term – up to 7 years.

Words that appear more than five times in indictments for anti-war criminal cases. Combine these words into sentences, and you place yourself outside the law:

Russia, Ukraine, Putin, war, call, kill, soldiers, liberators, crime, hero, violence, occupier, Russian, peace, world, destroy, country, shelling, inhabitants, terror, children, bombing, support, fascism, capture, Kyiv, set on fire, glory, freedom, die.

military censorship

We scrub down the door and wash the floor.
In her passport – a visa.
On my leg – a new ankle bracelet.
We haven't slept and the whole day has felt more surreal as a result. The March sun shone in the afternoon. We went together to the embassy. Went together across the square. Opposite on the square – the Supreme Court building. With a flagpole. The same building from the rainbow action. On the flagpole, the flag of Russia – the same flag, under which the Russian army is now killing people.

right now

– What have you done with the bracelet, where is it? asks Inspector Ekaterina.
– I cut it off and threw it out of the window.
– No more throwing away, Maria Vladimirovna.

I want to go on tour and help Ukraine. I write an explanation and argue with the inspector. 'If you jail me straight away, I'll serve my term. Twenty-one days in jail – not a problem.'

– We can't jail you now, Maria Vladimirovna. There is a procedure. We need to notify the court that you have committed a violation for the third time. Then two weeks before the hearing, the court has to notify you that it intends to put you in jail.
– Then I'll leave.
– Why are you telling ME this?
– So that you know the truth.

I am led into a room with a tall shelving unit. On the shelves are boxes. In the boxes are new ankle bracelets. A uniformed assistant to the inspector takes out one of the boxes. Puts a new bracelet on me. On the wall is a portrait of Dzerzhinsky.
'So you like Dzerzhinsky?' I ask.
'Of course I do.'

delivery club

A few minutes before Lucy walks out of that door and never walks through it again. The door that was broken down during the search, the door that I ran out of when I couldn't bear any more of her packing, the old sweet door that you could slip a power bank under. A red one.

Lucy is standing in a green uniform. 'Delivery Club'. A uniform for food delivery couriers. She bought it on a used goods website. It's the perfect disguise – you're visible from everywhere and invisible to all. Couriers go in and out of buildings, and nobody pays attention.

The uniform consists of a winter jacket with a hood, capable of withstanding freezing temperatures, a large thermal bag slung over the shoulder, and even a signature mask – made during the time of Covid. She wants me to follow her out of the country. To save me from prison.

In her hands a small crate with Mr Rat. Now Lucy puts him into a thermal bag on her back, walks through the door and is leaving Russia.

to go free

What is 'to go free'? It is to move from cell no. 12 to apartment no. 22.

I am left in this apartment alone.

At night, I see photos from Bucha – a suburb of Kyiv. Bodies.

Bodies of peaceful inhabitants. Someone had been riding a bicycle. Someone was mixed up with things. Children.

That's what to go free means – to become numb.

bucha

Putin was planning a blitzkrieg – to take 'Kyiv in three days'. Like Crimea. He was sure that resistance would be minimal. It was the opposite. As the Russian army advanced on the Ukrainian capital, President Zelenskyy gave the order to distribute weapons to everyone who was ready to take them and go to defend their country. Thousands signed up for the Territorial Defence Force. A month later, the Russian army retreated. The Ukrainians returned to their 'de-occupied' lands. What they saw was a shock. Something beyond words. One of these towns was Bucha.

road of death

Thirty-three days of Russian occupation. People not long before alive and peaceful – now bodies with hands tied behind their back. They were left lying in backyards. 'They gave us the order to shoot – civilians, not civilians, fuck it!' is how soldiers explained their killings to their relatives. They called them from the phones of the peaceful inhabitants they had killed. They called it 'cleaning up'.

I smoke the second pack unconsciously. And I look at the photos again. For hours. People call from various countries. We talk for hours about what happened to Russia. I'm afraid to say the most important thing out loud – a verdict. On all of us. I'm not sure Russia has the right to exist after this.

right to exist

Three days in the apartment and that's it – it's become frightening to leave it. Surveillance everywhere. Each grey and black car seems strange.

Before the war, Filipp and I used to go to the cinema. Now foreign film companies are, en masse, revoking licences to show their films in Russia. So Filipp and I watch films at home. We watch films, but I can't get rid of a feeling of shame. I can't get out of my head the dozens of tormented, raped, murdered people I saw in the photos from Bucha. God, how to see this. It's impossible not to look.

'They've got a carcass in the window of the shawarma shop, and I keep thinking it's a burnt body from a tank,' Olya, my nationalist friend from prison, says. I don't want to talk to her. She doesn't want to talk to me either. We can both see that we're enemies of each other. Horror and disgust. Words sticking in the throat. Some far-off part of my consciousness doesn't want to believe that the girl I met in the colony is really a fascist.

'They've also vandalized my door,' says Rita on the chat.

With the inscription 'We will end this war.' In white spray paint.

mark of a traitor

This is an order to pit people against each other. Once a full-scale war starts, it is especially important to prevent people from uniting against the war. So that neighbours can see who the 'traitor' is, so that the 'traitors' keep quiet, so that denunciations of new 'traitors' continue.

Activists' doors are marked all over Russia. Now if you don't support bombs falling on a neighbouring peaceful country, you are a traitor.

> *Don't betray the Motherland Dima – door of activist Dima*
> *Ivanov in Moscow*
> *A traitor lives here – door of journalist Oksana Akmaeva in*
> *Kaliningrad.*
> *Don't sell out the motherland bitch – door of activist Olga*
> *Misik in Moscow.*
> *A Finnish Nazi lives here! We will not forgive Nazism – door*
> *of activist Darya Kheikinen in St Petersburg*
> *Beware! A traitor to the MOTHERLAND lives here!!!! –*
> *door of shop owner Dmitri Skurikhin in the Leningrad region.*

here lives

I'm going to the funeral. It is forbidden. The crematorium is beyond the city limits. I'm being taken there by war journalist Masha – ten years ago she filmed our action in the cathedral.

Oksana's body has completed its journey. From Kyiv, where she was killed by a rocket, to Poland, where 'Ave Maria' was played at her farewell, to this crematorium beyond Moscow.

Employees in green jackets slide the coffin out of a white car. Service hall. A photo of Oksana. When they open the coffin, everyone is in tears and I am too. Although she is intact. Both of body and face. Despite the make-up and the occasion, I am not afraid. It's like she's been asleep a long time. Her mother in a black dress places flowers from her legs to her chest, covers her hair, as if she is wrapping her, wrapping her body so she doesn't get cold. Everyone is silent. 'You can now share your memories of Oksana,' the crematorium employee says, interrupting the silence.

very brave

– Did you know she became a journalist because of
  your court case? someone says to me at the entrance.
– I didn't.
– She said that she was bored of writing beauty blogs
  and went to cover the Pussy Riot trial.

I run to the stall to buy two candles – blue and yellow. I ask for them to be given to her mother. I say, 'Light these near her photograph.' By the evening, I can still see the hands of the employee twisting the screws into the coffin and Oksana's direct gaze from the photo in this scene.

a view onto the scene

Anything that resembles Ukraine – a blue-yellow fence or blue-yellow trainers – is banned. Fences are repainted, they issue a fine for trainers. Blue-yellow seats in stadiums and blue-yellow roofs are dismantled.

In occupied Crimea, a girl with a blue-yellow manicure was taken to the FSB. Also, there, a neighbour denounced girls who sang the Ukrainian folk song 'Chervona Kalyna' at home. The folk song was branded an anthem of 'Nazis'. The girls were fined and made to apologize on camera.

'Snitch first before they snitch on you' – the Soviet formula for survival from 1937 – multiplied by 'the war that doesn't exist'.

torture for poems

'These are the stickers we use on the metro,' says Sasha, and shows me small, square, black and white 'No to War' stickers.

The last time I saw her was in Sakharovo. Then we were in the same cell, but now we are sitting in the kitchen, drinking tea. The second guest in this kitchen is Dima Ivanov, the creator of the student Telegram channel Protest MSU.

In two weeks' time, Dima will be detained as he is leaving an exam. For this very channel. Sentenced to eight and a half years under the Article 'fake news about the army'.

Six months later, a crowd of Centre E cops, operatives and a film crew from Ren-TV channel will burst into the flat of Sasha and her boyfriend, the poet Artem Kamardin.

kill me, militia

They will arrest Artem for his poems. He will be tortured and raped in a room. Rape with dumbbells, filmed on camera. He will be forced to apologize for his poems on his knees in a semi-conscious state. Sasha will be locked in a room next door – she will listen to his screams. She will be shown the rape video, with threats to do the same to her. They'll superglue these anti-war stickers to her face. And then tear them off, along with her eyebrows and hair.

Artem will propose to Sasha in court, standing in a glass cage. They'll have their wedding in jail. He'll be sentenced to seven years for 'activities against the security of the state.'

I look at the anti-war stickers. We are sitting in this kitchen and none of us wants to leave Russia.

where have you been these eight years?

Now they send inspectors to the apartment every day. The inspector rings the intercom, comes into the flat and takes a photo of me. It's a confirmation that everything's okay. The bracelet is in place. The fsinphone is in place. The convicted is also in place. It will be insurance for the future: if she does escape – we did what we could, we checked.

One of them comes in the morning. He takes the standard photo – reports. I can't stand it:

'Do you realize what you're doing? There's a war going on.'

'It's not a war. It's true there's a special military operation going on, we've been putting up with it for eight years. Where have you been these eight years?'

'Where have you been these eight years?' is a question that propaganda repeats every day. And repeated by everyone who watches it. Every day since 24 February. Daily bombings and occupation of new territories – they explain this by saying that for eight years Ukraine has been oppressing Russians, and the whole world has been silently watching this, and now, finally (!), the Russian army has come to the rescue of those it did not rescue eight years ago. In 2014.

I don't have the energy to continue this conversation. I point the inspector at the door.

– Don't come here and don't call. I won't open the door.

I know where I've been for eight years.

i know where i've been

– Masha, you're very emotional. You have your opinion, I have mine.
– Do you get your news from the TV?
– Yes.
– Throw the TV away, please.

Dad's arguing with me about the war. Dad talks about eight years too. Dad walks with his legs bent almost halfway. Dad sees things that aren't there. He has Parkinson's. We're sitting across the table from each other.

There are different medications by the bed – there's a red pool on the floor, one of the medications has spilled. A red pool and red drops. I take the bleach, I take the rubbing alcohol and rub it. Red pool and red drops.

I rub and rub and rub at this pool. Like it's going to make a difference.

rub and rub

They steal hairdryers, tablets, washing machines – they go into the homes of civilians and rob them. They send them as parcels to Russia. By post. Air conditioners, TVs, stealing cars, even taking cosmetics. Lipsticks and baby clothes.

The feeling of horror is replaced by a feeling of abomination. Videos of queues at the Belarusian post office, where provincial Russian Guard looters pack stolen goods from Ukrainians to send to their wives and mothers-in-law. Intercepted conversations from stolen mobiles: 'It's all coming to the house, my sweet, to the family.'

They talk about the 'great victory', referring to the major feat of soldiers in the Second World War. But there is no major feat in occupation, in looting, in killing neighbours who you earlier shared the same history with. After this, the 'Russian soldier' will never be considered a hero.

– Maria Vladimirovna, stop with the depression, put the tracker on charge. Please! Maria Vladimirovna!

please!

I'm scared to leave the house again. I message mum, she arrives. We get in a taxi. We go to the verdict of editors of student media who are being prosecuted for calls to rallies in support of Navalny. Firstly, to support them; secondly, to see the Russia I love. Mum sees it is important to me and comes with me.

– Your laces are interesting! says the driver.
– They're made from napkins.

Mum tries to tell me to 'shush' when I talk about prison. But I reckon there's nothing to be embarrassed about – we will talk about it.

I'm very anxious about leaving. I don't know when to leave and if I should go at all. Mum sits opposite and listens. This rarely happens. When I go to get passport photos, she's waiting for me in the playground – on a big wooden dachshund dog. I look at her and remember this moment.

- What do they say in your courtyard? I ask my mum.
  Every morning and evening she walks there with her dog Nicole and with the dog owners of the neighbourhood.
- They don't talk about the war.
- At all?
- Who wants to admit that they are living under a new Hitler?

i watch and remember

Totalitarian societies are often depicted surrounded by a wall. A wall is one of the most simple, clear and easily understood metaphors. Now the feeling is not of a city, not of a country surrounded by a wall, now the feeling is of bricks in people's eyes. And in their mouth.

Mum tries to feed me. I can't eat, I can't sleep. I just lie there and watch. I can't decide which is best. I'm completely burnt out. The panic attack starts by night-time. I move boxes from our apartment to my mum's. And then I return to the fsinphone. Back to the Arbat.

The CIA says Putin might hit the nuclear button. I'm studying the radius of a nuclear strike.

News reports that the warship *Moscow* has been hit.
The Russian warship has finally been sent to hell.

moscow *at the bottom*

Russian warship: Snake Island, I, Russian warship,
repeat the offer: lay down your arms and surrender, or you will
be bombed. Do you understand? Do you copy?
Ukrainian border guard: Russian warship, go fuck yourself!

24 February. The first day of full-scale war. The Russian warship *Moscow* approaches Snake Island. The Black Sea. Doomed to captivity and torture, the Ukrainian border guard say a phrase that will become one of the main slogans of their nation for the next few years: Russian warship, go fuck yourself!

But warship *Moscow* will not be forgotten. Within a month and a half, Ukraine will sink the pride of the Russian naval fleet. Together with the ship, the crew will go to the bottom of the Black Sea. Including conscripts. Nineteen-year-old boys, about whom Putin lied when he said they would never be involved in military operations.

The Ministry of Defence will not admit that the 'pride of the Russian Navy' was sunk by Ukrainians. They will make up a version that a fire started on the warship, the crew was evacuated and there was no loss of life. Relatives will be told that their children are missing. On the high seas.

'And all this, all this hell, is just to restore the Soviet Union,' I say to Olya. 'But what has died cannot be brought back to life.'

And this seems to be the first thing she doesn't argue with.

what has died cannot be brought back

I take white paint and paint over the barrel of the gun. The black drawing that Olya did on the whole wall when we were renovating. To paint over the black barrel, which points straight at you, needs several coats of white paint. Each coat takes two hours to dry. That's what she said. I can't wait two hours. I do coat after coat until there's nothing left from the hand to the end of the barrel. I'm relieved. I don't know why. Maybe because, when I look up from my phone full of images of dead bodies, I no longer see the gun pointing at me, no matter what corner of the room I'm in.

The apartment needs to be rented out. The court date is coming up. After cutting off the bracelet, my punishment should be changed from forty-two days of limitations to my freedom to twenty-one days in jail. That's what I wanted when I cut it off. To reduce my punishment. To serve the rest of it and be free to leave. Leave in order to return. I never wanted to leave for ever.

leave for ever

'You do realize that all this makes no sense at all?' I say to Inspector Ekaterina.

Morning. The Inspectorate. Scheduled box-ticking. Feeling like I'm some idiot who's doing pointless shit. Ticking, paperwork, offices. At least they get paid for it and work towards their pensions. But with my own feet I stamp into this office, which now – in the second month of the war – seems to make no sense at all.

Afternoon. The embassy. The faces of those waiting in the

queue at the embassy are not the same as those of the pedestrians on the street – heavy faces. I have found out that the court won't return my passport. Even if I serve out my sentence. The embassy employees promise to print out a visa on A4 paper. A cop at the exit pretends to be conducting a 'document check' and tries to take away my only ID card. I try to hide in the embassy.

– We know who you are, we won't detain you, the cop tries to convince me.

But it's one of the few times when that line doesn't bring a smile to my face. Only disgust. I don't care who the man with the Russian epaulettes is. All I see are epaulettes.

z for a world without nazism

A Z rally at the stadium. One year later the hosts of the Nazi celebration will invite a fighter with the call sign 'Angel' to the stage, saying into the microphone that he 'saved' Mariupol children. One of the 'saved' – a girl, Anya. Her mother was killed by a Russian missile. 'Come on, go ahead, thank your saviour!' says the female host. The girl hesitates. 'I've forgotten a little bit.' 'Don't be shy! You can come up and give him a hug!' The presenter pushes a frightened Anya towards a man in military uniform.

This feeling of horror will never leave us, of not being able to believe that these men in your country's military uniform – your country – are doing what they are doing. In two years of full-scale war, several tens of thousands of children from Ukraine will be forcibly removed to Russia. Their parents were either killed by Russian weapons or are alive and looking for them. In Russia, Ukrainian children have their names and place of birth changed and are sent to orphanages and to foster families.

go on, thank him

The stories Ukrainian children tell of Russian institutions they were forcibly removed to are chilling. Every morning, they have to get out of bed to the Russian national anthem, just like in Petrovka prison. Ukrainian children are forced to learn this anthem – the Soviet tune with different words – by heart. Those who refuse have to write an explanation – like in a penal colony. If they speak in their native tongue, they are beaten with metal rods. The boy whom Ukraine managed to bring home remembered the name of one of the sadists – Astakhov. He turned out to be a former Berkut policeman, the Ukrainian riot police who shot protesters on the Maidan. Seeing a Ukrainian flag in one of the children's rooms, he burned it with the words, 'Watch how your country is burning!'

For kidnapping Ukrainian children, the International Criminal Court will issue arrest warrants for Putin and Russian children's ombudsman Maria Lvova-Belova – both international criminals who deserve to be tried and executed. Lvova-Belova is an 'Orthodox Christian' with ten children, one of whom was abducted from Mariupol. She will leave her priest husband for the Orthodox arms of the sponsor of the annexation of Crimea, the oligarch Malofeev.

watch it burn

- Are you coming to court?
- I don't know.
- What if I pick you up in the fsinmobile? I can wake you up!

- To be honest, I think I'll go and get drunk.
- But how will I get the equipment? Will anyone be there?

There are three days left, then two, then one. Tomorrow is the trial, the unfortunate trial to change my restriction measures that is driving me crazy. I have to either be present at it and serve twenty-one days or go on the run. 'Abandon Russia' is the expression for it now. Two words that don't fit in my head, tear at my heart, make my body clench in a corner – abandon Russia.

'Well?'

'Have you decided?'

'Mash, we have to decide.'

'WHAT'S IT LIKE OVER THERE?'

'I'LL ACCEPT ANY DECISION YOU MAKE. JUST DECIDE.'

I'm arguing with Lucy, I'm arguing with everyone; they're fed up with my mood swings. People are yelling and angry. They'd accept any choice, they just want me to make it. So I'd stop loading the responsibility for it onto them. But I can't make it. I can't decide. I don't know what's right.

two words

I packed a gym bag for jail and a suitcase for leaving the country. These two are the first things I see every time I walk into the room. From the kitchen, bathroom, toilet. Sitting there and reminding me of myself, reminding me of this unbearable choice. Inside I'm ready for both options. I'm ready to be in jail and I'm ready to leave. But I'm not ready to do either for ever.

The word 'to hide' in English and the Russian name for Hades, Аид – 'Aeed' – are similar. Hades is the god of the dead (and the realm of the dead itself was called Hades in Greek). Hades wore an invisible hat. For the ancient Greeks, the dead were just people whom we stopped seeing at some point.

hear me out

THE FOLLOWING DOES NOT CONSTITUTE A
RECOMMENDATION AND/OR GUIDE TO ESCAPE.
IF YOU ARE IN A DANGEROUS SITUATION AND ARE
BEING PERSECUTED BY THE STATE FOR POLITICAL
REASONS, CONTACT HUMAN RIGHTS DEFENDERS AND
SPECIALISTS.

Night, a lawyer in the kitchen and a bottle of wine. I'm trying to remove the cap on my ankle bracelet. Trying to prise it off with a knife to see what's underneath. A small black piece of plastic. To take the bracelet off and keep it. To take it off and put it on when I want to, not when the inspector wants me to. To perform with it.

Under the cap – two screws. If you loosen the screws, the strap of the bracelet will detach from the main part, the connection will break and the duty station will receive a signal. If you're intending to escape and you are wearing an ankle bracelet, do not touch the bracelet. I'm doing the exact opposite.

The connection's been broken. The fsinphone doesn't stop ringing. Ringing off the hook.

- So, duty officer, why are you calling me?
- Are you in place?
- Not in place! Everything is out of place. There's a war going on!
- Are you okay? What's happened with the bracelet?

- I'm okay, the bracelet's in place.
- Where is it?
- Like the whole country, gone to shit.
- What's happened to your bracelet?
- The bracelet is fine, perfect, intact, and says hi.
- You need to be patient. Everybody needs to be a bit patient.
- How long are you going to be patient? When are you going to give it all up?
- I can't give it up.
- Yes, you can. You are human.
- Maria Vladimirovna.
- Fuck, you can refuse, but please fucking hear me out. I believe in you. Hear me out, goddamn it, stop doing this.

connection is broken

Dawn is soon. The bracelet is twisted off, I'm holding it in my hand. The bracelet's twisted off, which means the cops will be here soon. So Olya and I have to get out of here. We go to my friend's apartment; the cops don't know her address – she didn't go to rallies or write protest posts, and she's not registered as my friend in the police files, so we still have some time.

The trial's in a few hours. It's the first goddamn time in my life I'm not going to my own trial. I'm going to sleep. If I could make tomorrow never come, I would. But tomorrow comes.

The trial goes on without me. The court changes my limitations to freedom to days in jail.

without me

To fulfil a punishment, you need a court order and you need a convict. Court order – here. Convict – not. The convict must be found.

I wake up. I switch on my phone, which means, in a matter of minutes, the phone's location can be tracked.

There's no simple way out from the apartment I'm hiding in. I can't just walk out and leave. I can only walk out and be jailed. Or find a way to walk out unnoticed – walk out dressed in the courier uniform Lucy left behind.

I'm dividing the page. Into two columns. One column is called 'courier', the other 'zone'.

It doesn't help.

'It would be a shame not to try "the courier",' messages Lucy.

courier / zone

Cops are surrounding the flat. Two cars. Also, a grey van. From the window, I watch the Centre E donut get out. The same one who detained us at the Bolshoi Theatre. It's obvious he's maximally upset. I think it's a rare moment when a Centre E cop feels exactly like my friends and family: Why can't you just do things normally?

The only normal way here is to be behind bars, help those who are in jail or become a partisan, and everything else against the backdrop of war is abnormal, wrong. People in cafés ordering iced lattes – that's what drives you crazy, but 'someone has to stay here'?

The cops start banging on the door. The doorbell goes off

like it did two days ago. Then they start banging on it with their fists. We need to figure a way out. In the meantime, I don't move. Not one part of my body.

And then Olya, who is in the apartment with me, writes a plan. On some sort of scrap of some sort of piece of paper.

The plan is as follows:

- switch off the phone, leave it in the flat
- get a clean mobile
- put on a courier's uniform.
- walk out of the back door
- get in a taxi round the corner
- go to flat X

'Go on, Mash. I want you to go and write that song that I'm going to hate.'

go on, mash

Night falls the moment the cops have left the lift and the stairs. I open the suitcase and bag for the detention centre. The balaclava, the black ankle bracelet, our petrol station animals, the forgotten perfume – I'm taking my whole life on a journey. I don't know when or where or how it will end. And if it will ever. I take shorts, T-shirts, coffee, cigarettes, all the things that might come in handy if I get detained. I put them into a green square bag – the food courier's branded bag. I put on the green jacket.

They call a taxi from another phone. It will be arriving round the corner. I need to leave. Just do it. I open the door and, without looking back, walk to the taxi.

not looking back

The car is meant to pick me up from apartment X and take me in the direction of the Belarusian-Lithuanian border. Take me in the direction of the West.

I'm sitting on the bed. My family and friends did everything to make an escape plan but without a plan for my crossing the border.

To the average resident of any of the Western countries, totalitarian regimes are scary black holes. A person who escapes from there simply materializes in their world. Materializes with their difficult, sometimes interesting but nevertheless scary story behind them. But it's the details and the specifics that often change everything. And this escape, however chaotic it may have been, would not have been possible without those details. Someone checked the stairs and the entrance to the building, someone else found a car by pulling a relative from his country house to drive several hundred kilometres to Belarus, someone devised the plan to leave dressed as a courier; ultimately some people let me into all these apartments, someone convinced the embassy to print out a visa (an official document, after all) on an ordinary sheet of paper, and someone else brought me blackberries and cheese.

The liminal state of night and day. Fog. Get in the car, drive through the fog that at one point on the road gathers and separates.

If time was wrapped in a coil – like wire or string can be – if you could unwrap a couple of coils and look inside . . .

while still alive

While I am travelling in the car – Navalny is still alive. As soon as it becomes clear that the war is long-term, they will try to exchange him and other political prisoners. Navalny is first on the list. Putin kills him the day before the supposed exchange date. To keep Enemy Number One from returning to action.

In the distant snow-covered Harp, close to the Arctic Circle, it's a dark night. February – the Lyuty month (the fierce month), as they call it in Ukraine – becomes the month Navalny dies. A motorcade drives along a narrow empty road between nothing and nothing. A motorcade of three cars – police and FSIN – is speeding away from the colony. A body lies in one of these cars.

His mother – Lyudmila Navalnaya – is flying to Harp. She is looking for the body of her son at the morgue. They hide the body and don't hand it over. Even Navalny's body is feared in the Kremlin. They're afraid of a public funeral.

> *'They want to take me to the outskirts of the cemetery to a fresh grave and say, "Here lies your son." . . . They want it done in secret, without a farewell. Looking into my eyes, they say that if I do not agree to a secret funeral, they will do something with my son's body. Investigator Vyrypayev openly told me, "Time is not on your side; the corpse is decomposing." I demand that my son's body be handed over.'*
> – Lyudmila Navalnaya, 22 February 2024

hand over the body

People carry flowers. Every day that the body is not released, people carry flowers. All over Russia – to monuments to victims of political repression; all over the world – to Russian embassies. The foot of the Solovetsky Stone in front of the Lubyanka is covered with flowers. At night, cops and communal workers rake them like locusts into black rubbish bags and take them to the dump. In the morning, the flowers reappear.

They twist arms, push along the snow, drag, push along, cops and more cops separated off by a cordon of avtozaks and barriers. In Surgut, a gun is put to the head of a man who brought flowers; questions are asked: 'Where did you buy the flowers?' 'Who owns Crimea?' 'Are you gay?' Hundreds of thousands of demands to hand over the body to the mother flood the Internet.

The body is being released. The only priest who agreed to perform Navalny's funeral will be deprived of his ministry. A queue of thousands of people to a cemetery on the outskirts of Moscow. Cops with video cameras. People from all over Russia, who came to say goodbye to the man who united them with a dream – the dream of a Beautiful Russia of the future. Because people are this Russia. There are so many bouquets of flowers that they completely cover a simple wooden cross.

do heroes die?

It is the biggest prisoner exchange since the Second World War. A plane carrying eight political prisoners will land in Ankara. Until the very end, none of them will know it was a plane to freedom. More are exchanged than planned because Navalny is not on the list. Because he's been murdered. And this murder – his death – turns into an opportunity to save more lives.

The price – of this plane of freedom – will be Russian spies and assassins jailed in Western prisons. The most valuable cargo is Putin's friend from the '90s, Killer Krasikov. In the noughties he killed unlucky businessmen and then shot dead a Chechen military commander in the centre of Berlin.

Russia's best people are being exchanged for hitmen and spies. That's who's needed. People who risked their lives and freedom to tell the truth are enemies, and those are heroes. A guard of honour and a red carpet will be rolled out to the plane. Putin will personally meet them. 'I want to thank you for your loyalty to the motherland.' Meanwhile, the plane of political prisoners in Germany will be met by ordinary people. Hundreds of Russian people whose stories of how they were forced to flee deserve separate books. They will come with flowers and placards. 'Alexei should have been with you,' reads one of the placards.

> *'For those who have become enemies, it's highly unlikely*
> *there'll be a place in our homeland.'*
>
> – Peskov, September 2023

green corridor

We don't choose where we're born. We don't choose the colour of our passport. But we do choose how we live our lives. To fight back or not to fight back against the system that makes cogs of humans.

Afternoon. Belarus-Lithuania border. Kotlovka border check-point. Lukashenko and Putin are dictator friends; to enter from Russia into the 'union state' of Belarus does not present a problem. You show your Russian ID and you are through. But to get into the European Union from there – a completely different challenge.

I approach the border in a white car driven by an elderly man. He doesn't know anything except that I need to be taken across the border. He tells me we need to get out of the car and show our papers to the border guard. Everything is fine, except that my papers are a Russian ID and a Schengen visa printed out on a piece of paper.

> – It's the first time I've ever seen a visa printed like that.
> I can't let you through with these documents.
> – But isn't this a green corridor?
> – What green corridor?

I've no experience of crossing borders without documents, so I think that the 'green corridor', through which Ukrainian refugees have been entering the European Union via Belarus, works for me as well. That the 'green corridor' is like a guest list – it is on the border guard's desk and people on it are let through.

> – I can explain everything. I am Masha, I'm an activist from Pussy Riot. They didn't warn you that I was coming?

wait here

The elderly man and I are not allowed to turn around and drive away. The car is shown to a designated area. Suddenly another border guard, about twenty years old, in a green uniform, approaches the car.

> – You need to get out, he says.

- Why? I ask.
- Come upstairs, to the office, he continues, and leads me out of the car. The elderly man waits. We go up the stairs, down the corridor. We enter one of the rooms at the very end.

The room is like a classroom. The desks are arranged in three rows. The chairs are turned upside down on the desks. The way we used to put the chairs upside down at school when we mopped the floor. On the wall in front of the desks is a plasma TV. I take one of the chairs off, sit down:

- Why am I here?
- We're going to watch a movie.
- Which movie?
- Us from the future.

He switches on a movie. A movie about guys getting drunk in the countryside, diving into a lake and ending up back in 1942. Second World War.

us from the future

I'm watching a film where blokes find military IDs in the sand with their names on them. That kind of dystopia.

In a few months, this will become a reality for Russia. After a Ukrainian counter-offensive, Putin will announce a 'partial' mobilization. Partial mobilization is a cover, so as not to scare, so as not to panic. But there will be panic.

Men with no military experience, with several children or with disabilities will be called up to the army. According to Mediazona, 527,000 people will be mobilized in just two months. Someone will break their own legs with a hammer to avoid conscription; someone will go to prison; someone will go to the military enlistment office and shout, 'Now we'll all go home,' and shoot the military officer twice. Their name is Ruslan Zinin, and the price of these shots is nineteen years in prison.

partial mobilization

The first mobilization since the Great Patriotic War. An order will be sent to the recruitment offices they'll be given a quota of how many people they need to catch. Those who fall into the trap of 'report to the recruitment office for a clarification of data' will be sent to the front – for a great victory with decrepit weapons.

The military draft will be presented as another great campaign against the Nazis. Mobilization will launch a new wave of people fleeing to airports, rather than military enlistment centres. Traffic jams kilometres long on the way out of the country.

For deserters – a new criminal Article 333, Part 3. For refusal to obey orders – up to fifteen years. Even if that doesn't scare them, the barrier detachment will. A machine-gunner, ready to shoot at any moment.

The mobilized must serve 'until the end of the special military operation'. Wives and mothers will unite to bring them home. They'll call the movement 'The Way Home'. They'll be labelled as foreign agents. In one action, desperate women will picket the Ministry of Defence. On their knees.

the way home

One man back from the special military operation killed someone in a restaurant and continued eating; another invited his
ex-wife to visit and beat her to death; another one, 'during an
argument triggered by hallucinations', stabbed his 77-year-old
grandmother several times; another, after being mocked for
his military service, killed an acquaintance on a playground;
another killed an acquaintance for 'rude words' about PMC
Wagner; another one stabbed a man, and then smashed his
head with an axe; another strangled with a cable an acquaintance who had borrowed money from him; another beat a
man with a wooden stick, and when his partner tried to protect him, killed her and threw her body into the river; another
one raped a fifteen-year-old boy; another raped his ten-year-old
stepdaughter; another killed a twelve-year-old girl and threw
her body into a well; and another beat his father with a mallet.

The prisoners recruited by Wagner will be pardoned in
exchange for a contract. They will return to their hometowns
as free people. Madmen and murderers will receive medals and
be called heroes.

'In Anapa rehabilitating after injury, 480 metres from the
sea. Awesome. Home soon,' Dmitry Karyagin will post. He
was previously convicted of murdering his grandmother. He
persuaded her to sell her apartment, took the money, lured her
into the garage and hammered her to death. The grandmother
was a veteran of the Great Patriotic War.

goida

'Goida!' the battle cry of the 'sovereign's hounds', the Oprich-niki guards of Tsar Ivan the Terrible. A cry for blood. A cry for execution. 'Goida!' shouts an actor – Putin's patriot – into the microphone from the stage on Red Square. A festival in honour of the annexation of new Ukrainian lands. A celebration of death in the centre of Moscow. The mausoleum with Lenin's corpse opposite the stage. 'This is a holy war!' the actor spits. In the crowd, thousands of people are waving Russian flags they've been handed out at the entrance. And bombs are drop-ping at the same time onto Ukrainian homes. Bombs that are being celebrated in the main square.

Funerals will be held, cemetery plots will be assigned. On prime-time TV there are reports of 'a new Lada in exchange for a son'.

They'll put desks for 'heroes' in schools. Journalists will be taken to the opening of these desks. A little boy of about seven will look at a desk with a picture of his dead father. And he'll cry. They have given him a military jacket with epaulettes to wear.

To look into the future of your country is scarier than any movie.

watch

– They've said the car needs to be checked. Let's go.

Two border guards get in the back seat and tell the elderly man to go to a special garage. In the garage they inspect

everything – the inside, the boot; they open my suitcase, care-
fully examine all my clothes, every little thing, look at the ankle
bracelet buried in my things. They look, but they don't see it.

- And now you go to a body search.
- Really?

The body search is a full strip search. Just the same as one in
a Russian prison. A Soviet-style woman without gloves. And,
as if in a dream: 'Take off your underwear. Quickly, please.'
I refuse with my last strength. Under the white, soulless 'daylight lamp'.

The border guard takes me to the office – the same one
where we watched the film. The door opens. The TV is
switched off, a man sits at the table. A typical Centre E cop. I'm
knocked sideways.

- Maria Vladimirovna, please sit down.

please sit down

A real Belarusian KGB cop. In jeans and pointy-toed shoes, just
like at home.

- What do you want? I ask him sharply.
- You are trying to cross the border illegally.

I answer like at school from behind a desk: 'I wasn't trying
to do anything illegal.' The KGB operative is opposite me – at
the 'teacher's desk' – hands in a lock, grinning: 'Well, how was
that not trying to, Maria Vladimirovna?' Perhaps the film was
better.

'What will you do next? Will you be going the green way?'
'What is the green way?'

'Don't you know?' A quiet sneer and a cynical look with which he tries to catch my eye. 'The green way is going through the woods, across the border. Do you know how many years you can go to prison for that?'

- Am I detained?
- No, you are not detained.
- That means I can go?
- No, it doesn't.

'What are you going to do next?' Fucking circular conversation. The more tired I get, the more he likes it. He asks questions, goes out, comes back, asks questions again. Exactly the same as before. There are no right answers. An hour goes by. An hour and a half goes by. I'm ready for anything. Arrest, search, cell, deportation, I just want out. And to never see this cop again. I pull out my phone. 'No phones allowed.' 'Am I under arrest?' 'No, you're not.' 'Then I'll record you.' 'That's not allowed.' 'Then confiscate the phone and arrest me now.' I press the record button, the cop runs out of the room. Never comes back.

They give me a document that explains the penalties for trying to cross the border illegally. And they let me go.

The old man, who's been waiting all this time, drives me away from the border. It's evening. What will happen next is uncertain.

coffee and nachos

The old man drives me to a hotel. The city of Ashmyany. I have to sleep and try again tomorrow. At another border checkpoint – Kamenny Log.

'Book the room under his name. And you are, well . . . his mistress,' advises Lucy. You can't flash an ID if you're on the run. They won't issue a room to the old man. No way. I hold out my ID at the reception desk – I'm tired. Tired, sleepy and cold.

In the morning, I'm hungry. Whether there are cops in the hotel or not, I don't know. I take my food out of my jail bag. Instant coffee and nachos. Breakfast in bed, it turns out.

It's twenty minutes from the hotel to the border checkpoint. I've got to find a car. The elderly guy won't repeat his mistake a second time. Lucy searches for a car online – the first one tricks her, takes the money and disappears; the second one is genuine. A black minibus. Just like the ones Centre E uses in Russia.

This time I'm just going to do it by the book. Not a word about activism. I'm travelling for work or to get medical treatment. I know they won't let me in, but I want to try. For the sake of others. For the sake of those who want me to cross this border.

to do it by the book

'It's a violation to travel with these documents, do you know that?' the driver asks. 'The driver's worried,' I write on the chat. 'He was paid to drive, don't worry.'

Kamenny Log border checkpoint. A three-hour queue. During these three hours, the driver repeats over and over again that they will not let me through. We reach the front. I go to the booth. I give my documents, I look at the camera pointed at my face.

'Wasn't it you who tried to get through yesterday at the other checkpoint?' the border guard smiles.

Please, not a body search. Not a car search. Not another conversation with the KGB. Please, please, please.

- Can I have my ID back? I answer, realizing that he won't let me through.
- Of course you can, the round Belarusian face in uniform continues, smiling. As soon as you call a taxi. You won't want to stay here, will you?

I'm standing in the middle of the border. With a suitcase and a bag for the detention centre. The driver's gone. No taxi, no cash.

- I'll give you the number of the taxi. You'll have to go to the desk for the cash.

I withdraw money from the cash desk, putting my card into the metal container, Soviet style. The border guard gives me my ID and says, 'Wherever you decide to go, good luck.'

- Where to? asks a cheery taxi driver, a woman with white hair.
- Can you take me to the border with Russia?
- No problem. As long as you're paying, I'll take you wherever you want.
- To the nearest motel.

golden horseshoe

I wake up in the Golden Horseshoe motel. A building standing alone in a field. The room has a bevelled ceiling, like in a village. A bar counter, artificial vines, double-glazed windows – a fairy tale adjusted for Belarus in the 21st century. A strange place in the middle of a green void. The girl at the front desk knows local guides. The ones who know how to drive through the woods.

- I'm going to the Russian border.
- So that means you've given up, right? asks a man who has dedicated his life to rescuing people fleeing post-Soviet dictatorships.

I'd be lying if I said it didn't spur me on. I don't have a problem with trying again. It's possible. But it'll be the last time. God loves a trinity. A horseshoe is good luck. I message the taxi driver that we're going to Grodno. To pay her, I must withdraw money from the nearest ATM.

I see a church, a white church, and I can't help but go in. There's no one in there. In the centre, a huge wooden cross lies on some red velvet squares. It's as if God left it there and then walked out. Priests who oppose the war will be banned from the ministry and imprisoned. Their parishioners will write denunciations against them.

god left it

When the Church is no more than an organ of propaganda, when love is exchanged for hate, when persecution, imprisonment, massacres and murders are carried out in the name of God, when two or three are gathered not 'in His name', then there is no one there. There is no God because they have banished Him.

The Belarusian Church is a daughter of the Russian Orthodox Church. Priests will be obliged to recite the so-called 'Holy Russia' prayer – the prayer that grants victory over the Antichrist. Antichrist is 'the collective West with gay parades'. A priest will later replace the word 'victory' with the word 'peace' in this evil prayer – and be deprived of his ministry.

They put collection urns for the army in churches, gather clothes and cigarettes for the military, sprinkle tanks with holy water; in Sunday School children weave camouflage nets. The Patriarch is filmed presenting an icon to the head of the Russian Guard. At the front priests baptise soldiers in black body bags. Three hundred priests sign a letter demanding a stop to the war. All of them are disgraced.

I will fear no evil

I wake up to the morning news. I'm on Russia's Federal Wanted list. I take a selfie in the kitchen. The city of Grodno.

I go to a café. A Belarusian woman who's taken me in for the night comes with me. If I talk politics, she starts whispering. 'Does everyone whisper like that here?' I ask. 'I hadn't even noticed,' replies the young woman. Her name is Masha too.

It's dangerous for me to stay in her flat. I need to find a new one. For one or two nights. Until the next – the last – attempt.

We find an apartment. 'Even brides stay here,' the landlady says proudly. Turquoise walls, white dressing table, blue curtains. The landlady comes back with the rental contract, takes my passport and gets scared. 'What is your permanent address? Are you homeless? No, I can't rent to you.'

Being on the Federal Wanted list means that soon my name and photo will appear in the Belarusian border-guard database.

federal wanted list

Belarus. A country with golden wheat fields and kind people, stamped with the seal of dictatorship. A bloody dictator, who looks like an ordinary farming man, year after year imprisons and kills dissenters. This year he opened the Belarusian border for Russian tanks to pass through. In Belarus they trained the very group that shot people in Bucha.

Without a passport, they don't let you book a hotel or rent an apartment here. It is forbidden. It's doubly dangerous to show your passport when you're a federal fugitive. I need an apartment. A director friend who wants to make a film about all of this is making up a cover story.

'You're not Masha, you're just an ordinary girl, Katya, who got drunk and came to the town without a passport, and your friends are on their way to bring it to you.'

It worked.

without a passport

Morning. An apartment in a dormitory neighbourhood. A very ordinary apartment in a panel block. With windows onto a kindergarten, a grocery shop and other high-rises. The kind of grey high-rise that seems to have been copied and pasted into every neighbourhood in every post-Soviet country.

I walk outside. It's sunny and there are very few people. In the playground there's a hut on chicken legs. In fairy tales a hut like this is a portal. The boundary between the living and the dead. It can rotate on its axis, turning the door to one world or the other. By default, it faces the forest, the world of the dead. Inside lives Baba Yaga – guardian and guide. If you ask the hut correctly, it will turn around. If you are not afraid of Baba Yaga, you can pass into the other world, accomplish tasks and return back to the world of the living. The entrance to this hut is blocked with a sheet of plasterboard. Children play nearby.

dementor's kiss

A country that has lived through and is still living through terrible violence. I remember how we stood outside the Belarusian embassy in Moscow, how we rehearsed in this country with the Belarus Free Theatre in a garage. The emptiness. As if everyone is walking around knowing that something terrible has happened.

It's like they're all survivors of a kiss from the demented.

Maybe that's how people who've had their hope taken away live.

axis of evil

By launching a full-scale war, Putin has done more than just launch a bloody attack on Ukraine. He has declared war on the West. He has declared war on the very possibility of freedom of choice and democracy – as one of the manifestations of that freedom.

And in this war, he has found and continues to find new allies. Drones from Iran, munitions from North Korea, land for storing missiles in Belarus, drones from China.

North Korea, Iran, China, Belarus – countries in which

dictators have consistently killed hope, where democracy does not exist either. Or has never existed. Where people are held hostage by their own country.

Countries where there are no human rights, countries where vice police beat women to death for not wearing a headscarf, where protesters are executed publicly in squares, where it is deadly dangerous to even think of protesting.

The world they are building is a world from which the soul has been sucked out.

expecto patronum

'I don't want to be like all those people who left and say they hate our country.'

I put owl from the petrol station on the table, take out a Vinegret salad from the supermarket. Soviet kitchen in a panel block. I don't know what will happen next.

'You're doing this for you. For yourself.'

I've heard those words many times. Words that hurt.

'Who am I?'

Maria is my great-grandmother's name; my mother named me after her. Three generations of women raised their daughters alone. Lived with the understanding that they could rely only on themselves. None of them spoke out against the authorities – they survived. Survived and lived. Largely thanks to their silence. And I'm writing this not to be silent. The only thing I can do for myself is not to keep silent about what I saw in the country of my birth. The country I love – trapped, brutal, embracing and repelling all at the same time. With untranslatable jokes. With endless dictators and donut cops, with priests who have blood on their hands, with brave girls who rebel against the regime – I want to save us as I have come to know and love us. To save us and all our adventures – so that it will be possible for you and us to have new adventures.

So that your freedom and ours can finally come to life.

not to be silent

Seven a.m. I'm going with cash to the bus station. The plan is to get on the bus, get lost in the crowd and get through. No more private cars or vans. Blue seats, blue curtains, green pine trees outside the window.

'Film it all. It's like in a movie!'

It's only a twenty-minute drive. A full shuttle bus of quiet morning sleepy people. They're talking, eating or catching up on sleep.

Privalka border checkpoint. The bus stops, people queue up at the border guard's hut. They let everyone through. They let everyone through except me.

– You need to get off the bus, says the border guard. With your things.

here we go

– How did you get to Belarus?
– With an ID.
– Which one?
– A Russian ID.
– And where is it?

A border guard in a green uniform is sitting at a table. He's holding a little book he's never seen before. When he opens it, my face looks out from the page. A selfie from a Belarusian kitchen. When he closes it, a golden emblem shimmers on the blue background. The border guard opens the book and closes it. But he doesn't recognize what's in his hands.

The border guard doesn't know that my bag contains a Russian ID. I can't let him find out.

'You see, I came to visit your country, to have a holiday. I went to a bar with my friends and I lost everything, all my documents.'

lost everything

– Wait here.

Small room. Soviet couch. I sit and look at my phone. I'm playing an actress. An actress from the Icelandic drama theatre who urgently needs to get to rehearsals. At first, the border guard works 'by the book' – entry without visa means a violation report: sit down at the computer, transcribe the information, issue a fine. Then something changes. He leaves. He gets up, goes out, comes back in.

> – Why don't I call the consul? I ask in the most timid voice possible.
> – What consul?

I need the Icelandic consul's phone number.
Any number.
What's his name?
What's the address of the theatre in Reykjavik?
CAN YOU JUST SEND ANY ADDRESS!!!

playing actress

The phone is hot. Heating up like a brick in the blazing sun. The border guard goes back and forth. Back and forth and back and forth. With a strange little book and a piece of paper with phone numbers.

He goes away again. And comes back again. This time he doesn't sit back down at the desk but hands me the blue passport. There will be no fine. The violation form remains on the table.

- You can go.
- Where to?
- Were you not going to a rehearsal?

We're going outside. A queue of cars. A border guard stops one of them. My bus left two hours ago.

- Take her. Quite frankly, we don't know what to do with her.

A middle-aged man is driving. He looks at the border guard. Then at me. He clearly doesn't want to take me but reluctantly agrees – he can't refuse a man in uniform. I put my suitcase and my bag for jail in the boot of his car. I get in the back seat: 'Hello.'

take the girl

I don't know why he let me through. The magic blue document. The power of hope of those who were rooting for it. A go-ahead from the special services. Being an actress. Or just the stupidity of the system. Or all of the above.

We're moving forward, we're driving along that wonderful neutral lane. Which belongs to no one. If you open the window and put your hand out, a breeze comes to meet it.

We're pulling up. The barrier. I give the Lithuanian border guard everything I have. My odd collection of documents. I get out of the car to smoke. I stand and look at the pine trees across the street. The morning pines. In essence the same but different to us, the people who created borders and dictatorships. I want to remember this moment. I say to the camera:

'Well, what's left behind are Belarusian pine trees, what's ahead is not clear but the important thing is that they're left behind.'

stop filming!

The border guard in a warm camouflage jacket runs towards me. 'Stop filming! It's forbidden!'

- Why? I was just filming myself and the pine trees, it's a selfie.
- Get your stuff out of the car.
- I came a long way to get here, people are waiting for me. I'll explain everything to you.
- What are you, Russian propaganda?

And later there will be pain and screams, indifference and delight, and there will be love and people will cry and applaud. And there will be the question: 'Mum, did you make it through?' Stop filming. We will go to a room with old windows, he will give me his warm camouflage jacket and offer me Ukrainian sweets. And then we won't be heard again, we will fall, get back up, show and tell. It's not a movie. Things from the jail bag will move to the suitcase. 'What is that strange bracelet on your ankle?' a girl will ask me on my birthday. In a warm country. Her face will change in a second after my reply. And a thousand more moments like that. 'Just take a look at me,' I tell the border guard. I really did live through it all.

take a look

P.S.

'Go on, Mash, write a song that I will hate.'

In 2024, a third criminal case is opened against Maria Alyokhina in Russia for 'fake news' about the Russian army, for the song 'Mama Don't Watch TV', and for anti-war performances.

The criminal case names other Pussy Riot members: Olga Borisova, Taso Pletner, Alina Petrova and Diana Burkot.

All of them are issued with international arrest warrants and charged in absentia. (The case is ongoing at the time of writing).

The same year, Lucy Shtein is convicted in absentia for 'fake news' about the Russian army and sentenced to six years imprisonment.

Anna Kuzminykh is placed on the international wanted list for an anti-war action.

Nadya Tolokonnikova is wanted and charged in absentia for 'insulting the religious feelings of believers'.

Peter Verzilov is convicted in absentia to over 8 years imprisonment for 'fake news' about the Russian army and is under investigation for treason.

Currently, if any of the people listed above appeared at the Russian border, they would face immediate arrest and long-term imprisonment.

 GO ON ♥